Nick Vandome

Laptops for Seniors

Windows 10 edition

In easy steps is an imprint of In Easy Steps Limited
16 Hamilton Terrace · Holly Walk · Leamington Spa
Warwickshire · United Kingdom · CV32 4LY
www.ineasysteps.com

In Easy Steps Limited supports The Forest Stewardship Council (FSC), the leading international forest certification organization. All our titles that are printed on Greenpeace approved FSC certified paper carry the FSC logo.

Printed and bound in the United Kingdom

ISBN 978-1-84078-647-7

Contents

3 Getting Up and Running 55

4 Working with Apps 71

5 Internet and Email 87

1 Choosing a Laptop

More and more computer users are now using laptops because of their convenience and portability. This chapter looks at some of the issues to consider when buying a laptop and how to ensure you buy the right one for your needs. It also covers the elements of a laptop and some of the accessories you will need.

A Brief History of Laptops

Modern computers have come a long way since the days of mainframe computers, which took up entire rooms and were generally only the domain of large educational establishments or government organizations. Before microprocessors (the chips that are used to run modern-day computers), these mainframe computers were usually operated by punch-cards: the operators programmed instructions via holes in a punch-card and then waited for the results, which could take hours or days.

Don't forget

Apple has an excellent range of laptops, running its OS X operating system. However, the majority of this book deals with "IBM-compatible" laptops, as they are known. These types of laptops are the most common and run on the Windows operating system.

The first personal computers, i.e. ones in which all of the computing power was housed in a single box, started to appear in the early 1970s and the first machine that bore any resemblance to modern personal computers was called the Datapoint 2200. The real breakthrough for personal computers came with the introduction of microprocessors – small chips that contained all of the necessary processing power for the computer. After this, the industry expanded at a phenomenal rate with the emergence of major worldwide companies such as Microsoft, Apple, IBM, Dell and Intel.

But even as personal computers were being developed for a mass-market audience, there was a concerted drive to try to create a portable computer so that people could take their own computer with them wherever they went. Even in the fast-moving world of technology, the timescale for shrinking a computer from the size of a large room to the size of a small briefcase was a dramatic one.

The New icon pictured above indicates a new or enhanced feature introduced on laptops with Windows 10.

First portable computers

With most types of technology, we are obsessed with the idea of making the item as small as possible, whether it is a music player, a telephone or a computer. However, the first portable computers bore little resemblance to the machines that we now know as laptops. At the beginning of the 1980s there were a few portable computers released, but most of them were bulky, had very small screens and could not run on internal batteries. The most popular of these was called the Osborne 1, which was released in 1981. Although this was the size of a small suitcase and had a minuscule amount of computing power compared with modern machines, it proved a big success as it enabled people to carry their computers around with them for the first time.

The machine that first used the term "laptop" was called the Gallian SC, which was developed in 1983 and introduced in 1984. This had the big advantage of being able to run on an internal battery, and it was also one of the first portable computers that appeared with the now-universal "clamshell" design, where the monitor folded down over the keyboard.

Because of their size and weight, the first portable computers, such as the Osborne 1, were known rather unflatteringly as "luggables".

In the late 1980s, companies such as Kyocera, Tandy, Olivetti, NEC, IBM, Toshiba, Compaq and Zenith Data Systems began developing fast and more powerful laptops, and it is in this period that the growth of laptops really began to take off.

In 1991, Apple introduced its PowerBook range of laptops and in 1995, the introduction of Windows 95 provided an operating system for IBM-compatible laptops.

Laptops have now become an integral part of the computer market and in many areas sales have outstripped those of desktop computers. Also, they are more than capable of comfortably meeting the computing needs of most computer users. Add to this, their portability (which has reached a stage where you no longer need to worry about causing yourself an injury in order to carry one around), and it is clear why laptops have become so popular.

Mobility is now an essential part of computing and when Windows 8 was released, it was aimed firmly at the mobile world. However, this caused some issues, particularly with users of desktop and laptop computers. Windows 10 has gone a long way to addressing these issues, partly by reinstalling a number of features that are aimed more at users with a traditional keyboard and mouse, such as the enhanced Start Menu. This shows that laptops still have an important role to play and will continue to do so.

Laptops v. Desktops

When considering buying a laptop computer, one of the first considerations is how it will perform in comparison with a desktop computer. In general, you will pay more for a laptop with similar specifications to a desktop. The reason for this is purely down to size: it is more expensive to fit the required hardware into a laptop than the more generous physical capacity of a desktop computer. However, with modern computing technology and power, even laptops with lower specifications than their desktop cousins will be able to handle all but the most intensive computing needs of most home users. The one situation where laptops will need to have as high a specification as possible is if you are going to be doing a lot a video downloading and editing, such as converting and editing old family movies.

Some of the issues to consider when looking at the differences between laptops and desktops are:

Don't forget

Another issue with laptops is battery power, which is required to keep them operating when they are removed from a mains electrical source. Obviously, this is not an issue that affects desktops.

- **Portability**. Laptops easily win over desktops in this respect, but when looking at this area it is worth thinking about how portable you actually want your computer to be. If you want to mainly use it in the home, then you may think that a desktop is the answer. However, a laptop gives you portability in the home too, which means that you can use your computer in a variety of locations within the home and even in the garden, if desired.
- **Power**. Even the most inexpensive laptops have enough computing power to perform most of the tasks that the majority of users require. However, if you want to have the same computing power as the most powerful desktops, then you will have to pay a comparatively higher price.
- **Functionality**. Again, because of their size, desktops have more room for items such as DVD writers, multi-card readers and webcams. These can be included with laptops but this can also increase the price and the weight of the laptop.

Types of Laptops

To meet the needs of the different types of people who use laptops there are several variations that are available:

- **Netbooks**. These are the ultimate in small laptops, but have less power and functionality than larger options. They generally have screens that are approximately 10 inches (measured diagonally from corner to corner) and are best suited for surfing the web and sending email, although they can also do productivity tasks.
- **Ultrabooks**. These are very light and slim laptops which still have significant power and functionality. They have screens of approximately 13 inches and weigh as little as 1.2 kg. They are an excellent option if you are going to be using your laptop a lot while traveling.
- **Notebooks**. These are the most common types of laptops as they have a good combination of size, weight and power. They generally have screens that are approximately 13-17 inches and weigh approximately 2-3.5 kg. Notebooks are an excellent option for using in the home and also while traveling.
- **Desktop replacements**. These are larger, heavier laptops that can be used in the home instead of a desktop computer. They are more powerful than other types of laptops but the downside is that they are not as portable. They generally have screens that are up to approximately 17-19 inches and weigh approximately 4-6 kg.
- **Hybrids**. With the proliferation of touchscreen mobile computing devices, such as smartphones and tablet computers, manufacturers have been looking at ways to incorporate this functionality into laptops. This has resulted in the development of touchscreen laptops and hybrid devices, which can be used both as a laptop and a tablet. This is done by including a keyboard that can be hidden (by having a sliding, detachable or revolving screen) so that the device can quickly be converted into a touchscreen tablet. These devices are becoming increasingly popular.

Netbooks usually have a slimmed-down version of the full Windows operating system, due to limits of their memory and architecture.

A lot of the weight in a laptop is taken up by peripherals such as DVD writers, card readers and webcams. The more of these that a laptop has, the heavier it is likely to be.

Laptop Jargon Explained

Since laptops are essentially portable computers, much of the jargon is the same as for a desktop computer. However, it is worth looking at some of this jargon and the significance it has in terms of laptops:

- **Processor**. Also known as the central processing unit, or CPU, this refers to the processing of digital data as it is provided by programs on the computer. The more powerful the processor, the quicker the data is interpreted.
- **Memory**. This closely relates to the processor and is also known as random-access memory, or RAM. Essentially, this type of memory manages the programs that are being run and the commands that are being executed. The more memory there is, the quicker programs will run. With more RAM, they will also be more stable and less likely to crash. In the current range of laptops, memory is measured in megabytes (MB) or gigabytes (GB).
- **Storage**. This refers to the amount of digital information that the laptop can store. In the current range of laptops, storage is measured in gigabytes. There are no external signs of processor or memory on a laptop but the details are available from within the This PC option, which is accessed from the File Explorer.

Memory can be thought of as a temporary storage device as it only keeps information about the currently-open programs. Storage is more permanent as it keeps the information even when the laptop has been turned off.

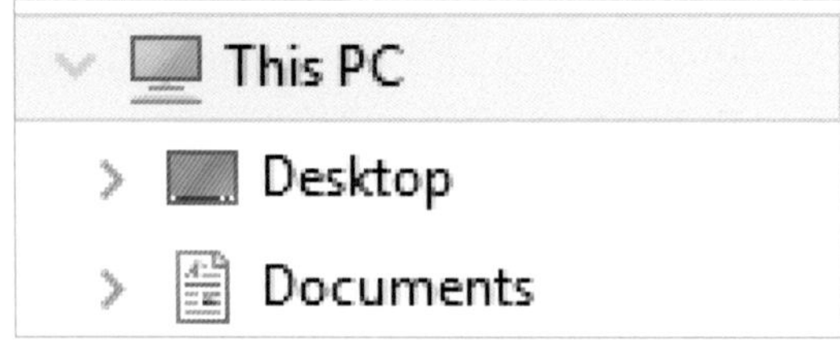

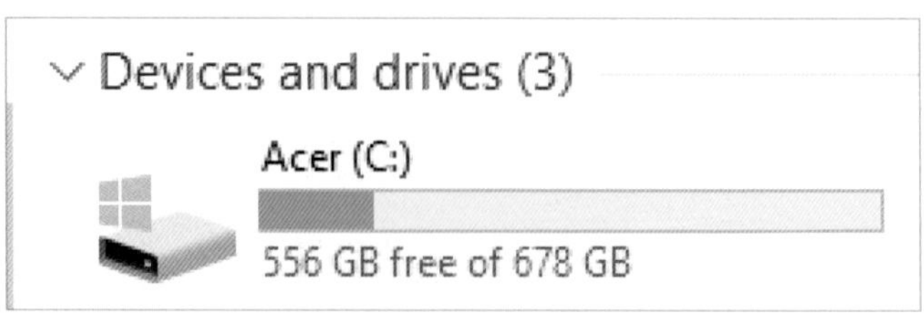

- **Optical drive**. This is a drive on the laptop that is capable of reading information from, and copying it to, a disc such as a CD or a DVD. Most modern laptops have internal optical drives such as CD writers or DVD writers.

External optical drives can also be connected to a laptop through a USB cable.

- **Connectivity**. This refers to the different types of media device to which the laptop can be connected. These include card readers for memory cards from digital cameras, USB devices such as music players, and FireWire devices such as digital video cameras.
- **Graphics card**. This is a device that enables images, video and animations to be displayed on the laptop. It is also sometimes known as a video card. The faster the graphics card, the better the quality the relevant media will be displayed at. In general, very fast graphics cards are really only needed for intensive multimedia applications such as video games or videos.

For more on using wireless technology see Chapter Nine.

- **Wireless**. This refers to a laptop's ability to connect wirelessly to a network, i.e. another computer or an internet connection. In order to be able to do this, the laptop must have a wireless card, which enables it to connect to a network or high-speed internet connection.
- **Ports**. These are the parts of a laptop into which external devices can be plugged, using a cable such as a USB. They are usually located on the side of the laptop and there can be two or three of each.

USB stands for Universal Serial Bus and is a popular way of connecting external devices to computers.

- **Pointing device**. This is the part of the laptop that replaces the traditional mouse as a means of moving the cursor on the screen. Most pointing devices are in the form of a touch pad, where a finger on a pad is used to move the cursor. An external mouse can also be connected to the laptop and used in the conventional way.
- **Webcam**. This is a type of camera that is fitted into the laptop and can be used to take still photographs, or communicate via video with other people.

Size and Weight

The issues of size and weight are integral to the decision to buy a laptop. In addition to getting a machine with enough computing power, it is also important to ensure that the screen is large enough for your needs and that it is light enough for you to carry around comfortably.

Size

The main issue with the size of a laptop is the dimensions of the screen. This is usually measured in inches, diagonally from corner to corner. The range for the majority of laptops currently on the market is approximately 12-17 inches, with some more powerful models going up to 19 inches.

When considering the size of screen it is important to think about how you are going to use your laptop:

- If you are going to use it mainly for functions such as letter writing and sending email, then a smaller screen might suffice.
- If you are going to use it mainly for functions such as surfing the web or editing and looking at photographs, then you may feel more comfortable with a larger screen.
- If you, or anyone else, is going to be using it for playing games and watching videos, then the larger the screen, the better.

Looking at material on a smaller screen can be more tiring on the eyes, as by default, it is displayed proportionally smaller than on a larger screen. It is possible to change the size of the screen display, but this will lead to less material being displayed on the screen. See pages 50-51 to see how to change the screen resolution, and text display size.

Weight

Unless you are buying a laptop to replace a desktop, weight should not be too much of an issue as most models are similar in this respect. However, make sure you physically feel the laptop before you buy it.

If you are going to be traveling a lot with your laptop then a lighter, ultrabook type, may be the best option. When considering this, take into account the weight of any type of case that you will use to carry the laptop, as this will add to the overall weight.

Getting Comfortable

Since you will probably be using your laptop in more than one location, the issue of finding a comfortable working position can be vital, particularly as you cannot put the keyboard and monitor in different positions as you can with a desktop computer. Whenever you are using your laptop try to make sure that you are sitting in a comfortable position, with your back well supported, and that the laptop is in a position where you can reach the keyboard easily and also see the screen without straining.

Working comfortably at a laptop involves a combination of a good chair, good posture and good positioning of the laptop.

Despite the possible temptation to do so, avoid using your laptop in bed, on your lap, or where you have to slouch or strain to reach the laptop properly:

If possible, the best place to work at a laptop is at a dedicated desk or workstation.

Seating position

The ideal way to sit at a laptop is with an office-type chair that offers good support for your back. Even with these types of chairs it is important to maintain a good body position so that your back is straight and your head is pointing forwards.

If you do not have an office-type chair, use a chair with a straight back and place a cushion behind you for extra support and comfort as required.

One of the advantages of office-type chairs is that the height can usually be adjusted, and this can be a great help in achieving a comfortable position.

...cont'd

Laptop position

When working at your laptop it is important to have it positioned so that both the keyboard and the screen are in a comfortable position. If the keyboard is too low then you will have to slouch or strain to reach it:

Take regular breaks when working with a laptop and stop working if you experience aches, or pins and needles in your arms or legs.

If the keyboard is too high, your arms will be stretching. This could lead to pain in your tendons:

The ideal setup is to have the laptop in a position where you can sit with your forearms and wrists as level as possible while you are typing on the keyboard:

Adjusting the screen

Another factor in working comfortably at a laptop is the position of the screen. Unlike with a desktop computer, it is not feasible to have a laptop screen at eye level, as this would result in the keyboard being in too high a position. Instead, once you have achieved a comfortable seating position, open the screen so that it is approximately 90 degrees from your eye line:

Find a comfortable body position and adjust your laptop's position to this, rather than vice versa.

One problem with laptop screens is that they can reflect glare from sunlight or indoor lighting:

Most modern laptops have screens with an anti-glare coating. However, even this will not be very effective against bright sunlight that is shining directly onto the screen.

If this happens, either change your position, or block out the light source using some form of blind or shade. Avoid squinting at a screen that is reflecting glare as this will quickly give you a headache.

Carrying a Laptop

As laptops are designed for mobility, it is safe to assume that they will have to be carried around at some point. Because of the weight of even the lightest laptops, it can be uncomfortable to carry a laptop for an extended period of time. To try to minimize this, it is important to follow a few rules:

If you are carrying your laptop for a long period of time make sure that you take regular breaks, otherwise you may cause yourself a strain or an injury.

- Carry the laptop with a carry case that is designed for this task (or a double-strapped backpack)
- Carry the laptop on one side of your body and move it from side to side if necessary

- Do not cross the strap over your shoulders and try not to carry too many other items at the same time

If you place your laptop with another piece of luggage, make sure that you keep it with you at all times, so as to minimize the chance of theft.

If you are traveling with your laptop you might be able to incorporate it into your luggage, particularly if it can be moved on wheels.

Keyboard and Touch Pad

Laptops have the same basic data input devices as desktop computers, i.e. a keyboard and a mouse. A laptop keyboard is very similar to a desktop one, although it is best to try the action of the keys before you buy a particular laptop, to ensure that they are not too "soft", i.e. that there is enough resistance when they are pressed.

One of the main differences between a laptop and a desktop computer is the mouse (or pointing device) that controls the on-screen cursor. In the early days of laptops, some of them had a small control stick to move the cursor. However, these have been almost universally replaced by touch pads, which are small, sensitive, square or rectangular pads that are activated by stroking a finger over them to move the cursor. It sometimes takes a bit of practice to get used to them but after a little experience they can be as effective as a traditional mouse. When using a keyboard or touch pad, avoid having your fingers too high:

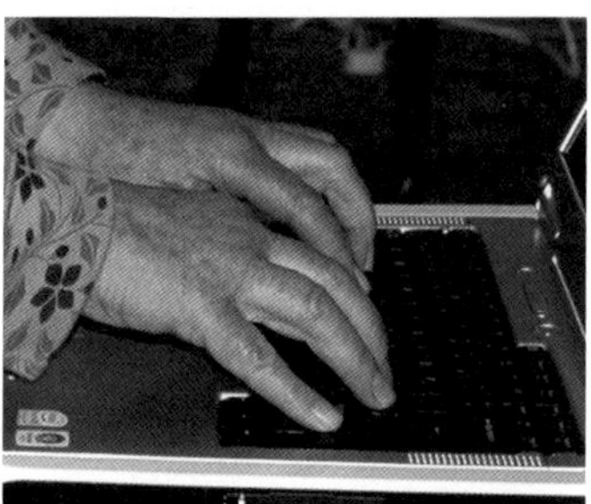

Instead, keep your hands and fingers as flat as possible over the keyboard and the touch pad:

Laptop keyboards contain the same functionality as any standard computer keyboard. However, most manufacturers have keyboards with functions that are specific to their own laptops. If this is the case, the functionality will be explained in the laptop's manual.

Using an External Mouse

Not everyone likes touch pads as a means of moving the cursor on a laptop, and it is true they can sometimes be slightly fiddly and prone to erratic movement if the control is too jerky. The good news is that it is possible to use a conventional mouse with a laptop to move the cursor.

A mouse can be connected to a laptop via one of the suitable sockets (ports) at the back or side of the laptop. These are usually in the form of USB ports:

It is certainly worth persevering with a laptop's touch pad, even if it seems very frustrating at first. Once you have found the correct pressure to apply, it will become much easier to control.

Once the mouse has been connected to the laptop it can be used in exactly the same way as with a desktop computer. In some cases it is possible to add a wireless mouse, which can be used without the need for a cable:

Ports and Slots

Most laptops have a slightly bewildering array of sockets and slots for connecting external devices. These sockets are known as ports, and they come in a variety of shapes and sizes for different devices and uses:

- **USB**. This is a method for connecting a variety of external devices such as digital cameras, MP3 music players, scanners and printers. The latest standard in widespread use is USB 2.0, and this has largely replaced parallel and serial ports in terms of connecting devices such as printers or an external mouse.
- **FireWire**. This is a similar method of data transfer to a USB but it is much faster. For this reason it is generally used for devices that need to transfer larger amounts of data, such as digital video cameras.
- **Ethernet**. This can be used as a cable connection to your internet router, rather than using a Wi-Fi connection.
- **HDMI (High-Definition Multimedia Interface)**. This can be used to connect to compatible digital devices, including high-definition TVs. This enables you to view whatever is on your laptop screen on a television, and is a good option for watching movies or displaying photos.
- **Memory card readers**. These are used for downloading photos from memory cards from digital cameras or smartphones. Some laptops only have an SD card slot, since these are most commonly used. If you need to attach a multi-card reader for different types of memory card, this can be done using a USB port.

The main slot on a laptop is:

- **CD/DVD players or re-writers**. These can be used to play music CDs or watch videos on a DVD. They can also be used to copy data to blank CDs or DVDs. This is a good option for backing up items that you want to keep, such as photos.

Some laptops now come equipped with USB 3.0 ports. These can still be used with USB 2.0 (or earlier) devices but they will also work with any USB 3.0 devices.

Not all laptops have a CD/DVD player, although external CD/DVD drives can be connected.

The Wonder of Wireless

For anyone who has struggled with a tangle of computer cables and wires, the advent of wireless technology has been one of the great computing breakthroughs of recent years.

Wireless technology does exactly what the name suggests: it allows a wireless-enabled computer to communicate with other similarly-enabled devices, such as other computers, printers or an internet connection. First of all, the devices have to be set up as a network, i.e. they have to be linked together so that they know they should be communicating with each other. Once this has been done, files can be shared or sent to the printer, and the internet browsed, all without the need to connect the devices using a cable.

One concern about hotspots is security. This is because if you can access a network wirelessly, someone else could then also access your laptop and data. Many hotspots have software in place to try to stop this.

In order to be part of a wireless network, a laptop must have a wireless capability. Most modern laptops come with wireless cards already installed; otherwise, they can be installed in any available expansion slot.

Hotspots

One of the great growth areas of wireless technology is hotspots. These are public areas that have been set up to distribute the internet wirelessly. This means that anyone with a wireless card in their laptop can, if they are within a certain range, access the internet in a variety of public places. These include:

- Coffee shops
- Airports
- Hotels
- Libraries
- Supermarkets

For more details about Wi-Fi and networks, see Chapter Nine.

Hotspots operate using Wi-Fi technology, which is the method by which the signal from the network is transferred to individual users. Most hotspots have a limited range of approximately 100 yards. Some are free to use, while others charge a fee, depending on usage.

Cleaning a Laptop

Like most things, laptops benefit greatly from a little care and attention. The two most important areas to keep clean are the screen and the keyboard.

Cleaning the screen

All computer screens quickly collect dust and fingerprints, and laptops are no different. If this is left too long it can make the screen harder to read, causing eye strain and headaches. Clean the screen regularly with the following cleaning materials:

- A lint-free cloth, similar to the type used to clean camera lenses (it is important not to scratch the screen in any way).
- An alcohol-free cleaning fluid that is recommended for computer screens.
- Screen wipes, again that are recommended for use on computer screens.

The outer casing of a laptop can be cleaned with the same fluid as used for the screen. Equally effective can be a duster or a damp (but not wet) cloth and warm water. Keep soap away from laptops if possible.

Cleaning the keyboard

Keyboards are notorious for accumulating dust, fluff and crumbs. One way to solve this problem is to turn the laptop upside down and very gently shake it to loosen any foreign objects. Failing this, a can of condensed air can be used with a narrow nozzle to blow out any stubborn items that remain lodged in the keys.

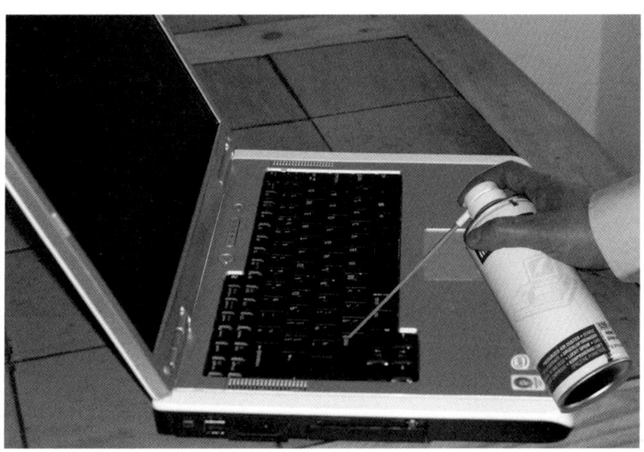

Choosing a Carry Case

When you are transporting your laptop it could be placed in any convenient bag, such as a backpack, a duffle bag or even a large handbag. However, there are several advantages to using a proper laptop carry case:

- It will probably be more comfortable when you are carrying it, as it is designed specifically for this job.
- The laptop will be more secure, as it should fit properly in the case.
- You should be able to keep all of your laptop accessories together in one case.

When choosing a carry case, look for one that fits your laptop well and has a strap to keep it secure inside:

A laptop case should also be lockable, either with its own internal lock, or with a fastening through which a padlock can be put.

Also, make sure that there are enough additional spaces and pockets for accessories, such as cables and an external mouse. Finally, choosing a case with a padded shoulder strap will be of considerable benefit if you have to carry your laptop for any length of time.

Spares and Accessories

Whenever you are going anywhere with your laptop, there are always spares and accessories to consider. Some of these are just nice things to have, while others could be essential to ensure that you can still use your laptop if anything goes wrong while you are on your travels. Items to consider for putting in your laptop case include:

For more information on batteries see Chapter Ten.

- **Spare battery**. This is probably the most important spare if you are going to be away from home for any length of time, and particularly if you think you may be unable to access a power supply for a period of time, and so be unable to charge your laptop battery. Like all batteries, laptop batteries slowly lose power over time and do not keep their charge for as long as when they are new. It is a good idea to always keep an eye on how much battery power you have left and, if you are running low, try to conserve as much energy as possible. Although laptop batteries are bulky and heavy, carrying a spare could mean the difference between frustration and relief, if you are left with no battery power and no charging options.
- **Power cable**. This is the cable that can be used to power the laptop when it is not being run on battery power. It usually consists of a cable and a power adapter, which makes it rather bulky and heavy. Whenever possible, this should be used rather than the internal battery, and it should be kept with the laptop at all times.

...cont'd

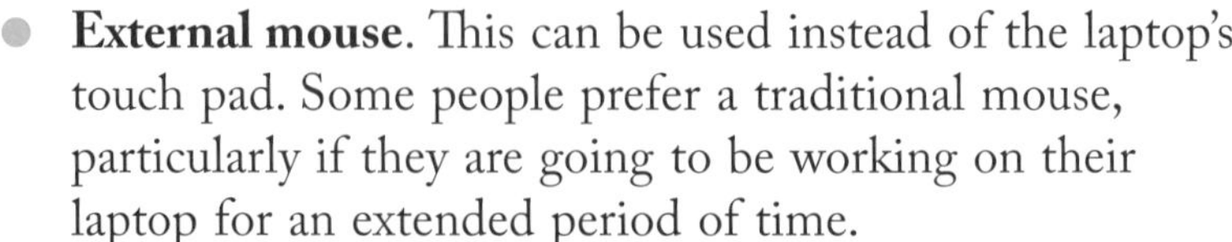

- **External mouse**. This can be used instead of the laptop's touch pad. Some people prefer a traditional mouse, particularly if they are going to be working on their laptop for an extended period of time.
- **Multi-card reader**. If you do not have a built-in multi-card reader (see page 21) an external one can be used to download photos from a digital camera memory card. This will connect via a USB port.

It is important that headphones are comfortable to wear for an extended period of time. In general, the types that fit over the ears are more comfortable than the "bud" variety that is inserted into the ear.

- **Headphones**. These can be used to listen to music or films if you are in the company of other people and you do not want to disturb them. They can also be very useful if there are distracting noises coming from other people.
- **USB flash drive**. This is a small device that can be used to copy data to and from your laptop. It connects via a USB port and is about the size of a packet of chewing gum. It is an excellent way of backing up files from your laptop when you are away from home.

Backing up (see pages 180-181) is the process of copying folders and files from your laptop onto an external device for safekeeping in case the folders and files on the laptop are deleted or corrupted.

- **Cleaning material**. The materials described on page 23 can be taken to ensure your laptop is always in tip-top condition for use.
- **DVDs/CDs**. Video or music DVDs and CDs can be taken to provide mobile entertainment, and blank ones can be taken to copy data onto, similar to using a USB flash drive.

2 Around a Laptop

This chapter shows how to quickly become familiar with your laptop, and Windows 10. It gives an overview of Windows 10 so that you can become comfortable with this new environment and confidently use the reinstalled Start Menu and the Windows apps. It also looks at personalizing Windows 10 to exactly the way you want it.

Opening Up and Turning On

Open the screen of your laptop carefully, so as not to put any unnecessary pressure on the connection between the screen and the main body of the laptop.

The first step towards getting started with a new laptop is to open it ready for use. The traditional clamshell design keeps the screen and keyboard together through the use of an internal clip or connector. This can be released by a button on the exterior of the laptop, which is usually positioned at the front or side. Some laptops have a magnetic connection between the screen and the main body.

Once the screen has been opened it can then be positioned ready for use. The screen should stay in any position in which it is placed:

Press the power button with one firm, definite motion. If you accidentally press it twice in quick succession, the laptop may turn on and then shut down immediately afterwards.

The power button for turning on a laptop, ready for use, is usually located near to the keyboard:

The laptop can be turned on by pushing this button firmly. The laptop will then probably make a sound, to indicate that it has been turned on, and begin loading the operating system (the software that is used to run and manage all of the laptop's apps, folders and files). Once the laptop has completed its startup procedure the opening screen should be displayed. At this point the laptop is ready for use.

Most laptops will take a couple of minutes to start up and be fully ready to use.

Touchscreen Laptops

Windows 10 is the latest operating system from Microsoft and this will be installed on most new laptops. It is optimized for touchscreen use, so it is ideal for using with laptops with touchscreen capability and also with Windows 10 tablets.

Touchscreen laptops still have a traditional keyboard but navigation can also be done by tapping, swiping and pinching on the screen. Some of the functions that can be performed on a touchscreen laptop are:

- Activate a button, such as Done or OK, by tapping on it. Apps on the Windows 10 interface can also be accessed by tapping on them from the Start Menu.
- Move up and down long pages by swiping in the required direction, e.g. to navigate around web pages.
- Zoom in and out of pages by pinching inwards, or outwards, with thumb and forefinger (if the open app has this functionality). It is most commonly used for zooming in and out of web pages.

The Microsoft Surface Pro 4 tablet also runs on Windows 10, and it is a realistic option in terms of replacing a regular laptop.

Touchscreen laptops are a realistic option for users who want to get the most out of the functionality of Windows 10. Some laptop manufacturers to look at are:

- Acer
- Dell
- HP
- Lenovo
- Sony
- Toshiba

A number of touchscreen models can also be converted into tablet mode, either by revolving the screen, or detaching the keyboard. There are also some hybrid models, with a detachable screen that can be used as either a tablet, or a traditional laptop with the keyboard attached.

About Windows 10

Windows 8 was one of the most significant changes to the Windows operating system since Windows 95 helped redefine the way that we look at personal computers. It aimed to bring the desktop and mobile computing environments together, principally with the brightly colored Start screen and Charms bar. However, this proved to be awkward for a lot of users, with Windows 8 not fully meeting the needs of the devices they were using.

With Windows 10, it is possible to synchronize Windows 10 so that all of your settings and apps will be available over multiple devices through an online Microsoft Account.

The Windows 10 interface has been redesigned so that it looks as similar as possible, regardless of whether it is being used on a desktop computer with a mouse and keyboard, or on a mobile or touchscreen device (and most of the underlying functionality is still the same).

Windows 10 will look more familiar to users of pre-Windows 8 versions of Windows. It opens at the Desktop, where shortcuts to items can be placed, and the Taskbar is at the bottom of the screen. The Start screen format and the Charms bar have also been replaced with more traditional elements of the Windows operating system, including the reinstated Start Menu.

Start Menu

The Start Menu has also been reinstated in Windows 10. This will be more familiar to pre-Windows 8 users, although it has been redesigned so that it also includes a range of colored tiles, which can be pinned to the Start Menu, and then used to access the most commonly-used apps. The left-hand side of the Start Menu contains links to some of your most frequently used functions (such as the Power button) and most used apps.

For users of laptops, the version of Windows 10 used is much more similar to the interface for earlier versions, such as Windows 7 and earlier. There is also a version for touchscreen devices, such as the Microsoft Surface, where much of the screen navigation can be done by tapping, swiping and pinching on the screen.

Obtaining Windows 10

Windows 10 is a departure by Microsoft in that it is being promoted as an online service, rather than just a standalone operating system. This means that, by default, Windows 10 is obtained and downloaded online, with subsequent updates and upgrades provided on a regular basis.

The three main options for obtaining Windows 10 are:

- **Upgrade** – Replace an older version of Windows, retaining the installed applications and settings. This can only be done with Windows 7 and later: for earlier versions you will need to install a new, full, copy of Windows 10. **If you already have Windows 7 or 8.1 it is free to upgrade to Windows 10**.
- **Clean Install** – This has to be done if you have Windows XP or Windows Vista and you want to upgrade to Windows 10. (See tip.)
- **Pre-install** – Buy a new PC or laptop with Windows 10 already installed, then install the required apps.

For users of Windows 7 or 8.1, Windows 10 is a free upgrade (as long as you upgrade within a year of its release on 29 July 2015). Ensure Windows Update is turned on within Settings to ensure you are informed about the upgrade. When it is available you will be notified and you will be able to download and install the free upgrade. Once it has been installed you will receive updates as they become available. (In some cases, there may be a Get Windows 10 app located at the right-hand side of the Taskbar that can be used to obtain the upgrade to Windows 10).

Two of the steps that the installation will go through are:

- **Personalize**. These are settings that will be applied to your version of Windows 10. You can choose to have express settings applied, or customize them.
- **Microsoft Account**. You can set up a Microsoft Account during installation, or once you have started using Windows 10.

Windows 7 Enterprise and Windows 8/8.1 Enterprise are excluded from the free upgrade.

If you have a version of Windows that is earlier than Windows 7 (e.g. Vista or XP) you will have to pay for the upgrade to Windows 10. This will be with a DVD and cost US$119 (£99). This requires a clean install which means that your files and settings will be removed. It is essential that these are backed up before the installation is started.

You may need your license number for the free upgrade from Windows 7 or 8.1.

The Start Button

The familiar Windows Start Button was removed in Windows 8, but it has returned in Windows 10. It is also the point for accessing the Start Menu, which has also returned, in an enhanced format.

Using the Start Button

The Start Button provides access to the apps on your Windows 10 laptop, frequently accessed items and also the enhanced Start Menu:

1. Click on the **Start Button** in the bottom left-hand corner of the screen

2. The **Start Menu** is displayed

3. The left-hand side of the Start Menu contains links to frequently used apps and a list of quick links to items such as the Power button and All apps (these can be customized within the **Personalization > Start** section of the Settings app)

4. The right-hand side of the Start Menu is where apps can be pinned so that they are always available. This is displayed as a collection of large, colored tiles

5. Other items can also be accessed from the Start Button by right-clicking on it

Hot tip

Tiles on the right-hand side of the Start Menu are displayed in groups. Tiles can be dragged in and out of different groups. To change the name of a group, double-click on its name and overtype with a new one. Whole groups can be moved by dragging their top title bar to a new position on the Start Menu.

Start Button functionality

Although the Start Button is different to earlier versions of Windows, it still has a range of functionality:

1. Right-click on the **Start Button** to view its menu

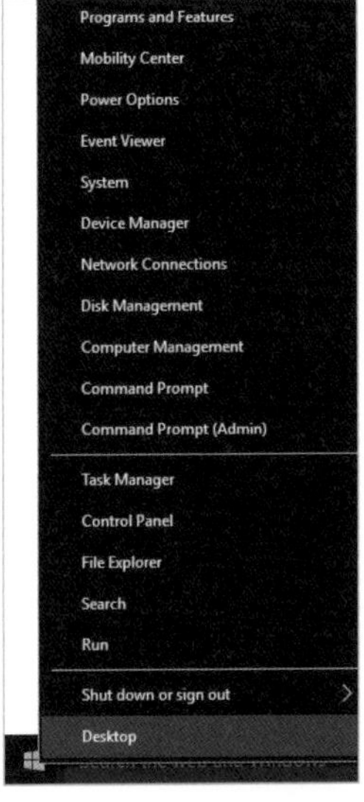

The Start Button menu in Step 1 has a number of options for accessing system functions, such as Command Prompt and Disk Management.

2. Click on the relevant buttons to view items including the **Desktop** and **Control Panel**

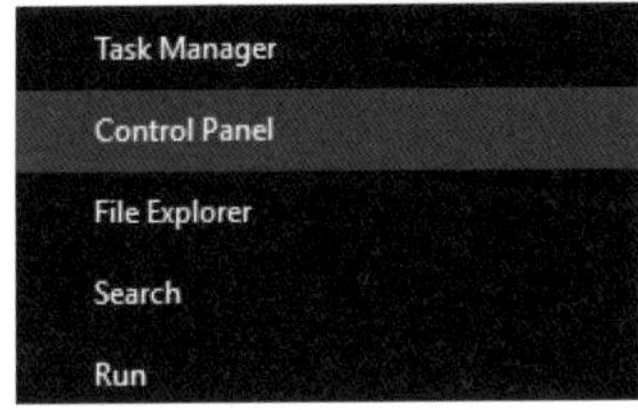

Click on the **Power** button on the Start Menu to specify actions to be taken when you press your computer's power button.

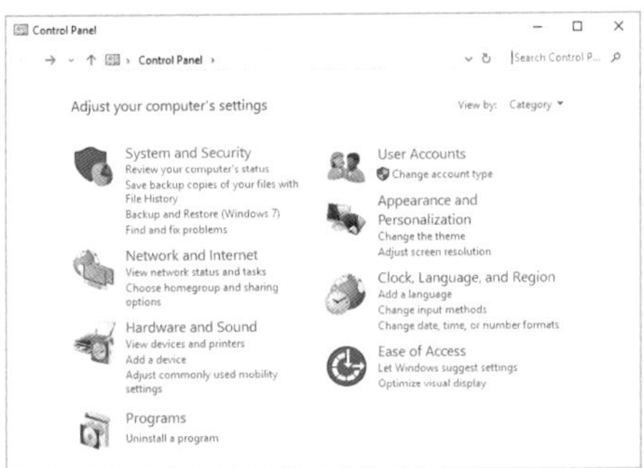

3. Shut down options are also available from the **Start Button** (see page 41)

The Start Menu

The reinstated Start Menu in Windows 10 is where you can access areas within your computer, perform certain functions and also access all of the apps on your laptop:

1. Click here to access your own account settings or sign out from your account

2. Your most frequently used apps are displayed here. Click on one to open it (these items will change as you use different apps)

Apps can also be pinned to the Start Menu so that they remain there permanently, see page 36 for details.

3. Click here to access items including the **File Explorer**, your **Documents** library within File Explorer and the Windows 10 **Settings**

4. Click on the **Power** button for options to **Sleep**, **Shut Down** or **Restart** your computer

5. Click on the **All apps** button to access a list of all of the apps on your computer. Use the scroll bar at the right-hand side to move through the list of apps

6. Click on a letter heading to view an alphabetic grid. Click on a letter to move to that section

7. Click on the **Back** button to return to the standard Start Menu view

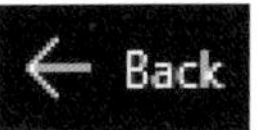

If there is a down-pointing arrow next to an app this means that there are additional items that can be accessed. Click on the arrow to view these.

Pinning Items

In most cases, you will want to have quick access to a variety of apps on the Start Menu and also the Taskbar at the bottom of the screen. To do this:

1. Click on the Start Button and click on the **All apps** button

2. Right-click on an app and click on the **Pin to Start** button

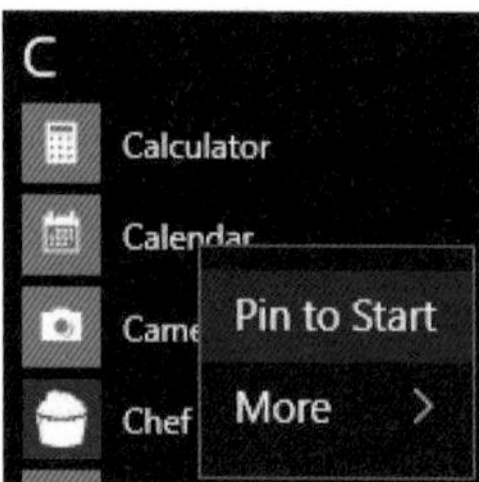

3. The apps tile is added to the Start Menu)

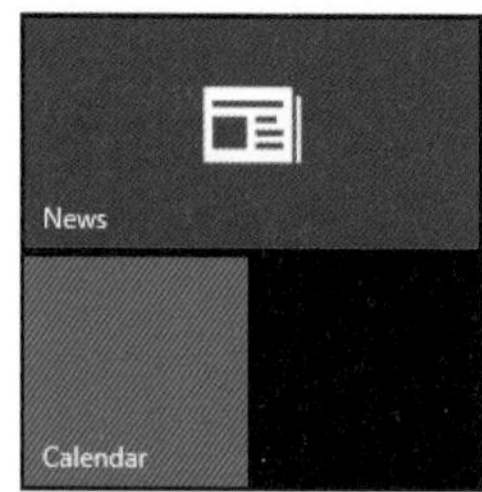

4. Right-click on an app and click on **More > Pin to taskbar**

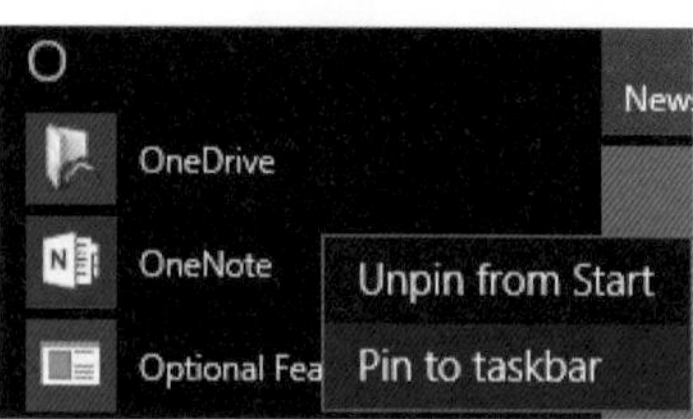

5. The app's icon is added to the Taskbar and it can be opened directly from here

Tiles on the Start Menu can be resized by right-clicking on them and clicking on the **Resize** button. The resizing options are **Small**, **Medium**, **Wide** and **Large**, although not all options can be applied to all apps.

Using Live Tiles

Before any of the Windows 10 apps have been used, they are depicted on the Start Menu with tiles of solid color. However, once you open an app it activates the Live Tile feature (if it is supported by that app). This enables the tile to display real-time information from the app, even when it is not the app currently being used. This means that you can view information from your apps, directly from the Start Menu. To use Live Tiles:

The apps with Live Tile functionality include: Mail, People, Calendar, Photos, Groove Music, News, Sport and Money. Some of these, such as Mail, require you to first set up an account before Live Tiles can be fully activated.

1. Right-click on a tile to select it. If it has Live Tile functionality, click on the **Turn live tile on** button to activate this feature

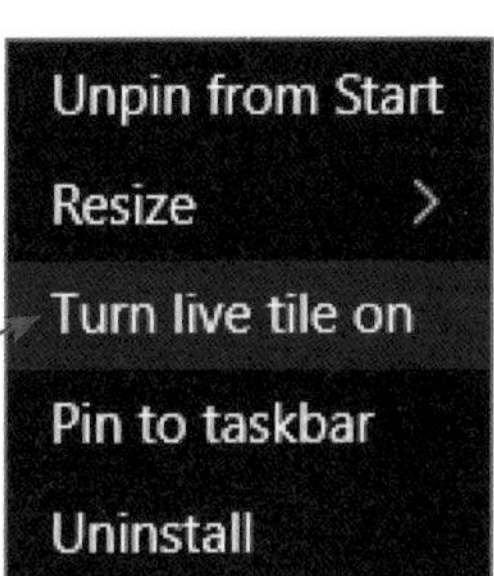

2. Live Tiles display real-time text and images from the selected apps. These are updated when there is new information available via the app

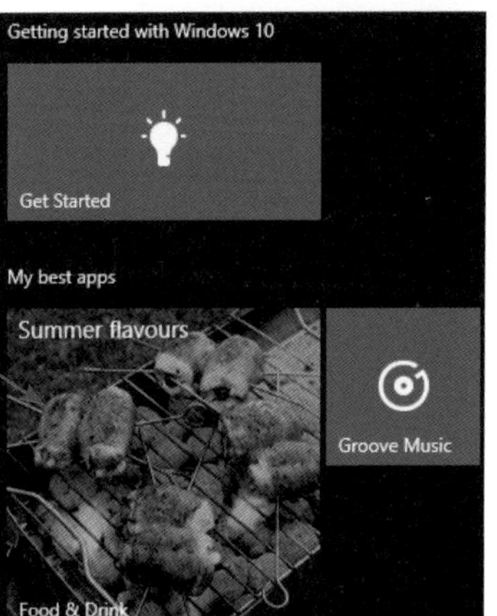

3. To turn off a Live Tile, right-click on a tile to select it and click on the **Turn live tile off** button

If you have too many Live Tiles activated at the same time it can become distracting and annoying, with a lot of movement on the Start Menu.

The Desktop and Taskbar

The Windows Desktop is once again an integral part of Windows and is visible when you turn on your laptop. This also displays the Taskbar, at the bottom of the screen.

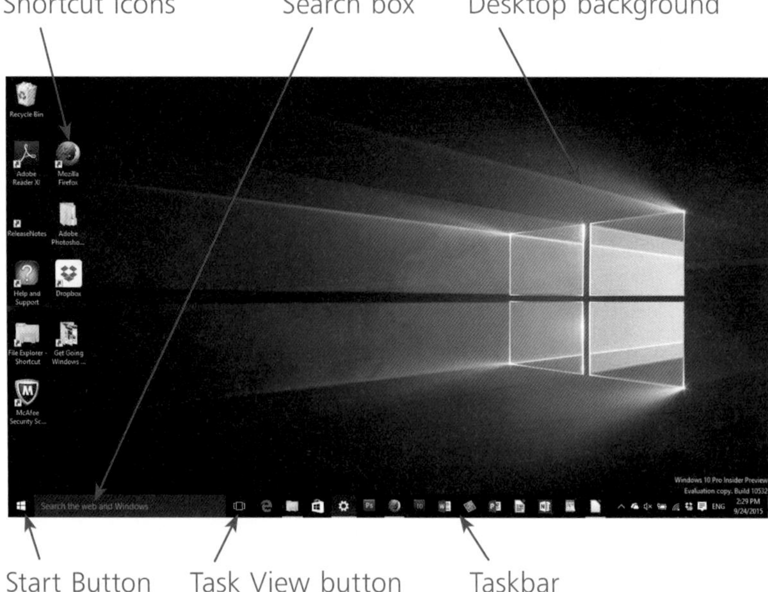

1. Click on this button on the Taskbar to access Task View, which displays minimized versions of the currently open apps

2. To show and hide the Task View button, right-click on the button and check On or Off the **Show Task View button** option

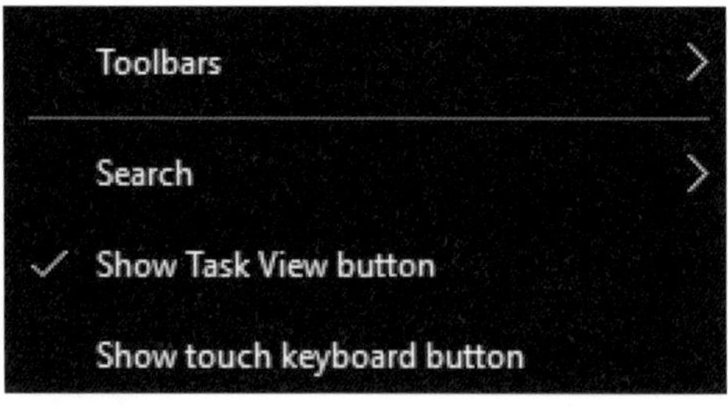

Hot tip

The Desktop can also be accessed by pressing the **WinKey** + **D** or by right-clicking on the Start Button and selecting **Desktop**.

The WinKey can be used to access the Start Menu at any time and also perform a number of tasks in conjunction with other keys.

If an app has two or more windows open, each of them will be displayed when you move the cursor over the app's icon on the Taskbar.

3. The Task View displays minimized versions of the currently open apps and windows

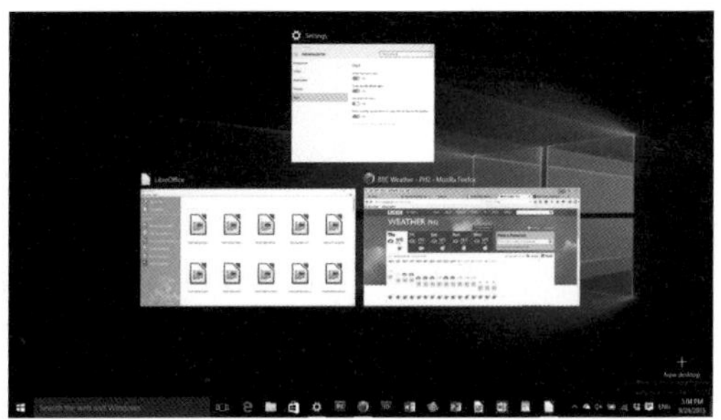

4. As more windows are opened, the format is arranged accordingly

5. If an app has more than one window open, e.g. File Manager, each window is displayed within Task View

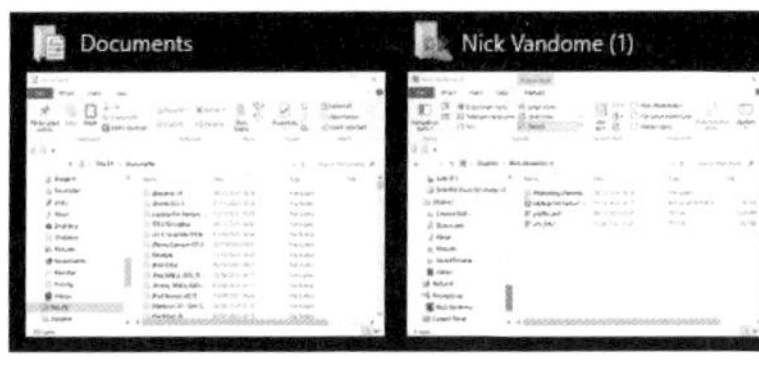

Apps can only be open on one desktop at a time. So if an app is open on one desktop and you try to open it on another, you will be taken to the already open app (see page 40 for multiple desktops).

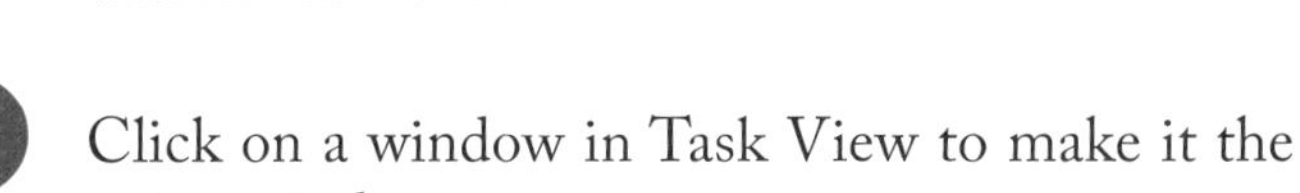

6. Click on a window in Task View to make it the active window

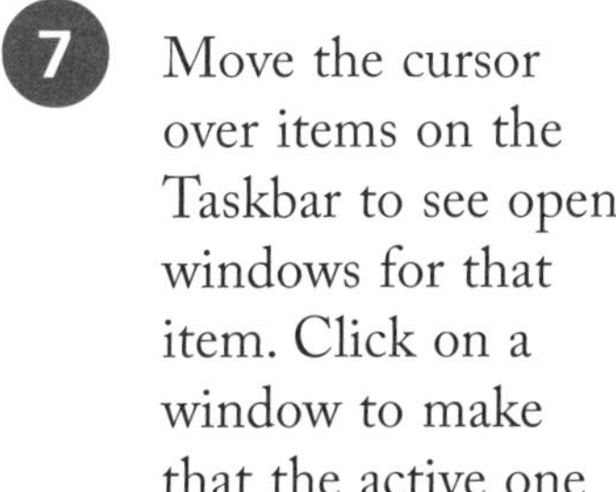

7. Move the cursor over items on the Taskbar to see open windows for that item. Click on a window to make that the active one

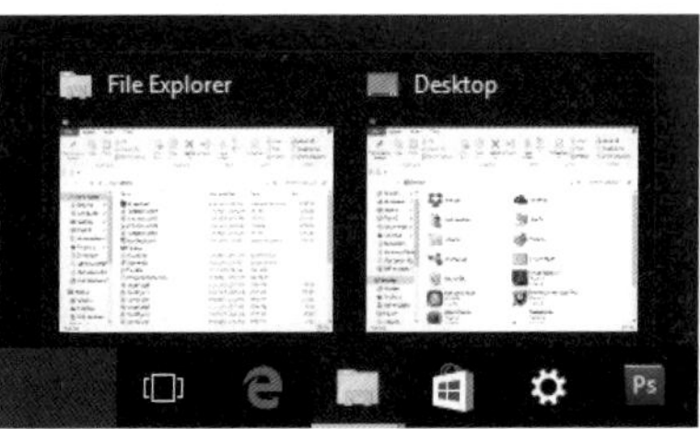

8. The notifications area at the right-hand side of the Taskbar has speaker, network and other system tools. Click on one to see more information about each item

Adding Desktops

Another function within Task View is for creating additional desktops. This can be useful if you want to separate different categories of tasks on your computer. For instance, you may want to keep your open entertainment apps on a different desktop from your productivity ones. To create additional desktops:

1. Click on the **Task View** button on the Taskbar

2. The current desktop is displayed with the open windows

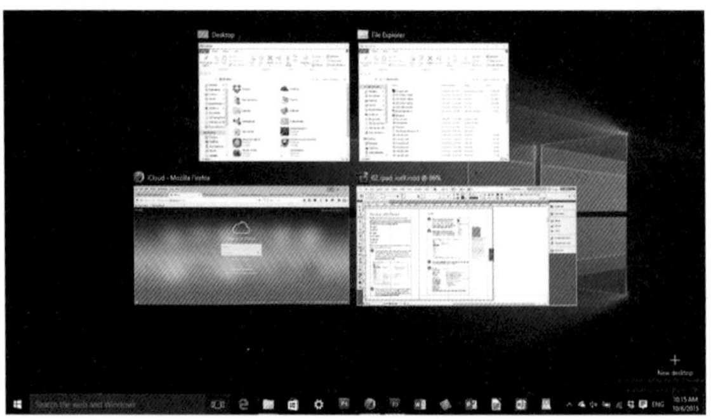

If you add too many desktops it may become confusing in terms of the content on each one.

3. Click on the **New desktop** button

4. The new desktop is displayed at the bottom of the Task View window

When you open an app on a new desktop, this is where it will be located, until it is shut down. It can then be opened on a different desktop, if required.

Shutting Down

The method of shutting down in Windows 8 was another contentious issue, and one which has been addressed in Windows 10 by adding this functionality to the Start Menu.

Shutting down from the Start Menu

1. Click on the **Start Button** 
2. Click on the **Power** button 

3. Click on either the **Sleep**, **Shut down** or **Restart** buttons

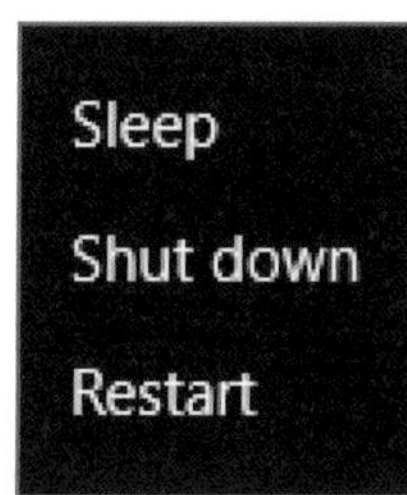

For some updates to Windows, you will need to restart your computer for them to take effect.

Shutting down from the Start Button

To shut down directly from the Start Button:

1. Right-click on the **Start Button > Shut down or sign out** and select either **Sign out**, **Sleep**, **Shut down** or **Restart**

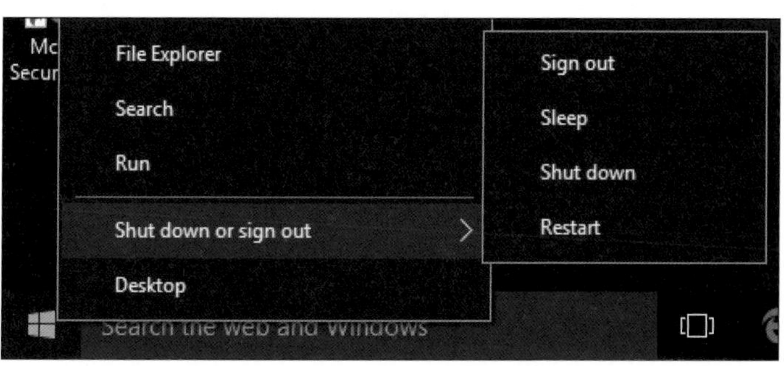

Using a Microsoft Account

We live in a world where computer users expect to be able to access their content wherever they are and share it with their friends and family in a variety of ways, whether it is by email, messaging or photo sharing. This is known as cloud computing, with content being stored on online servers, from where it can be accessed by authorized users.

In Windows 10, this type of connectivity is achieved with a Microsoft Account. This is a registration system (which can be set up with most email addresses and a password) which provides access to a number of services via the Windows 10 apps. These include:

Beware

Without a Windows Account you will not be able to access the full functionality of the apps listed here.

- **Mail**. This is the Windows 10 email app which can be used to access and manage your different email accounts.
- **Skype**. This is the text messaging and video calling app.
- **People**. This is the address book app.
- **Calendar**. This is the calendar and organizer app.
- **The Windows Store**. This is the online store for previewing and downloading additional apps.
- **OneDrive**. This is the online backup and sharing service.

Creating a Microsoft Account

It is free to create a Microsoft Account and can be done with an email address and, together with a password, this provides a unique identifier for logging into your Microsoft Account. There are several ways in which you can create and set up a Microsoft Account:

Hot tip

Microsoft Account details can also be used as your sign-in for Windows 10.

- During the initial setup of Windows 10. You will be asked if you want to create a Microsoft Account.
- When you first open an app that requires access to a Microsoft Account. When you do this you will be prompted to create a new account.
- From the **Accounts** section of the **Settings** app (for more information about the Settings app see page 58).

Whichever way you use to create a Microsoft Account, the process is similar:

1. When you are first prompted to sign in with a Microsoft Account you can enter your account details, if you have one, or

Sign in with your Microsoft account. You can use this account with other apps on this device. Learn more.

someone@example.com

Password

Forgot my password

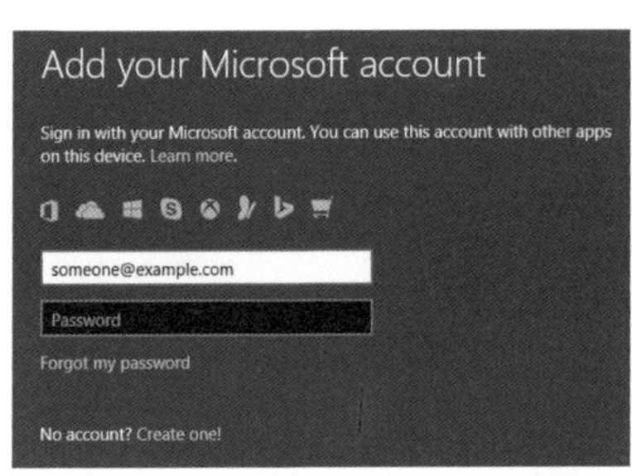

2. Click on the **No account? Create one!** link

3. Enter your name, an email address and a password for your Microsoft Account

Windows, Office, Outlook.com, OneDrive, Skype, Xbox. They're all better and more personal when you sign in with your Microsoft account.* Learn more

Nick | Vandome

✓ After you sign up, we'll send you a message with a link to verify this user name.

nickvandome2@gmail.com
Get a new email address

••••••••

United States

Birth month | Day | Year

Back | Next

4. Click on the **Next** button to move through the registration process

5. Enter your password again to confirm your account

6. Click on the **Next** button to move to the final window to complete setting up your Microsoft Account

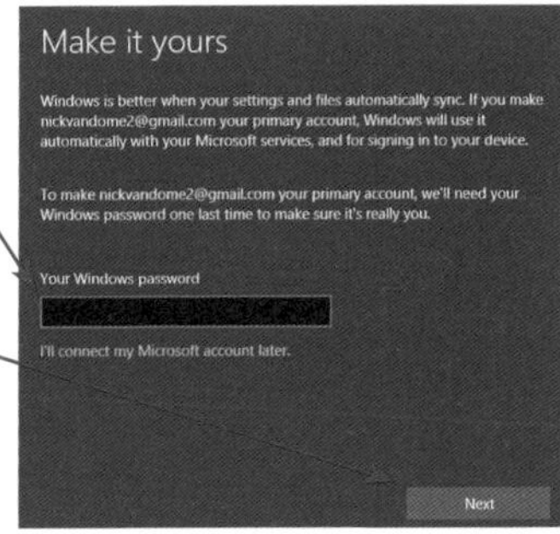

Make it yours
Windows is better when your settings and files automatically sync. If you make nickvandome2@gmail.com your primary account, Windows will use it automatically with your Microsoft services, and for signing in to your device.
To make nickvandome2@gmail.com your primary account, we'll need your Windows password one last time to make sure it's really you.
Your Windows password
I'll connect my Microsoft account later.
Next

If you create a Microsoft Account when accessing a related app, the sign-up process will take you to the online Account Live web page, but the process is similar. In both cases you will be able to log in to the Account Live web page too, at **https://login.live.com** You can also access your account details at **https://account.live.com**

You can manage your Microsoft Account, and add other users, within the **Accounts** section of the **Settings** app.

Personalizing Windows 10

The Settings app in Windows 10 can be used to customize certain elements of your system's appearance, so that you can give it your own look and feel. There are also several other options within the Settings app and these are looked at on pages 58-59. To personalize the look of Windows 10:

1. Click on the **Settings** app (from either the Start Menu or on the Taskbar)

2. Click on the **Personalization** button

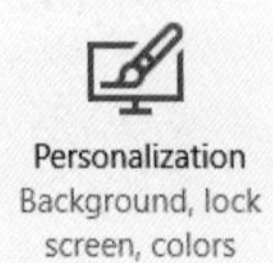

Background

To set the Desktop background:

The Desktop background can also be a solid color or a slideshow of photos. This is selected in the **Background** box in Step 1.

1. Click on the **Background** button (on the left panel) to select a desktop background. Select **Picture** in the Background box and click here to select a picture, or

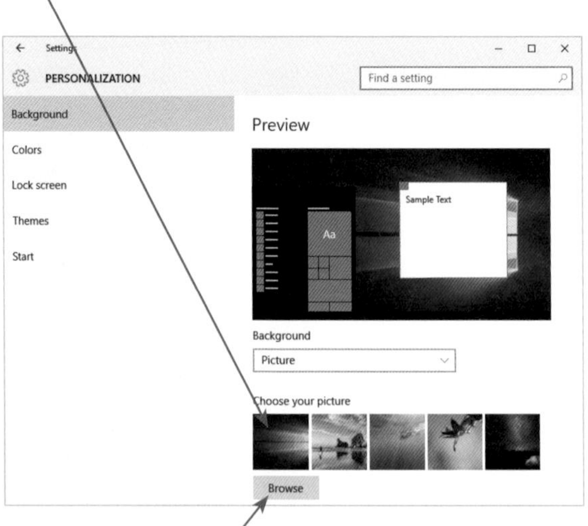

2. Click on the **Browse** button to select one of your own pictures

3. The background selected in Steps 1 or 2 is applied as the Desktop background

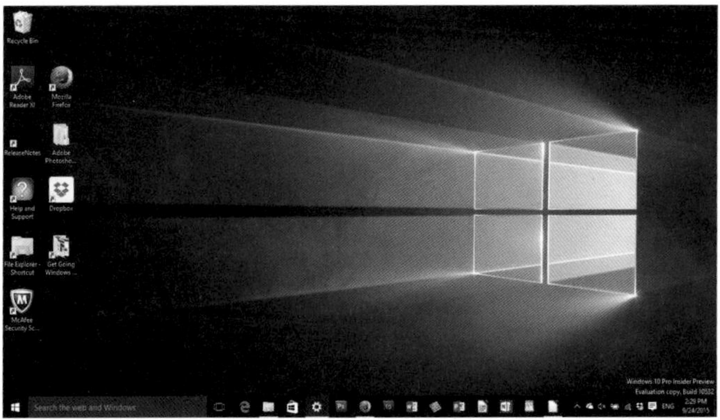

In Windows 10, more of the personalization options have been moved into the Settings app. However, there are still some options within the Control Panel, including themes, sounds and the screen saver.

Colors

To select colors for various Windows 10 elements:

1. Click on the **Colors** button to select an accent color for the current background, Start Menu and Taskbar

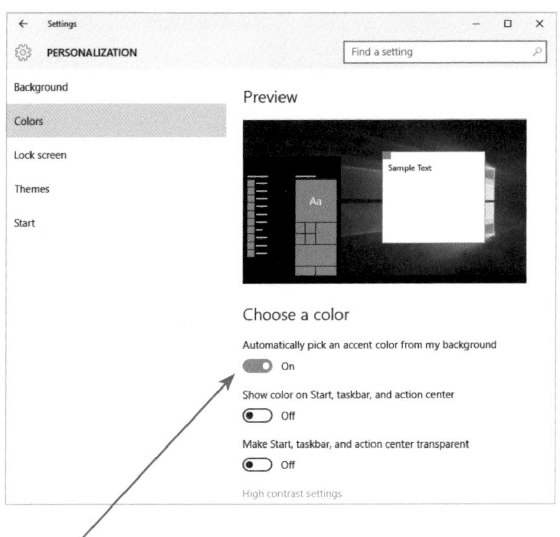

2. Drag this button to **Off** to disable the automatic selection for the accent color

...cont'd

3. Click on one of the colors to select it for the accent color. A preview is shown in the top panel

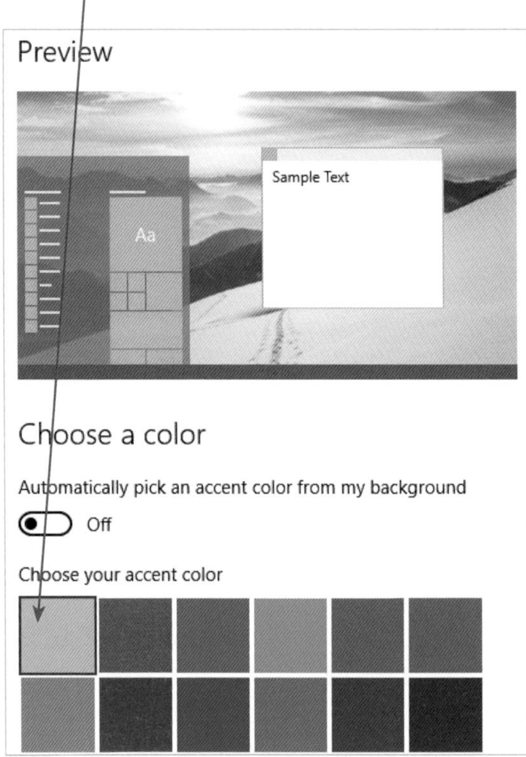

4. Drag this button **On** to use the color selected in Step 3 on the Start Menu, Taskbar and Action Center

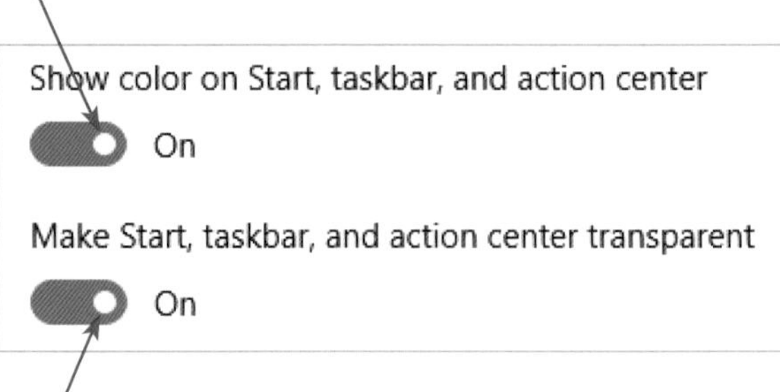

5. Drag this button **On** to make the Start Menu, Taskbar and Action Center transparent

The Action Center can be accessed from the Notifications icon on the Taskbar.

Lock screen

Settings can also be applied to the Lock screen (which is the screen that is visible when the screen locks because the laptop is not in use). To do this:

1. Click on the **Lock screen** button to select a background picture for the Lock screen
2. Click here to select a type of background

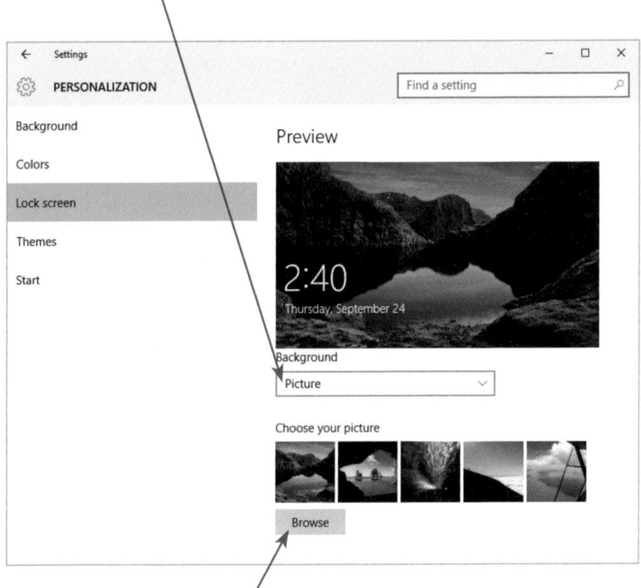

3. Click here to browse your own files to select one of your own pictures as the Lock screen background
4. Scroll down the Lock screen page and click on these buttons to select apps to show their quick or detailed statuses on the Lock screen

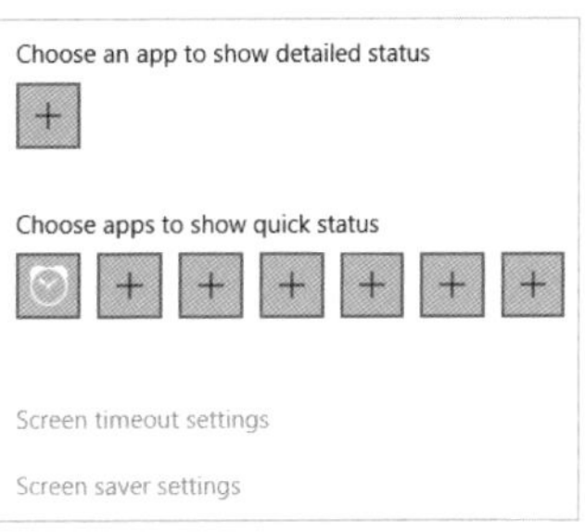

Another option for the background of the Lock screen in Step 2 is Windows Spotlight. This is a selection of photos selected by Windows and you can select whether you want to keep looking at similar photos or choose a new style.

Add the Mail or Calendar apps to the Lock screen in Step 4 so that new messages or calendar events are visible here (only one app can be added to the Lock screen in this way).

...cont'd

Themes

Color themes can be applied to a range of items, such as the color of buttons and scroll bars. This is done through the Control Panel, but this can still be accessed from the Settings app. To do this:

One of the related settings in the Themes section of the Settings app is for Desktop icons, where you can select specific icons to appear on the Desktop, or restore the default icon set.

1. Click on the **Themes** button to select a color theme for Windows 10. Some of these will be available from the **Theme settings** button, which links to themes used in previous versions of Windows

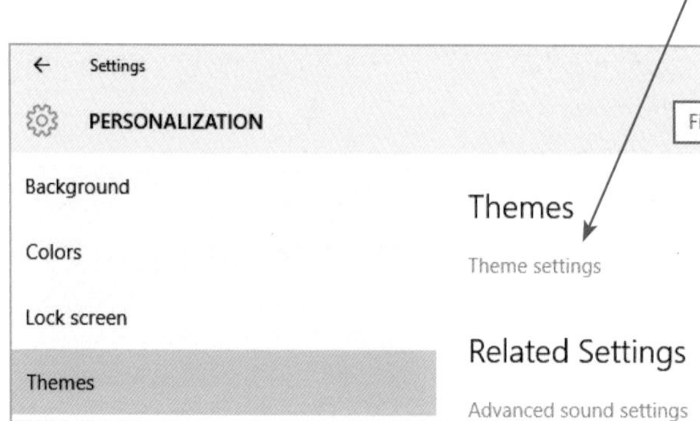

2. Click on one of the themes to view and apply it, or click on the **Get more themes online** link

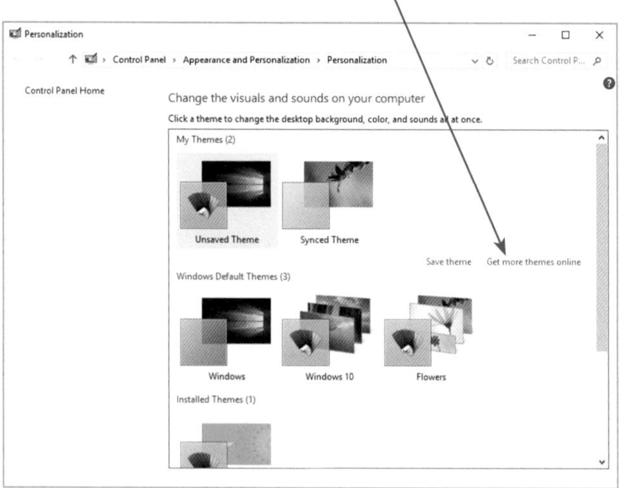

Start

The final personalization option is for the Start Menu.

1. Click on the **Start** button to select items that appear on the Start Menu. Click here to show most used and recently used apps on the Start Menu

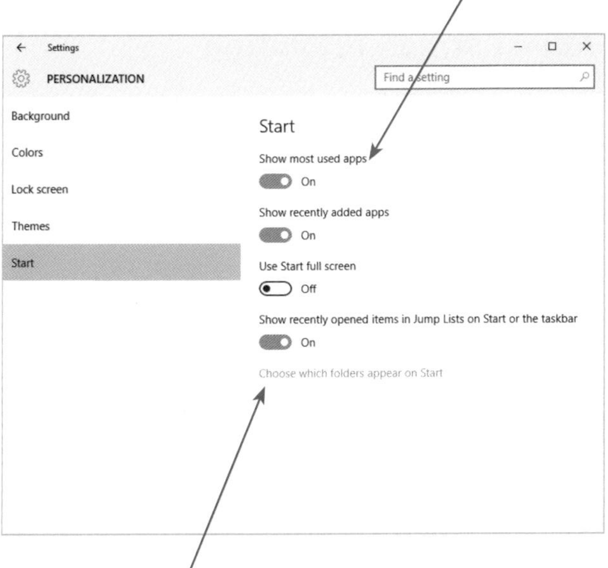

2. Click on **Choose which folders appear on Start** to select folders for the Start Menu

3. Drag these buttons **On** or **Off** to show or hide folders on the Start Menu

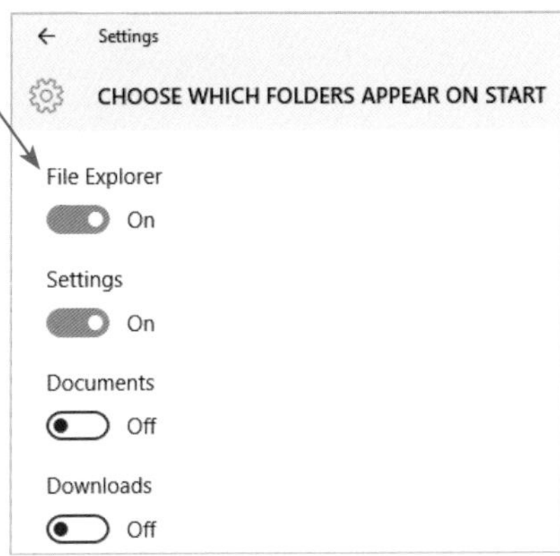

The **Use Start full screen** option in Step 1 is best used for tablet computers, and by default it is **Off**.

Folders appear at the bottom of the Start Menu, just above the Power button.

Screen Resolution

If you have a high resolution screen, you may find that the text as well as the icons are too small. You can increase the effective size by reducing the screen resolution.

To access the Control Panel, right-click on the **Start Button** and select it from the menu that appears. Right-click on the Control Panel button and select **Pin to Start** or **More > Pin to taskbar** to add it to these areas.

1. Access the Control Panel and select **Appearance and Personalization** and select **Adjust screen resolution**

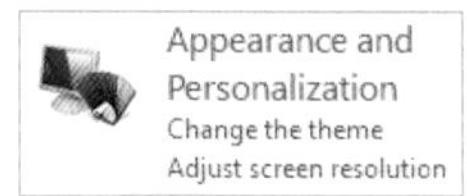

2. Click the down arrow next to **Resolution**

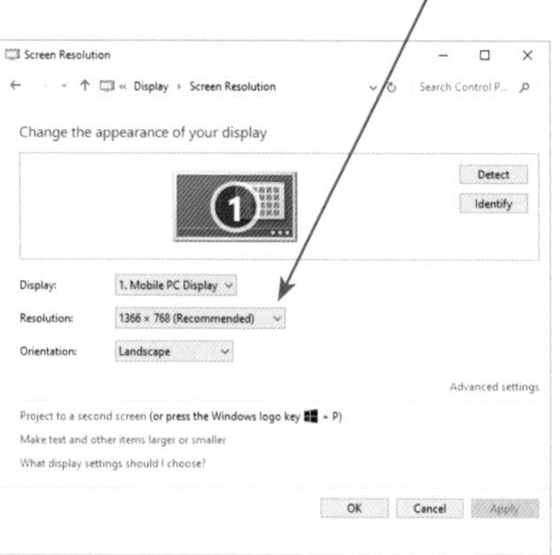

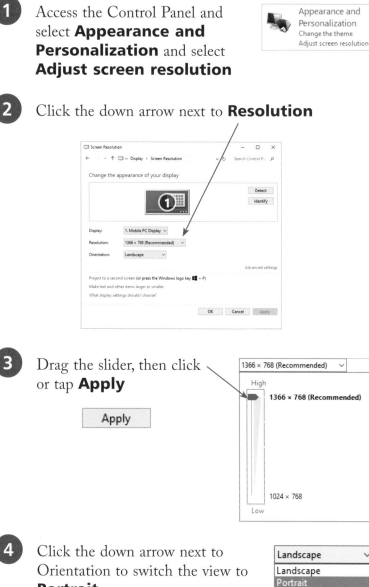

3. Drag the slider, then click or tap **Apply**

Apply

1366 × 768 (Recommended)
High
1366 × 768 (Recommended)
1024 × 768
Low

4. Click the down arrow next to Orientation to switch the view to **Portrait**

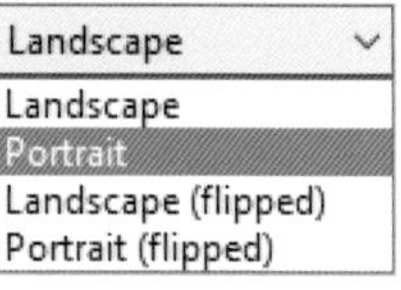

Adjusting Text

As well as changing the overall screen resolution, it is also possible to adjust the size at which text is displayed on the screen. To do this:

1. Access the Control Panel and select **Appearance and Personalization > Display > Make text and other items larger or smaller**

Display
Make text and other items larger or smaller
Adjust screen resolution

2. Click on **use these display settings** to change the size of text, apps and similar items. Click under the **Change only the text size** section to make changes to this

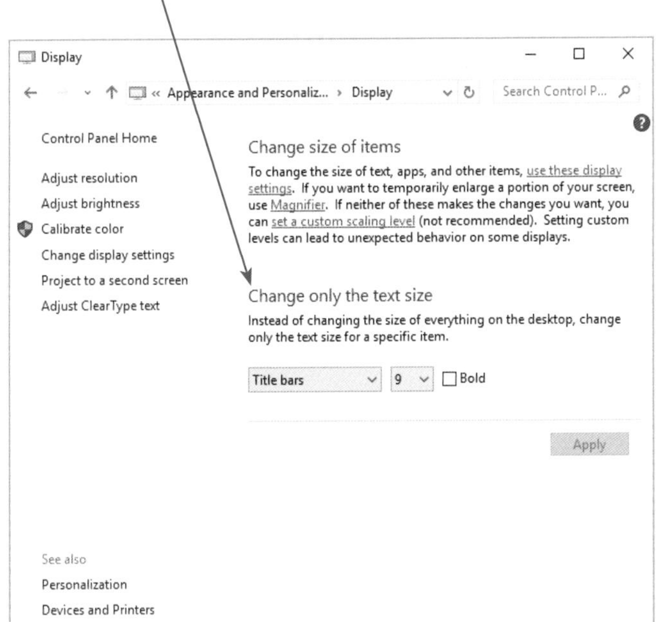

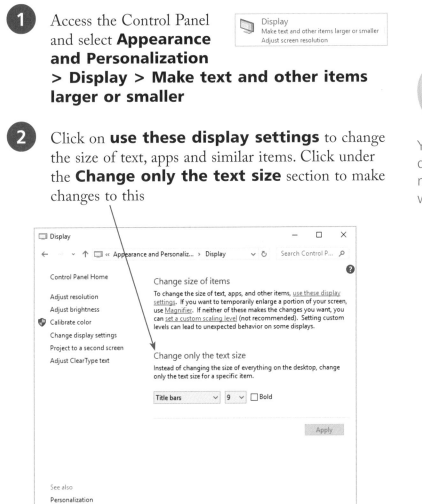

3. Click on the **Apply** button to apply the changes

Apply

You can change your display settings to make it easier to read what is on the screen.

Adjusting Volume

There are different sources of sounds on a laptop. The main two are:

- Sounds from the speakers
- Sounds from the Windows system

The volume for each of these can be adjusted independently of the other. To do this:

If you are going to be using your laptop near other people, and without headphones, make sure the volume controls are set at a reasonable level, so as not to annoy people.

1. Access the Control Panel and click on the **Hardware and Sound** link

2. In the Sound section, click on the **Adjust system volume** link

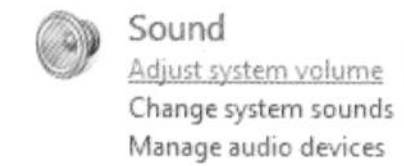

3. In the Volume Mixer window, drag the sliders to adjust the volume for a particular item

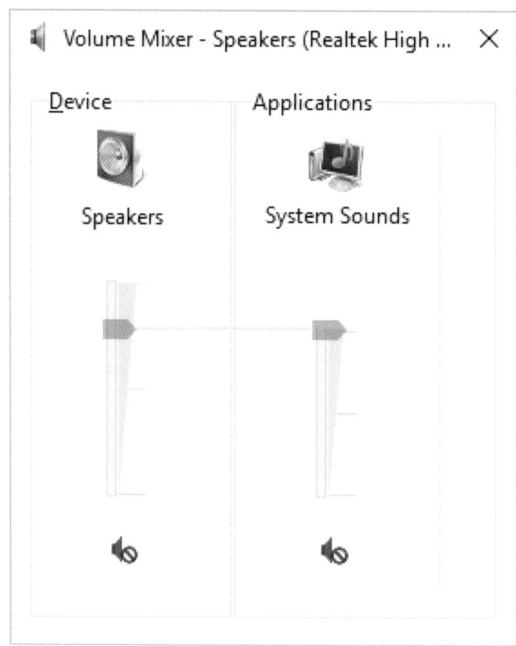

You can adjust the volume of your laptop's speakers, or mute them, by clicking on this icon in the notifications area at the right-hand side of the Taskbar.

Loading CDs and DVDs

CDs and DVDs are an important aspect of life with a laptop. They can be used to store information and also for playing music or movies, particularly when traveling. To load CDs or DVDs:

1. Locate the CD or DVD drive. This will be a slot that is located at the side or front of the laptop

2. Press the button on the front of the drive once, to eject the tray

3. Insert the CD or DVD into the tray and press the button again to close it, or push it in gently

4. To view the location of the CD or DVD, click the **This PC** button in the File Explorer. The CD or DVD will be shown as a separate drive

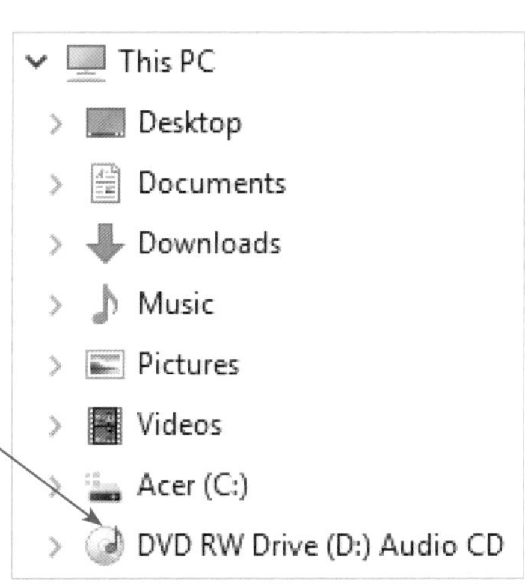

By default, movie DVDs cannot be played on Windows 10 laptops. To do this you have to download and buy an enhanced version of the Windows Media Player from the Microsoft website.

Not all laptops have a CD or DVD drive, but external CD/DVD drives can be purchased and connected separately.

USB Flash Drives

USB flash drives are small devices that can be used for copying files and then transferring them between computers. In some ways they are the natural successor to floppy discs. To connect a flash drive to a laptop and use it:

Because of their size, USB flash drives can be lost quite easily. When traveling, attach them to something like a keyring or keep them in a small pocket in your laptop case.

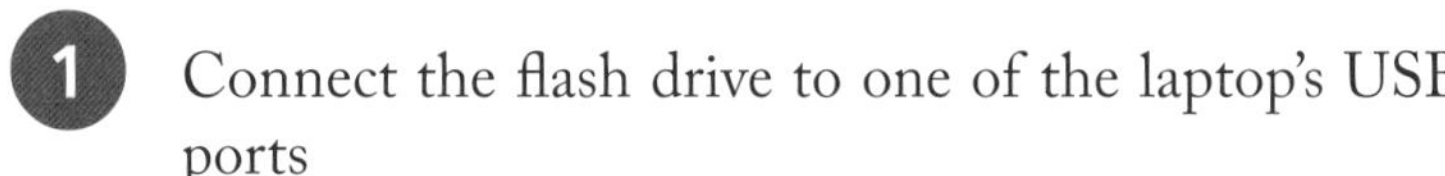

1. Connect the flash drive to one of the laptop's USB ports

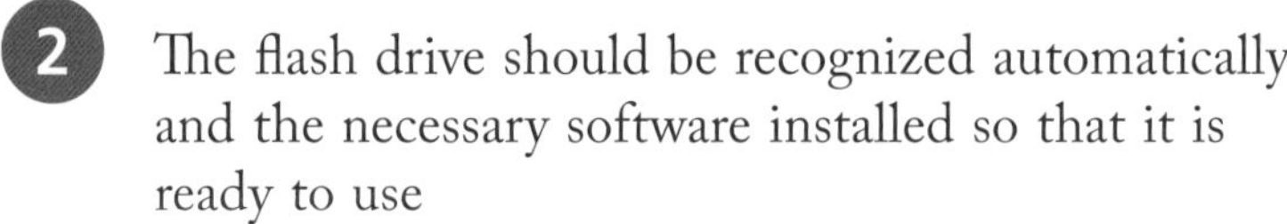

2. The flash drive should be recognized automatically and the necessary software installed so that it is ready to use

3. Access the Desktop and click on the **File Explorer** button on the Taskbar

4. The flash drive should appear as a removable drive under This PC. (Flash drives can also be known as pen drives and can be renamed in Windows Explorer by right-clicking on the name and selecting Rename.)

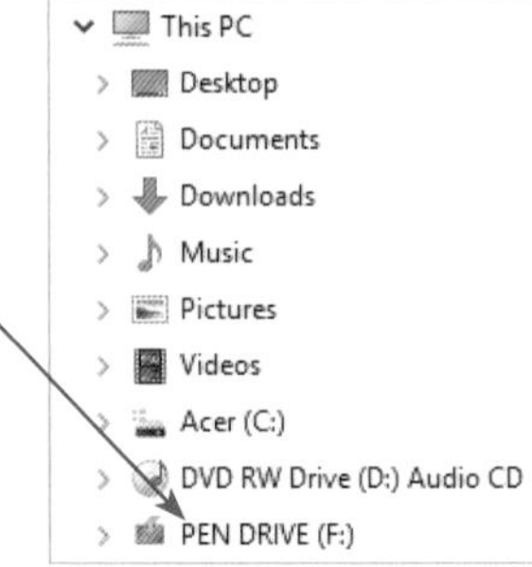

5. Double-click on the flash drive to view its contents. The files can then be used in the same way as any others on your laptop

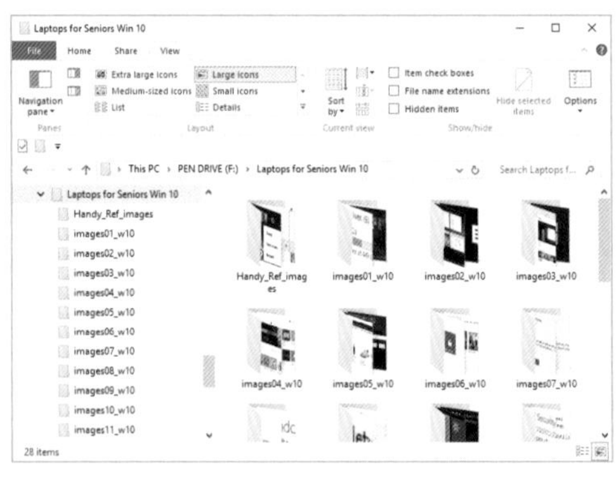

The File Explorer can also be accessed from the **All apps** option on the Start screen. See Chapter Four, page 79 for details about accessing All apps.

3 Getting Up and Running

This chapter looks further into Windows 10, focusing on the new search facility, Cortana. It also shows how to access the File Explorer for organizing your files.

Sign-in Options

Each time you start up your computer you will need to sign in. This is a security feature so that no-one else can gain unauthorized access to your account on your laptop. The sign-in process starts with the Lock screen, and then you have to enter your password.

Don't forget

For details about personalizing the Lock screen see page 47.

1. When you start your laptop the Lock screen will be showing. This is linked to the sign-in screen

You can lock your laptop at any point by pressing the **WinKey** + **L**.

2. Click on the **Lock screen**, or press any key, to move to the sign-in screen. Enter your Microsoft Account password (see page 43) and press **Enter** or click on this arrow

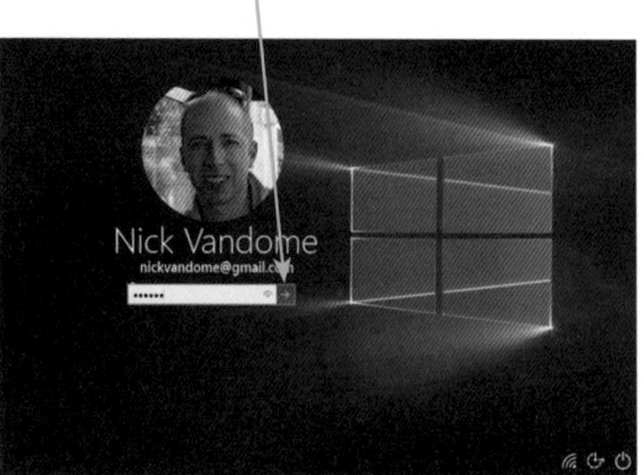

You will get an error message if you enter the wrong password, or if you simply mis-key and cause an incorrect character to be added.

3. On the sign-in screen, click on this button to select Ease of Access options

4. Click on this button to select Power off options including Shut down and Restart

5. If there are other users with an account on the same laptop, their names will be displayed here

6. Click on another user to access their own sign-in screen

You can sign in with a Local Account or a Microsoft Account. If you sign in with the latter you will have full access to the related services, such as Mail and People. Also, you will be able to sync your settings and use them on another computer with your Microsoft Account.

Sign-in settings

Settings for how you sign-in can be accessed from the Accounts section in the Settings app:

1. Access the **Settings** app and click on the **Accounts** button

2. Under **Sign-in options**, select options to change your password, create a picture password or create a PIN instead of a password

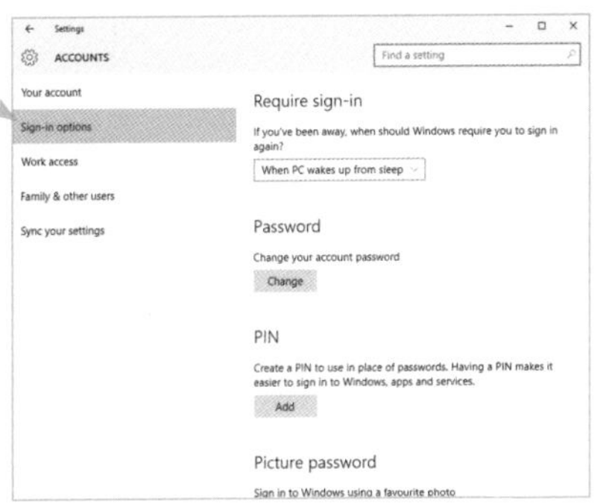

3. The picture password option is designed primarily for touchscreen devices but can also be used with a mouse. Select a picture and draw a pattern to use as your sign-in

Windows Hello, is a function that uses biometric authentication for signing in to Windows 10. This is either done by scanning your face or with a fingerprint reader. However, specialist hardware is required and this is not available on many devices at present.

Settings

Accessing Settings

The Settings in Windows 10 provide options for how you set up your computer and how it operates. There are nine main categories of Settings, each of which have a number of sub-categories. The Settings app can be accessed in a number of ways:

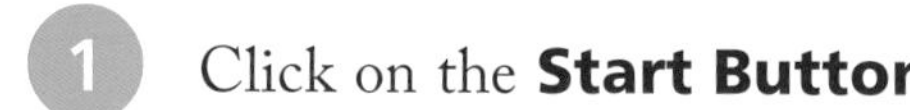

1. Click on the **Start Button**

2. Click on the **Settings** button on the Start Menu or the **Settings** tile on the Start Menu; or

3. Click on the **Notifications** button on the Taskbar

4. Click on the **All settings** button; or

5. Enter **settings** into the **Search** box and click on the **Settings** button

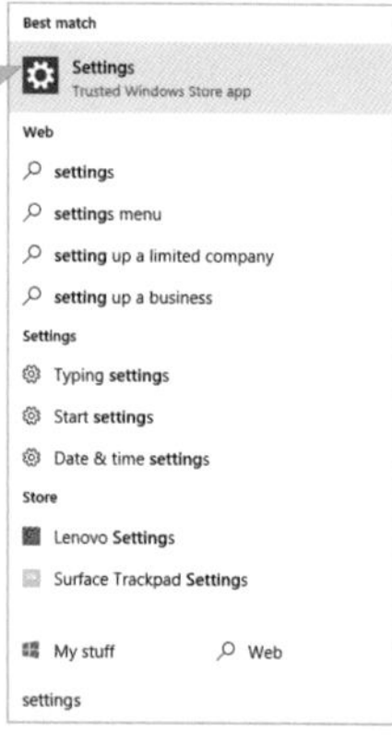

Add the Settings app to the Taskbar for quick access. To do this, access it from the Start Menu, right-click on it and click on **More > Pin to taskbar**.

Settings categories

In the **Settings** app, click on one of the main categories to view the options within that category:

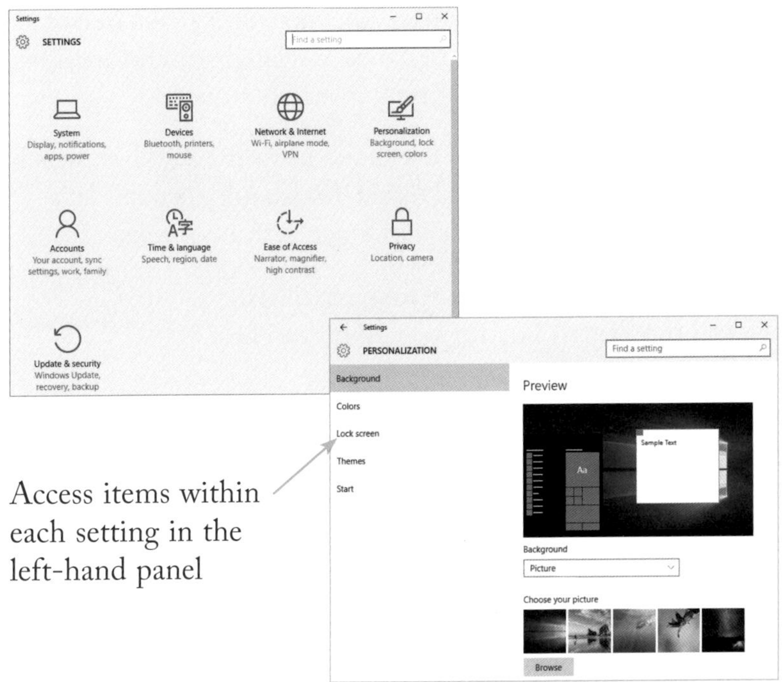

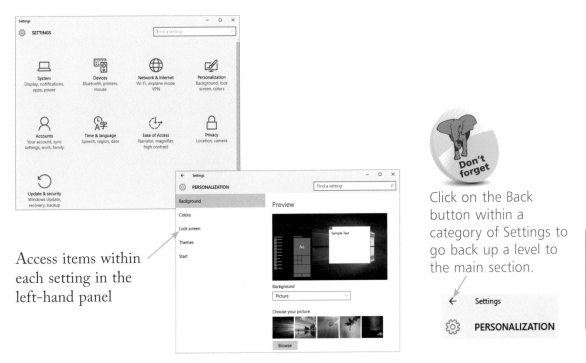

Access items within each setting in the left-hand panel

Click on the Back button within a category of Settings to go back up a level to the main section.

The main Settings categories in Windows 10 (and covered throughout the book) are:

- **System**
- **Devices**
- **Network & Internet**
- **Personalization**
- **Accounts**
- **Time & language**
- **Ease of Use**
- **Privacy**
- **Update & security**

Searching

Searching for items and information on computers and the internet has come a long way since the first search engines on the web. Most computer operating systems have sophisticated search facilities for finding things on your own computer and on the web. They also now have Personal Digital Assistants, which are voice activated search functions that can be used instead of typing search requests.

Windows 10 has a Search box built-in to the Taskbar, which also includes the Personal Digital Assistant, Cortana. This can be used for a wide range of voice activated tasks.

Using the Search box for text searching

To use the Search box for text-only searches:

1. Click in the Search box

2. Enter a search term (or website address)

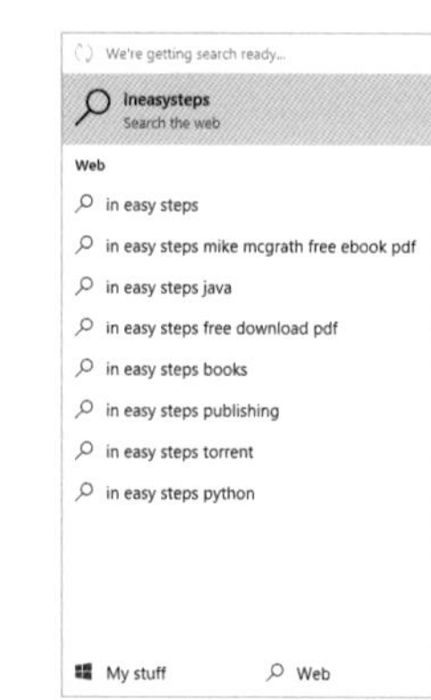

3. Click on one of the results, or on the **Web** button, to view the search results in the Microsoft Edge browser

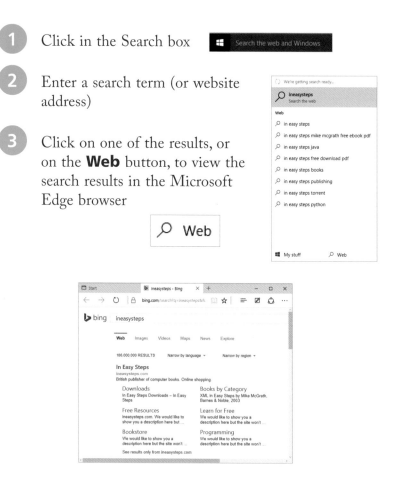

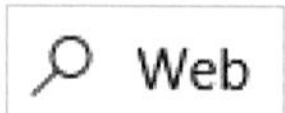

The top search result is displayed at the top of the window in Step 2.

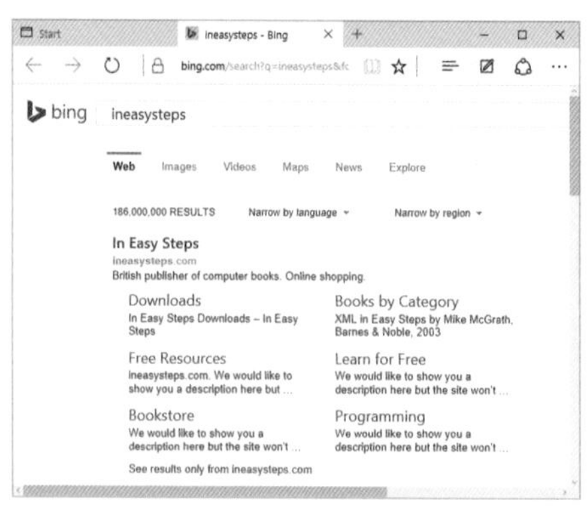

Asking a question

The Search box can also be used to ask specific questions:

1. Enter a question in the Search box

2. Click on the **Search the web** button at the top of the search box to view the results in the Microsoft Edge browser

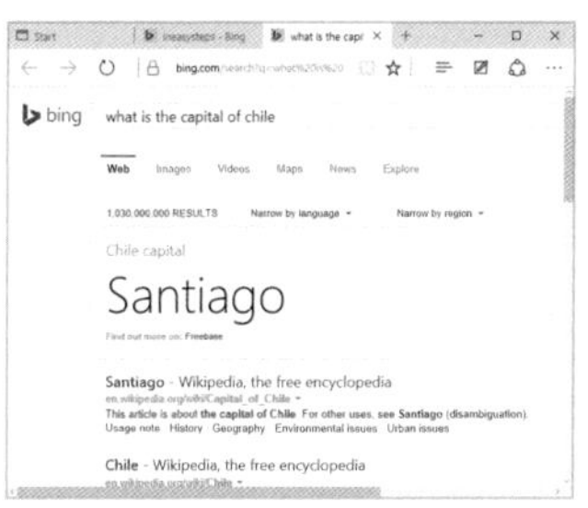

The magnifying glass icon indicates that a search is going to be undertaken on the web, and this will be displayed on a search results page, as in Step 2.

Searching over your computer

As well as searching over the web, the Search box can also be used to find items on your computer:

1. Enter a search query into the Search box and click on the **My stuff** button

My stuff

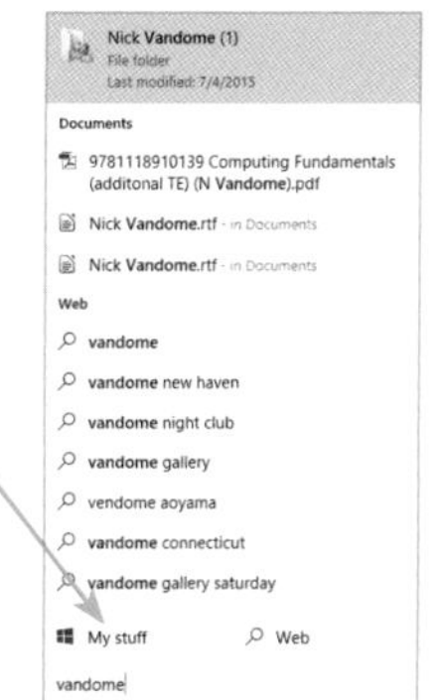

2. Click on one of the results to open the item on your computer

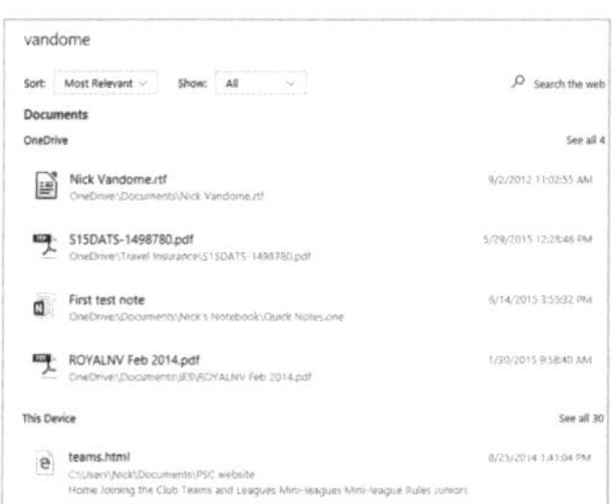

If you are searching for a keyword over files on your computer, the search will be conducted over the text in documents, and folders, not just the document titles. It will also search over the online backup and storage facility, OneDrive.

Setting Up Cortana

To ensure that you can use Cortana to perform voice searches and queries, the language settings on your Windows 10 laptop have to be set up correctly. To do this:

1. Open the **Settings** app and click on the **Time & language** button

2. Click on the **Region & language** button

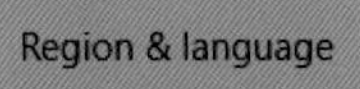

3. Click here to select a country or region

4. Click on the required display language and click on the **Set as default** button

5. Click on the **Speech** button under **Time & language**

6. Select the same **Speech language** as the one used as the display language in Step 4

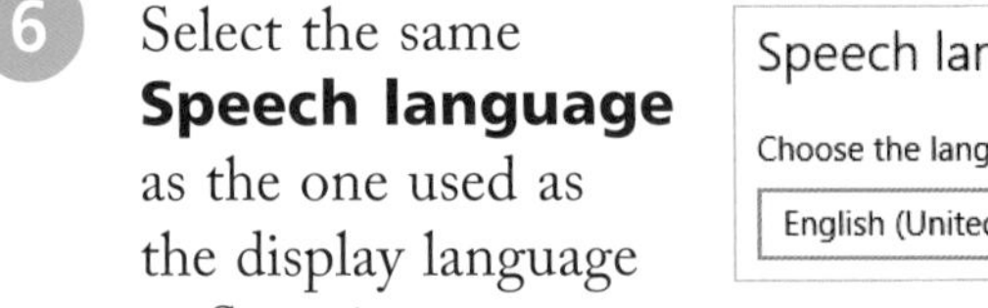

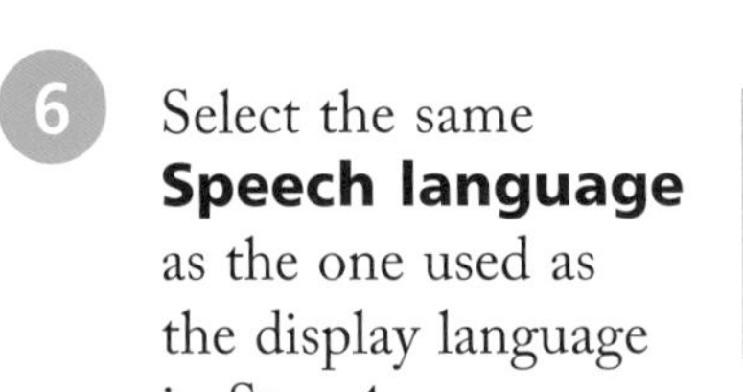

The county or region, display language and speech language should be the same in order for Cortana to work.

If the Cortana Search box is not displayed once the languages have been set, restart your computer to apply the changes.

Using Cortana

Once the correct languages have been selected for Cortana, you have to ensure that your computer's microphone is working properly, since it will be used for voice queries with Cortana. To set up your laptop's microphone:

1. Open the **Settings** app and click on the **Time & language** button

2. Click on the **Speech** button

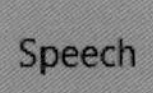

3. Under the **Microphone** section, click on the **Get started** button

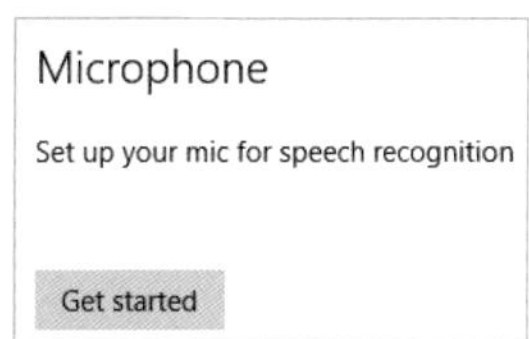

Most modern laptop computers have built-in microphones, but an external one can also be attached.

4. In the microphone wizard, click on the **Next** button

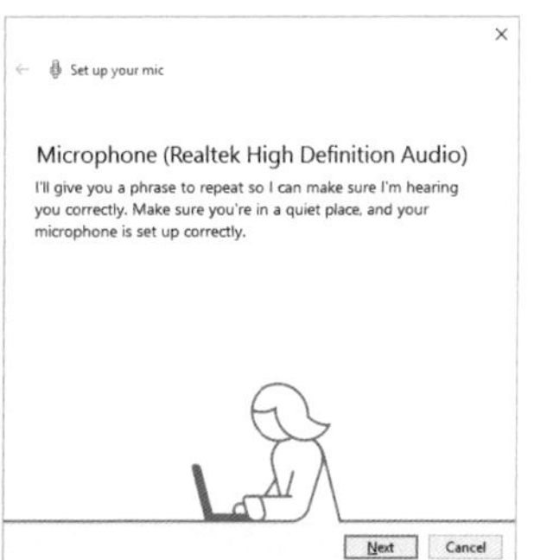

Set up your mic
Microphone (Realtek High Definition Audio)
I'll give you a phrase to repeat so I can make sure I'm hearing you correctly. Make sure you're in a quiet place, and your microphone is set up correctly.
Next
Cancel

It can take Cortana a bit of time to fully recognize your voice and style of speech. Make sure that there is no loud background noise when you are using Cortana.

5. Repeat the phrase in the wizard window to complete setting up your microphone. (If the setup is successful, the wizard will move to the completion page automatically)

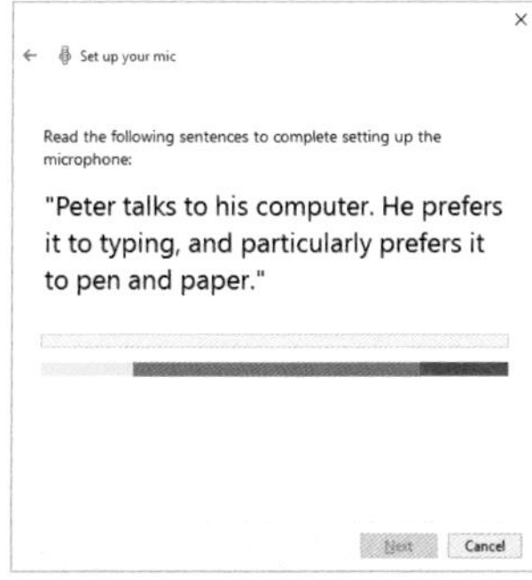

6. Click on the **Finish** button

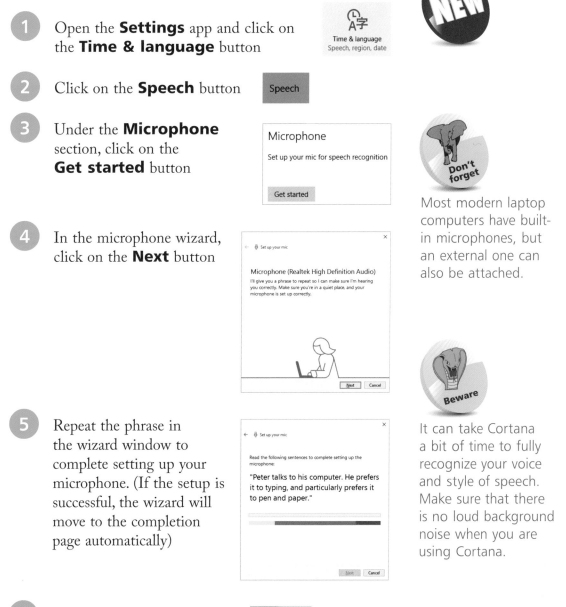

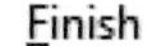

...cont'd

Searching with Cortana

As with text searches, Cortana can be used to search over various places and for different items:

Click on this button on the Cortana sidebar to set reminders, based on time, places or people.

1. Click on the microphone button in the Search box to begin a voice search

2. The Cortana symbol is displayed in the Search window with the word **Listening** in the Search box. Speak what you want to find

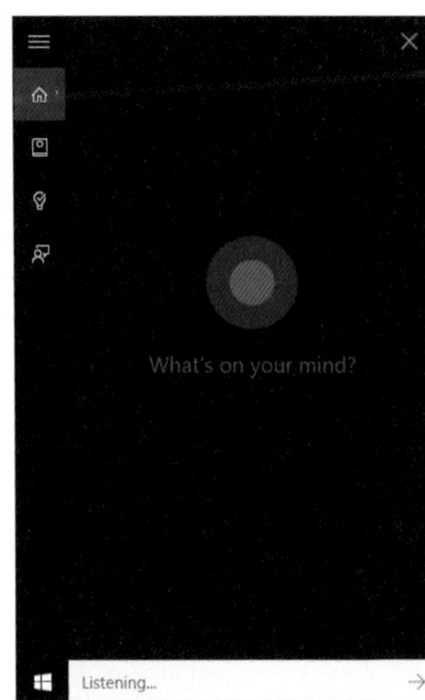

3. Cortana can be used to open specific apps, e.g. by saying **Open Mail**

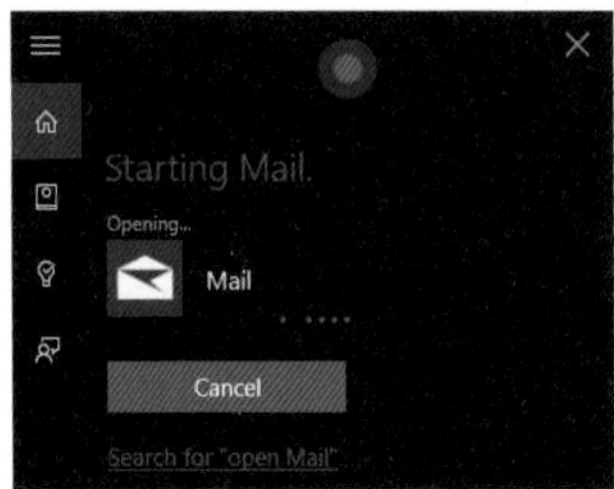

Settings for Cortana can also be accessed from the Search window. Click in the Search box and click on the **Notebook** button and then the **Settings** button.

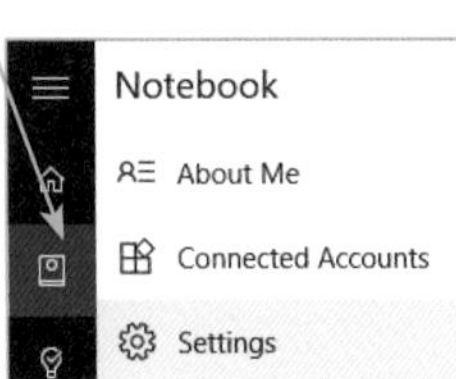

4. If the query is general, e.g. **Open Microsoft**, various options will be displayed

5. For a specific request, e.g. **Open Microsoft Edge**, the required app will be opened

Viewing Notifications

In the modern digital world, there is an increasing desire to keep updated about what is happening in our online world. With Windows 10, the Notifications panel (Action Center) can be used to display information from a variety of sources, so that you never miss an update or a notification from one of your apps. To view your notifications:

1. Click on the **Notifications** button on the Taskbar

2. New notifications appear at the top of the panel. Click on one to view its details and take any action

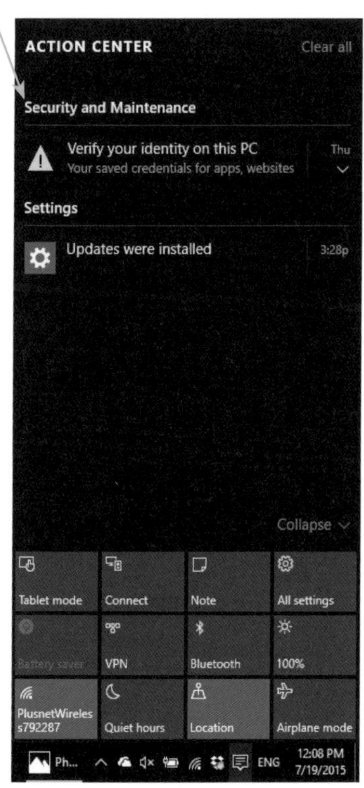

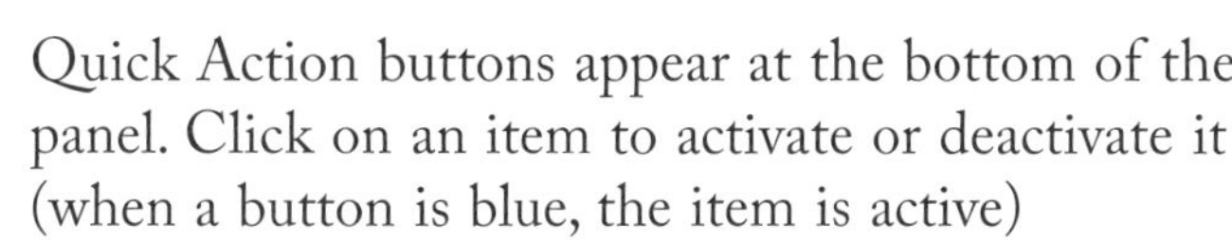

3. Quick Action buttons appear at the bottom of the panel. Click on an item to activate or deactivate it (when a button is blue, the item is active)

Settings for the Notifications/Action Center can be applied within **Settings > System > Notifications & actions**. This includes options for selecting the Quick Action buttons that appear on the Taskbar, and specifying notifications to appear on the Lock Screen and from specific apps.

Opening File Explorer

Although File Explorer (formerly called Windows Explorer) is not necessarily one of the first apps that you will use with Windows 10, it still plays an important role in organizing your folders and files. To access File Explorer:

You can right-click on the Start Button and access File Explorer from here too.

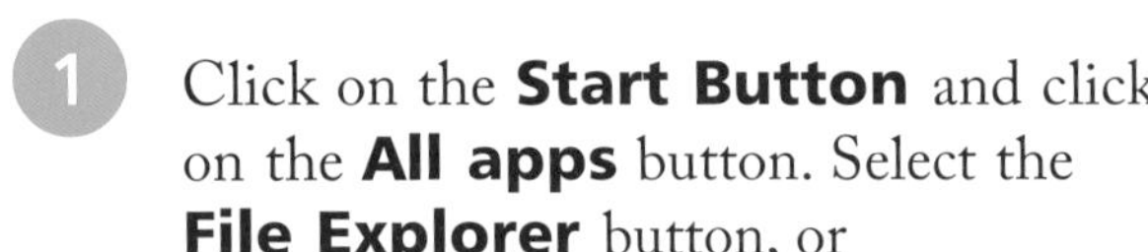

1. Click on the **Start Button** and click on the **All apps** button. Select the **File Explorer** button, or

2. From the Desktop, click on this icon on the Taskbar, or

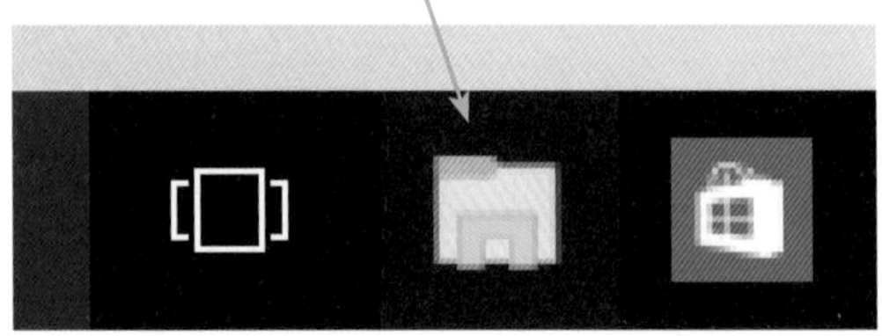

This PC displays files from different locations as a single collection, without actually moving any files.

3. Press **WinKey** + **E**, and File Explorer opens with the **Quick access** folder

4. When File Explorer is opened, click on the **This PC** link to view the top level items on your computer, including the main folders, your hard drive and any removable devices that are connected

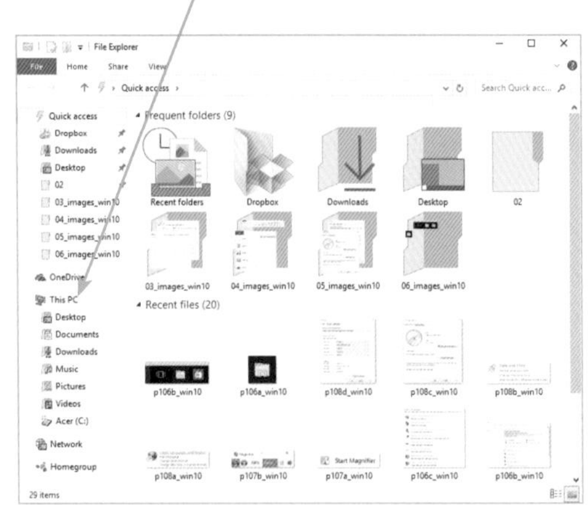

Quick Access in File Explorer

When working with files and folders, there will probably be items which you access on a regular basis. The Quick access section of the File Explorer can be used to view the items that you have most recently accessed, and also to pin your most frequently used and favorite items. To use the Quick access section:

1. Click on the **Quick access** button in the File Explorer navigation pane so that the right-pointing arrow becomes downwards-pointing

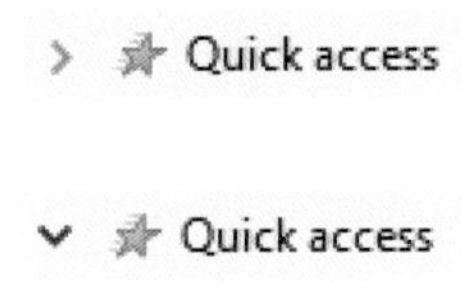

2. In the main window, your frequently used folders and most recently used files are displayed

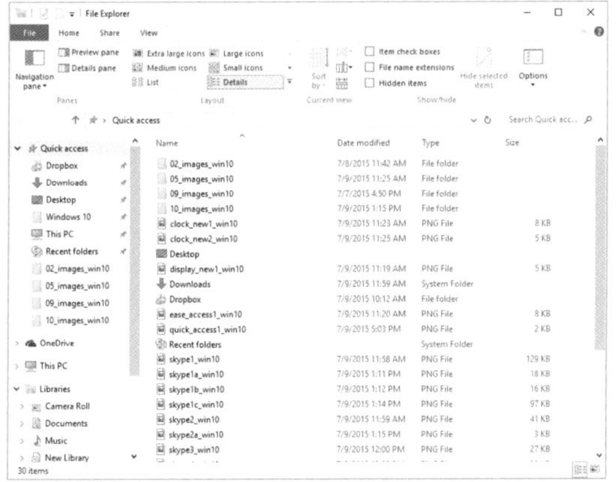

3. The folders are also listed underneath the **Quick access** button in the Navigation pane

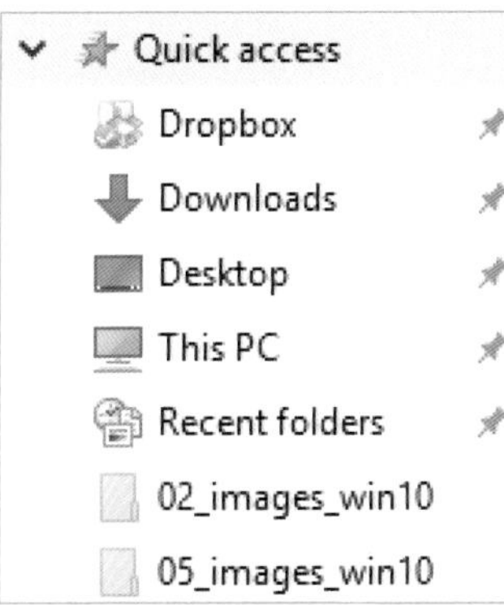

The items displayed under Quick access are not physically located here; the links are just shortcuts to the actual location within your file structure.

...cont'd

Adding items to Quick access

The folders that you access and use most frequently can be pinned to the Quick access section. This does not physically move them, it just creates a shortcut within Quick access. To do this:

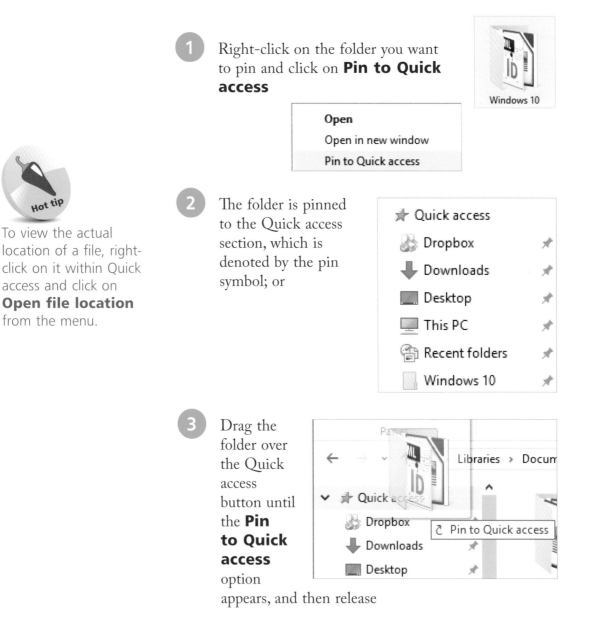

1. Right-click on the folder you want to pin and click on **Pin to Quick access**

Open
Open in new window
Pin to Quick access

To view the actual location of a file, right-click on it within Quick access and click on **Open file location** from the menu.

2. The folder is pinned to the Quick access section, which is denoted by the pin symbol; or

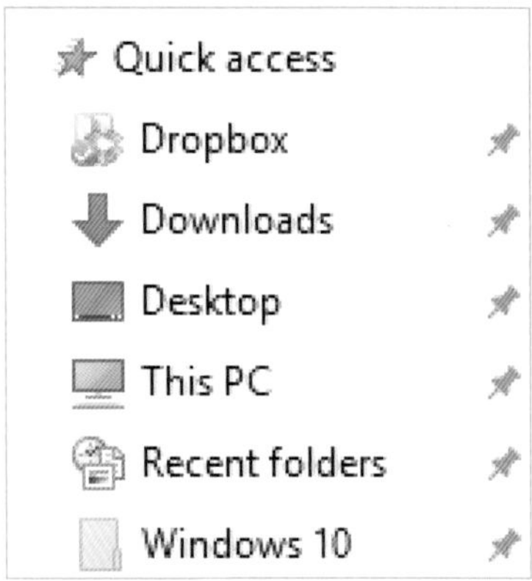

3. Drag the folder over the Quick access button until the **Pin to Quick access** option appears, and then release

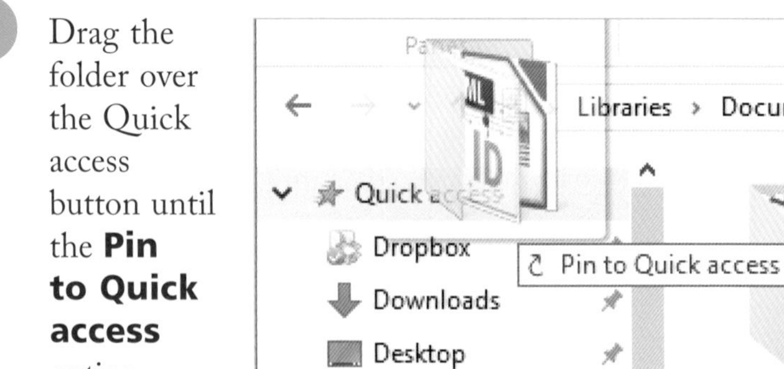

Scenic Ribbon

The navigation and functionality in the Libraries is done by the Scenic Ribbon, located at the top of the window. This has options for the Library itself, and also the type of content that is being viewed:

1. Click on the tabs at the top of the Library window to view associated tools

Library Tools Picture Tools

2. Click on the Library Tools tab to view the menus for the whole Library

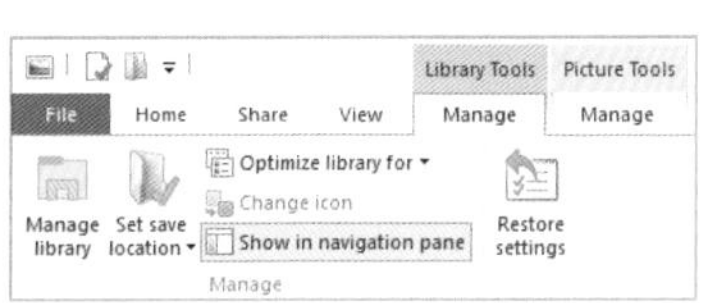

3. Click on the content tab (Picture Tools in this example) to view menus for the selected content

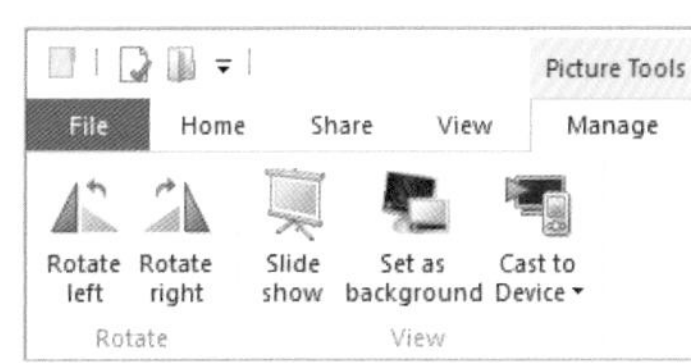

Library File Menu

This contains options for opening a new window, closing the current window or moving to a frequently-visited location in the Library.

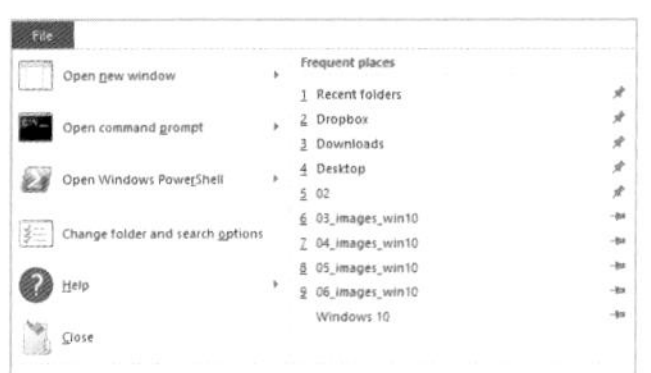

Library Home Menu

This contains options for copying and pasting, moving, deleting and renaming selected items. You can also create new folders, view folder properties and select folder items.

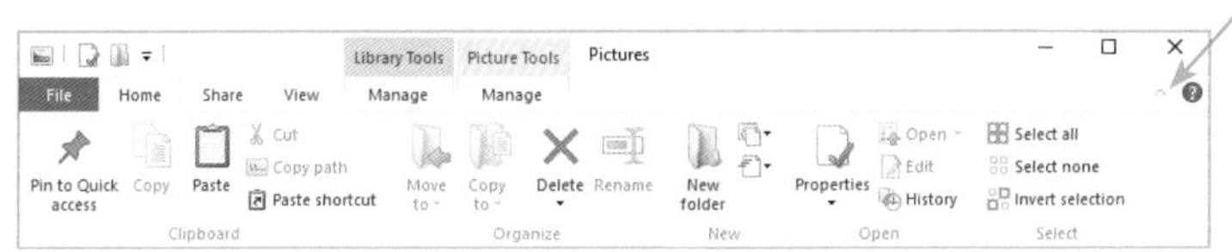

The Scenic Ribbon can be minimized by clicking on this button at the right-hand side of the top toolbar, or by pressing Ctrl + F1.

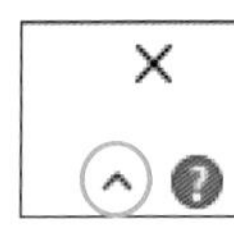

...cont'd

Library Share Menu

This contains options for sharing selected items, by sending them to the HomeGroup or another user on the computer, burning them to a CD or DVD, creating a compressed Zip file or sending the items to a printer.

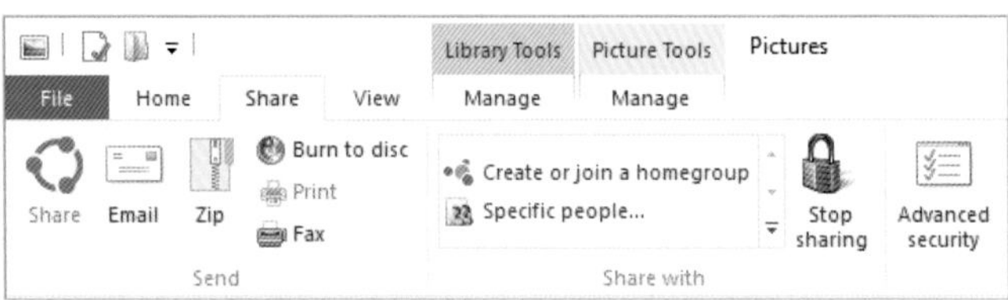

Click on the **Options** button on the View Menu to set additional options for the operation of a folder and how items are displayed within it.

Library View Menu

This contains options for how you view the items in the current active folder.

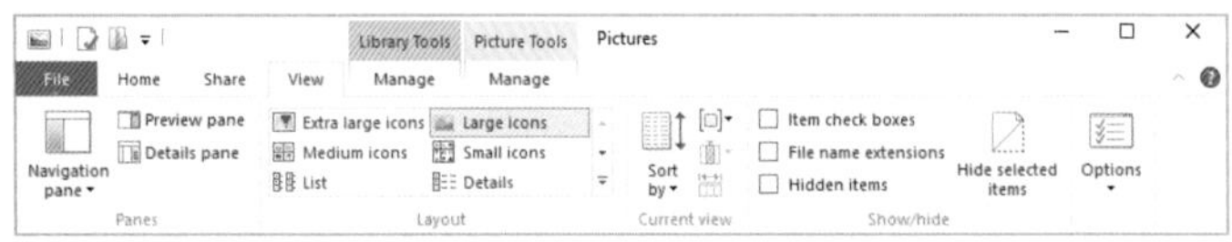

Library Manage Menu

This contains options for managing specific libraries. Click on the **Manage library** button to add additional folders to the one currently being viewed.

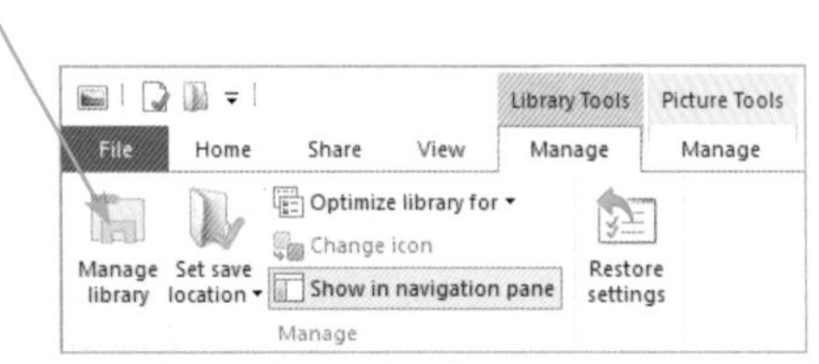

When a folder is optimized, the items at the top of the folder window are relevant to the type of content that has been selected.

Library menu options

If there is a down-pointing arrow next to an item on a Library menu, click on it to see additional options such as the **Optimize library for** button, which optimizes the folder for specific types of content.

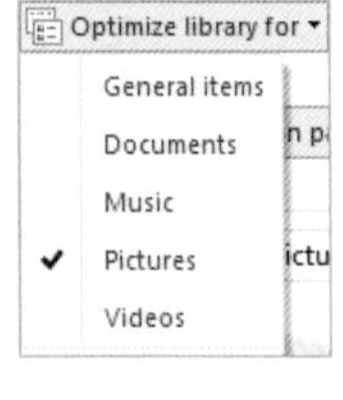

4 Working with Apps

In Windows 10, some apps are pre-installed, while hundreds more can be downloaded from the Windows Store. This chapter shows how to work with and organize apps in Windows 10.

Starting with Apps

The word "app" may be seen by some as a new-fangled piece of techno-speak. But, simply, it means a computer program. Originally, apps were items that were downloaded to smartphones and tablet computers. However, the terminology has now been expanded to cover any computer program. So, in Windows 10 most programs are referred to as "apps", although some legacy ones may still be referred to as "programs".

There are three clear types of apps within Windows 10:

- **Windows 10 apps**. These are the built-in apps that can be accessed from the Start Menu. They cover the areas of communication, entertainment and information, and several of them are linked together through the online sharing service, OneDrive. In Windows 10, they open in their own window on the Desktop, in the same way as the older-style Windows apps (see below).
- **Windows classic apps**. These are the older-style Windows apps that people may be familiar with from previous versions of Windows. These open in the Desktop environment.
- **Windows Store apps**. These are apps that can be downloaded from the online Windows Store, and cover a wide range of subjects and functionality. Some Windows Store apps are free, while others have to be paid for.

In Windows 10 all apps open directly on the Desktop and their operation is more consistent, regardless of the type of app.

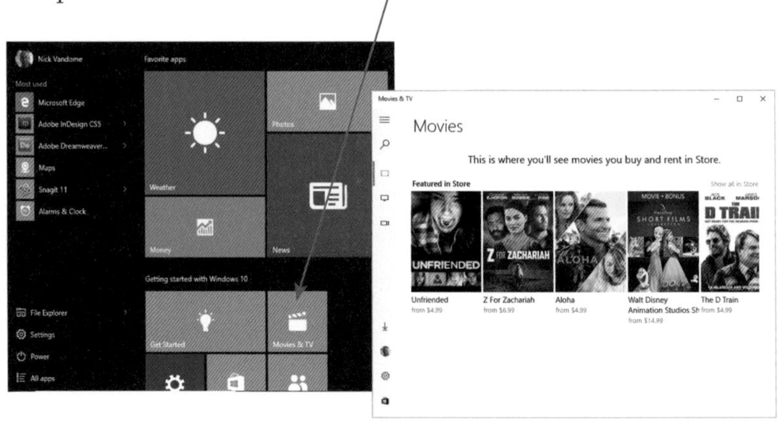

Windows 10 apps

Windows 10 apps are accessed from the brightly-colored tiles on the Start Menu (or All apps section). Click on a tile to open the relevant app.

Windows classic apps

The Windows apps are generally the ones that appeared as default with previous versions of Windows and would have been accessed from the Start button. The Windows apps can be accessed from the Start Menu by clicking on the **All apps** button. Windows apps have the traditional Windows look and functionality. Windows apps open on the Desktop.

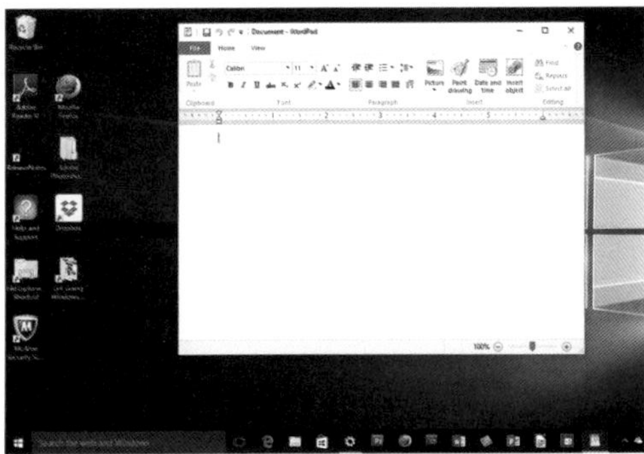

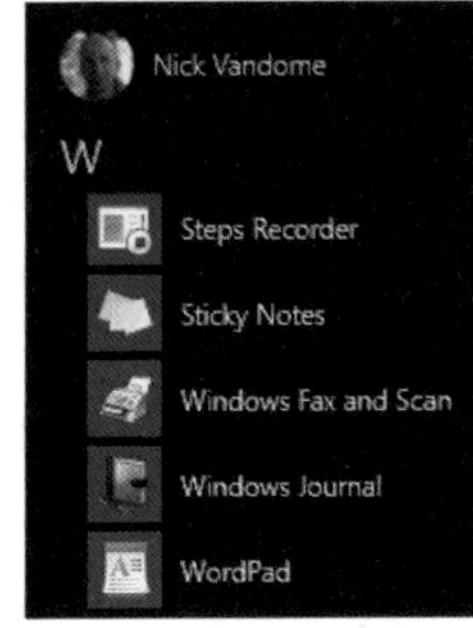

The Windows Store is accessed by clicking on the **Store** tile on the Start Menu or on the Taskbar.

Windows Store apps

The Windows Store apps are accessed and downloaded from the online Windows Store. Apps can be browsed and searched for in the Store, and when they are downloaded they are added to the All apps section of the Start Menu.

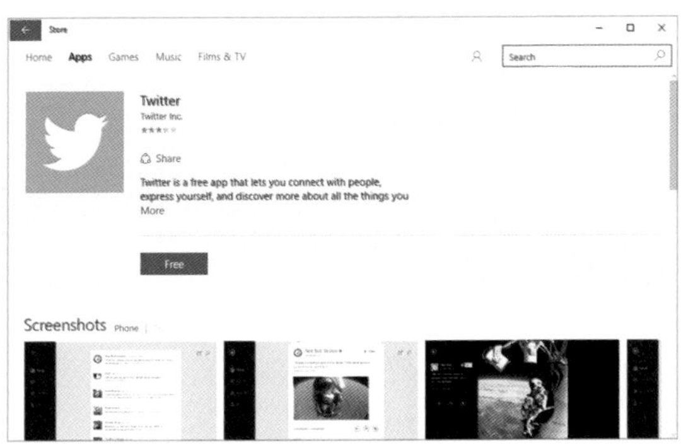

Windows 10 Apps

The Windows 10 apps that are accessed from the All apps option on the Start Menu cover a range of communication, entertainment and information functions. The apps include:

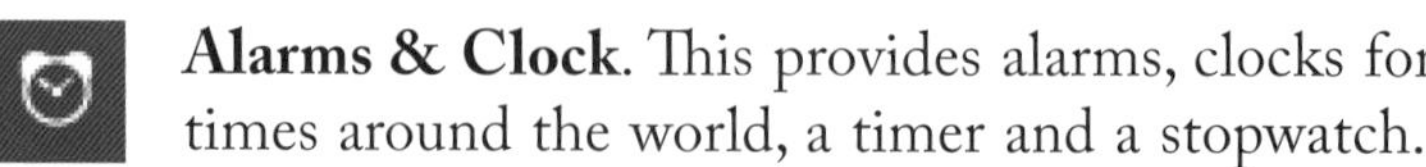
Alarms & Clock. This provides alarms, clocks for times around the world, a timer and a stopwatch.

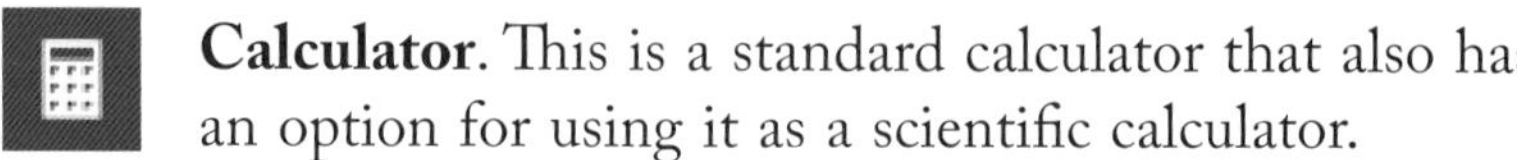
Calculator. This is a standard calculator that also has an option for using it as a scientific calculator.

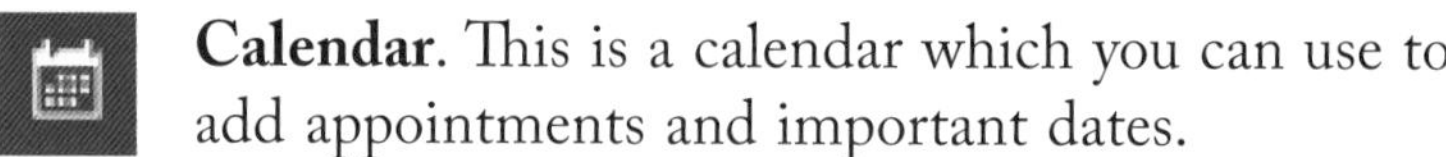
Calendar. This is a calendar which you can use to add appointments and important dates.

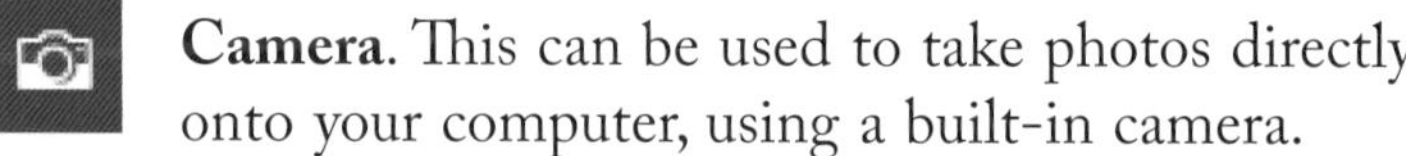
Camera. This can be used to take photos directly onto your computer, using a built-in camera.

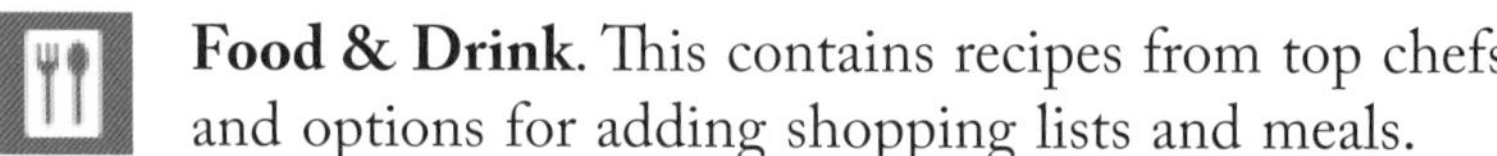
Food & Drink. This contains recipes from top chefs and options for adding shopping lists and meals.

Fresh Paint. An app for creating your own artwork and also viewing photos.

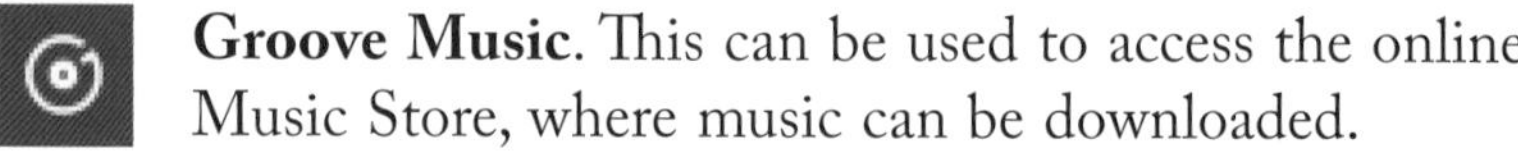
Groove Music. This can be used to access the online Music Store, where music can be downloaded.

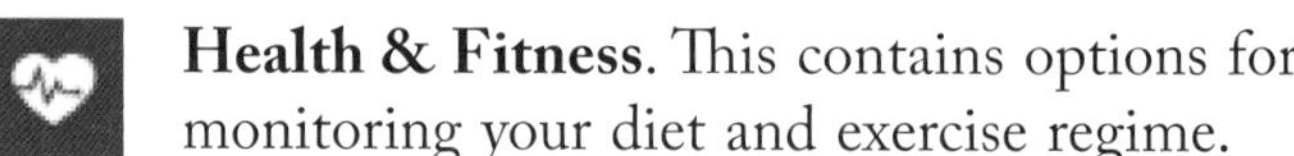
Health & Fitness. This contains options for monitoring your diet and exercise regime.

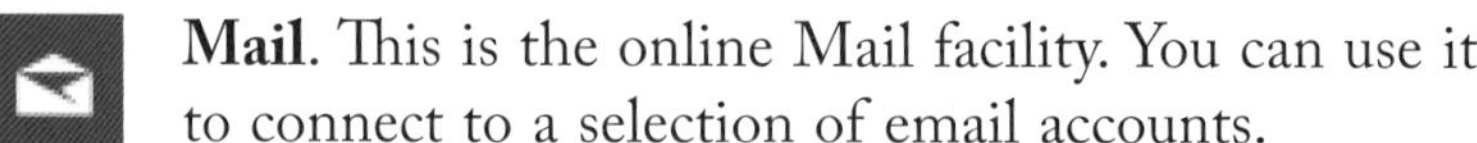
Mail. This is the online Mail facility. You can use it to connect to a selection of email accounts.

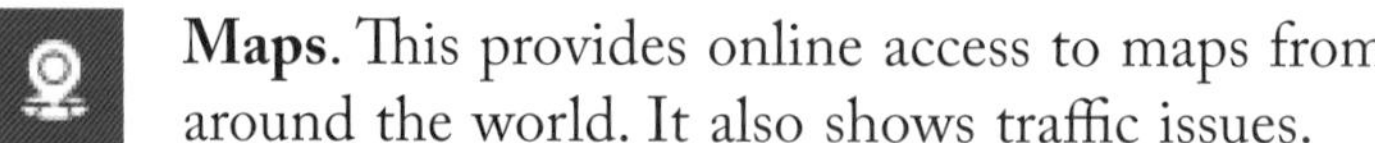
Maps. This provides online access to maps from around the world. It also shows traffic issues.

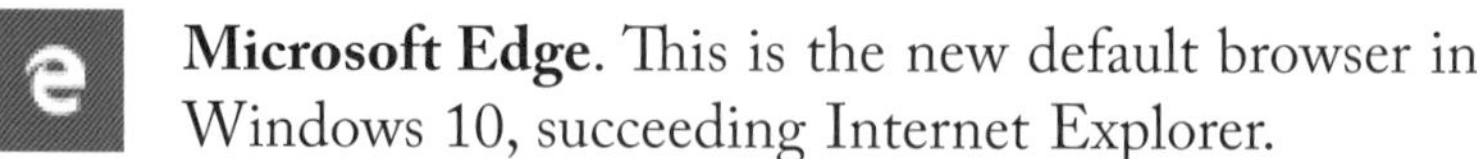
Microsoft Edge. This is the new default browser in Windows 10, succeeding Internet Explorer.

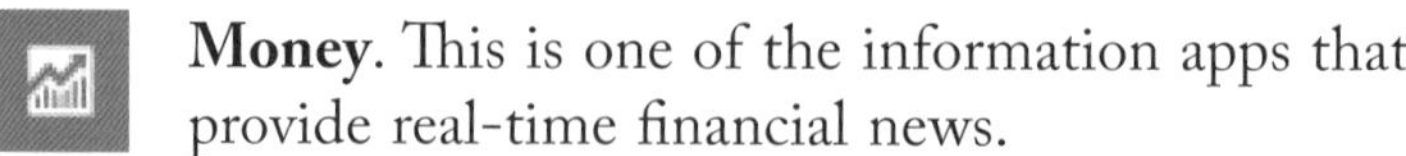
Money. This is one of the information apps that provide real-time financial news.

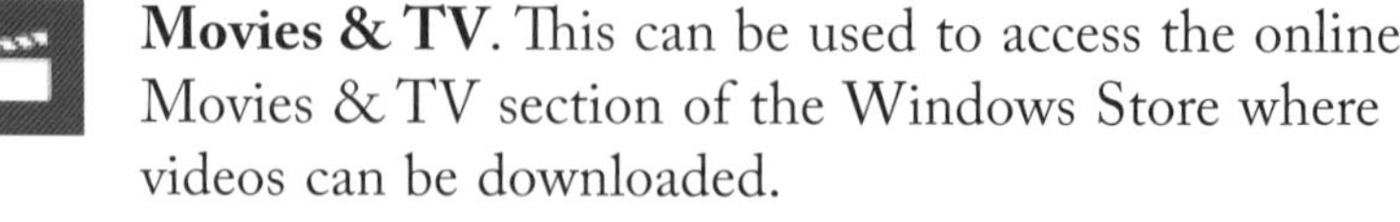
Movies & TV. This can be used to access the online Movies & TV section of the Windows Store where videos can be downloaded.

See pages 90-99 for more information about working with Microsoft Edge.

News. This is one of the information apps that provide real-time news information.

OneDrive. This is an online facility for storing and sharing content from your computer. This includes photos and documents.

OneNote. This is the Microsoft note-taking app, part of the Office suite of apps.

People. This is the address book app for adding contacts. Your contacts from sites such as Facebook and LinkedIn can also be imported into this app.

Photos. This can be used to view, organize, share and print your photos.

Reader. This can be used to open documents in different file formats, such as PDF and TIFF.

Reading List. This can be used to save web pages for reading at a later time, and even when you are offline.

Settings. This can be used to access all of the main settings for customizing and managing Windows 10 and your computer. (See pages 58-59 for details.)

Sport. This is one of the information apps that provide real-time sports news.

Store. This provides access to the online Windows Store, from where a range of other apps can be bought and downloaded to your computer.

Weather. This provides real-time weather forecasts for locations around the world. By default, it will provide the nearest forecast to your location as entered when you installed Windows 10.

Xbox. This can be used to download and play games and also play online Xbox games.

The information for the Money, News, Sports, Travel and Weather apps is provided by Bing.

Using Windows 10 Apps

In Windows 8 and 8.1, the newer style Windows apps had a different look and functionality. However, in Windows 10, all of the apps have been created with a more consistent appearance, although there are still some differences.

Windows 10 apps

Windows 10 apps now open in their own window on the Desktop (in Windows 8 and 8.1 they only opened in full-screen), and they can be moved and resized in the same way as older-style apps:

In Windows 10 there has been a conscious effort to achieve a greater consistency between the newer-style apps and the old, classic style apps.

1. Click and drag on the top bar to move the app's window

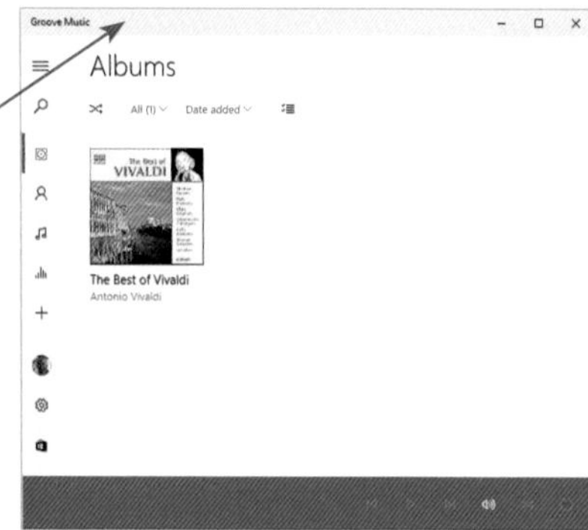

2. Drag on the bottom or right-hand border to resize the app's window (or the bottom right-hand corner to resize the height and width simultaneously)

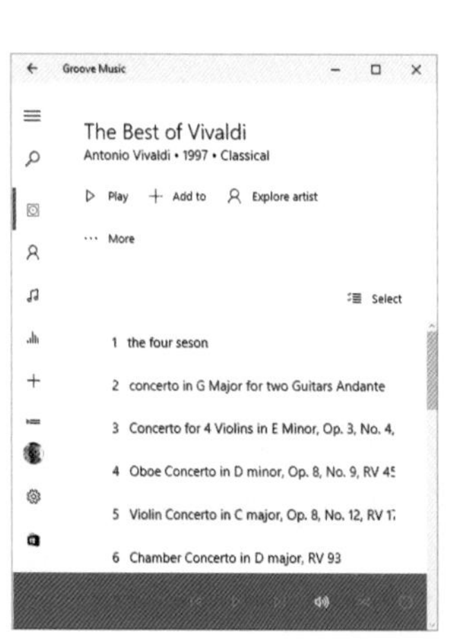

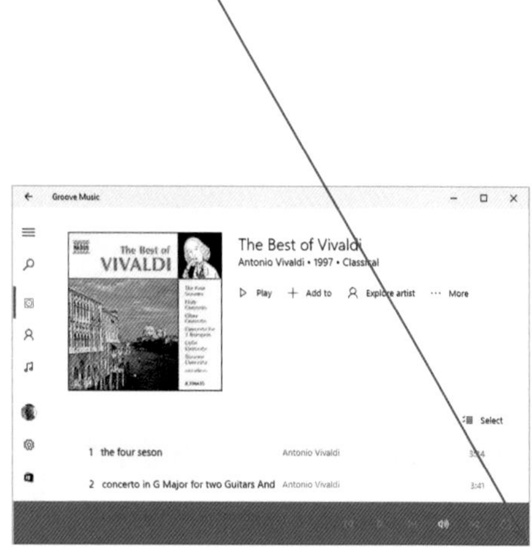

Windows 10 app's menus

Some Windows 10 apps have their own menus:

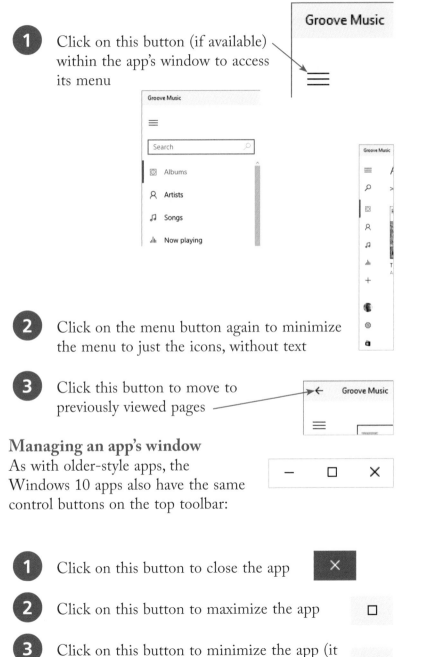

1. Click on this button (if available) within the app's window to access its menu

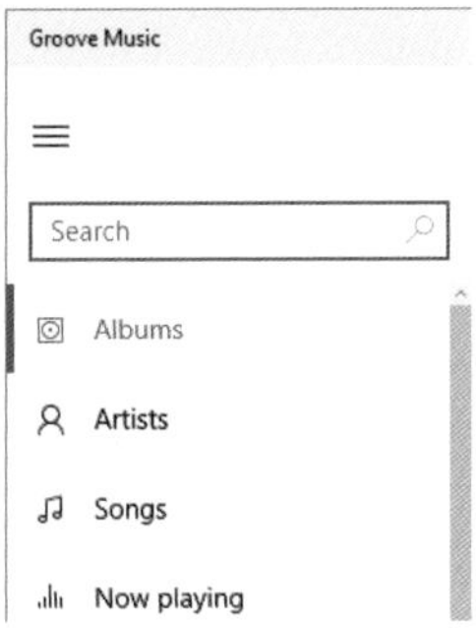

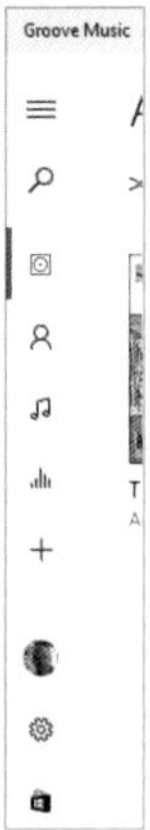

2. Click on the menu button again to minimize the menu to just the icons, without text

3. Click this button to move to previously viewed pages

Managing an app's window

As with older-style apps, the Windows 10 apps also have the same control buttons on the top toolbar:

1. Click on this button to close the app

2. Click on this button to maximize the app

3. Click on this button to minimize the app (it will be minimized onto the Taskbar)

Apps that are installed from a CD or DVD are automatically included in the All apps section, but not necessarily on the Start Menu.

Closing Apps

There are several ways to close an app:

1. Click on the red **Close** button in the top right of the window

2. Select **File > Exit** from the File menu (if available)

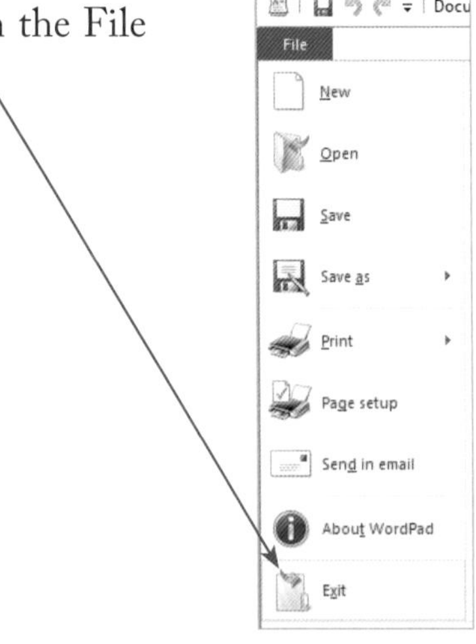

3. Press **Alt** + **F4**

It is always worth saving a new document as soon as it is created. It should also be saved at regular intervals as you are working on it.

4. Right-click on the icon on the Taskbar and select **Close window**

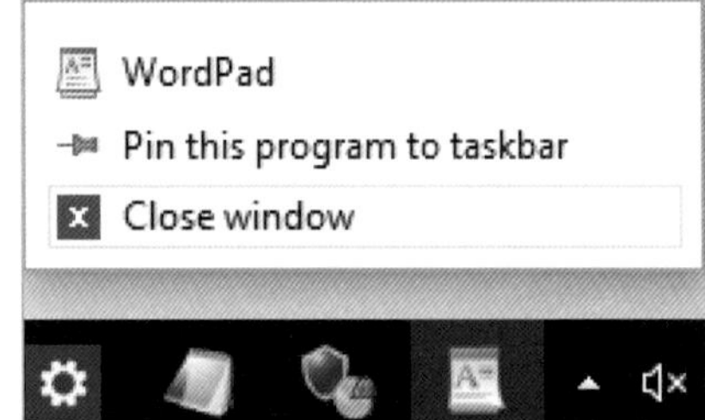

5. If any changes have been made (to a document in this case), you may receive a warning message advising you to save the associated file

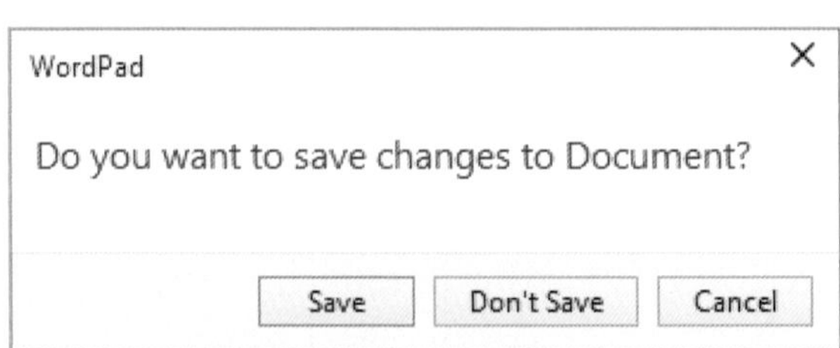

Viewing All Apps

There is a lot more to Windows 10 than the default Windows 10 apps. Most of the Windows system apps that were available with previous versions of Windows are still there, just not initially visible on the Start Menu. However, it only takes two clicks on the Start Menu to view all of the apps on your laptop.

1. Click on the **Start** button

2. Click on the **All apps** button

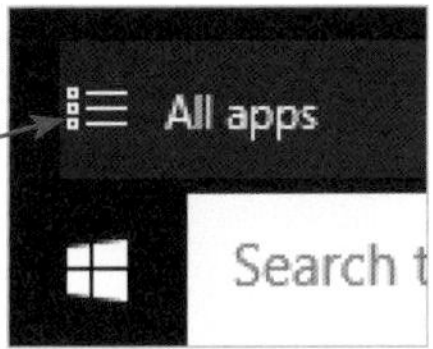

3. All of the apps are displayed. Use the scroll bar to move through all of the apps

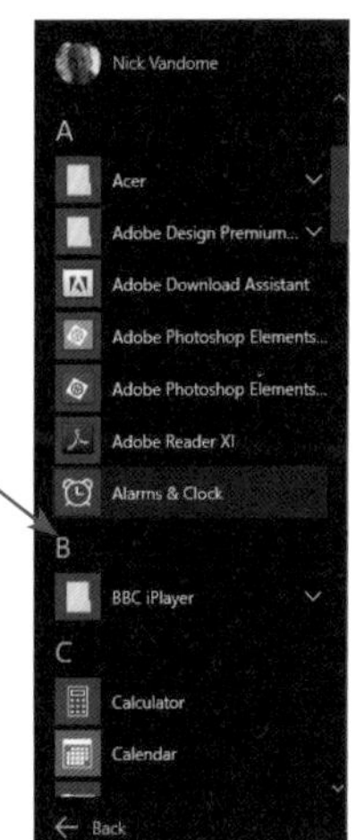

4. Click on a letter heading to view an alphabetic grid for finding apps. Click on a letter to move that section

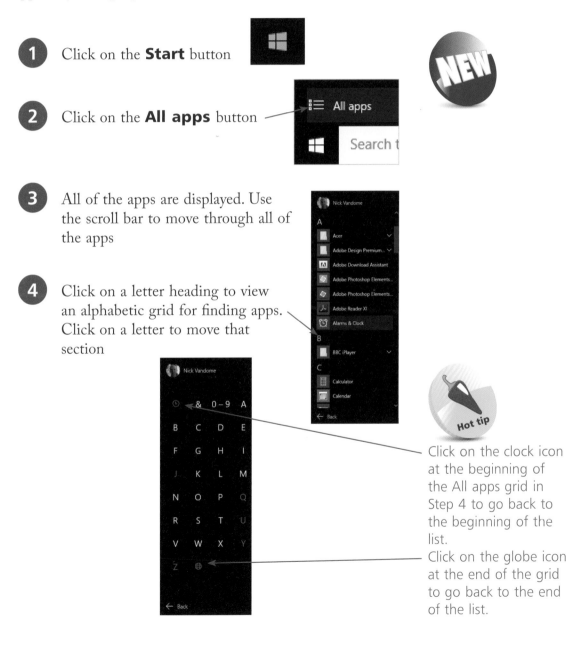

Click on the clock icon at the beginning of the All apps grid in Step 4 to go back to the beginning of the list. Click on the globe icon at the end of the grid to go back to the end of the list.

Searching for Apps

As you acquire more and more apps, it may become harder to find the ones you want. To help with this, you can use the Search box to search over all of the apps on your laptop. To do this:

1. Click in the Search box on the Taskbar

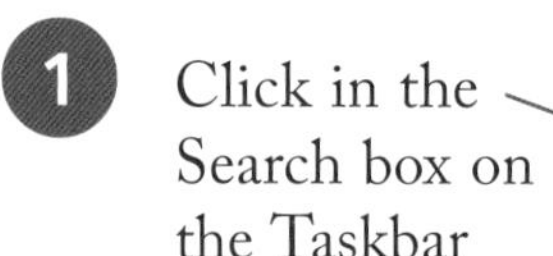

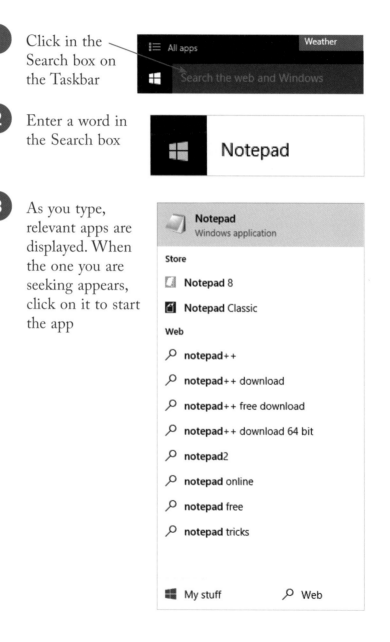

2. Enter a word in the Search box

3. As you type, relevant apps are displayed. When the one you are seeking appears, click on it to start the app

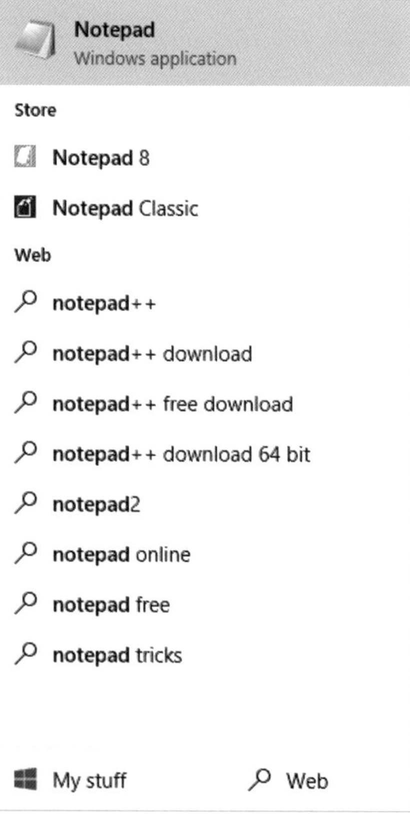

You just have to put in the first couple of letters of an app name and the search will automatically suggest results based on this. The more that you type, the more specific the results become. Case does not matter when you are typing a search query.

Using the Windows Store

The third category of apps that can be used with Windows 10 are those that are downloaded from the Windows Store. These cover a wide range of topics and it is an excellent way to add functionality to Windows 10. To use the Windows Store:

1. Click on the **Store** tile on the Start Menu

2. The currently-featured apps are displayed on the Home screen

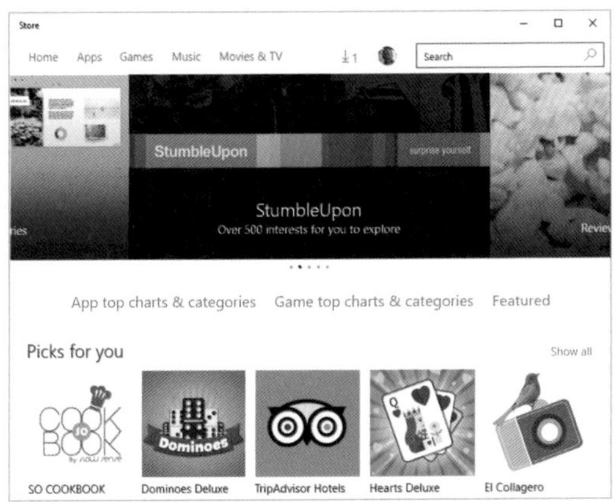

The Windows 10 apps can all be downloaded from the Windows Store.

3. Scroll up and down to see additional featured apps

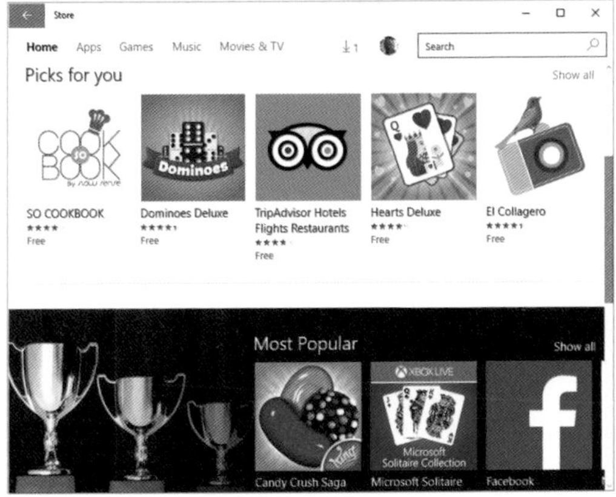

...cont'd

4. Click on the **App top charts & categories** button on the Homepage and select apps under specific headings, e.g. **Best rated** apps

App top charts & categories

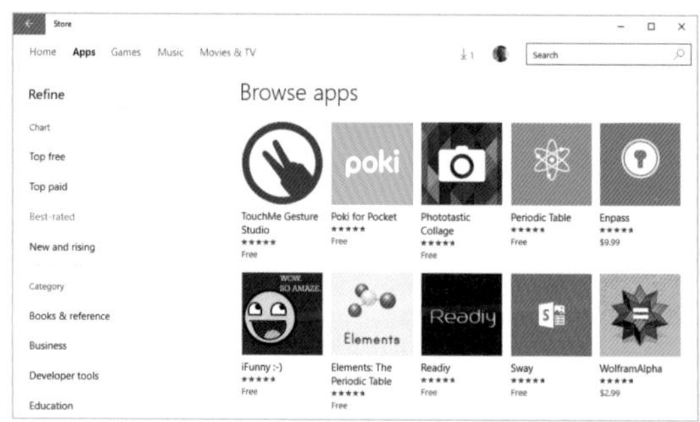

5. Click on options in the **Refine** section to view apps according to certain criteria, e.g. **Top free**

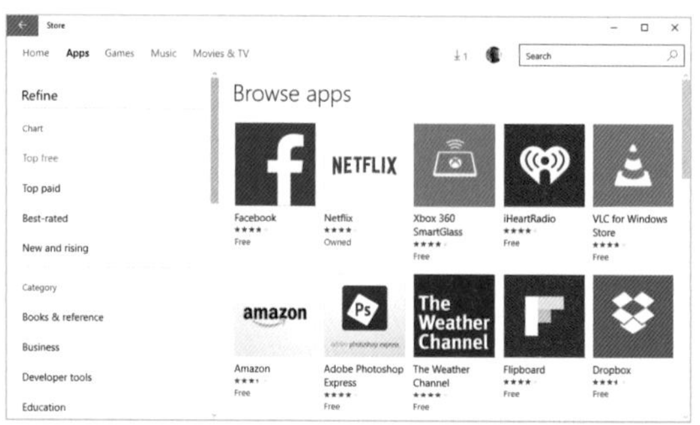

6. Click on an app to preview it

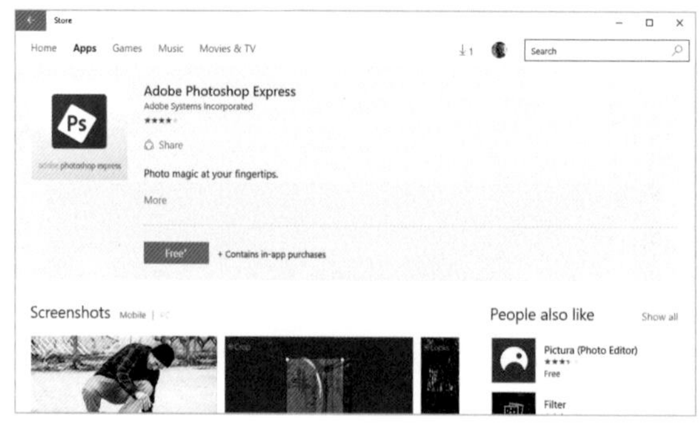

Scroll up and down in Step 6 to view ratings and reviews about the app and also any additional descriptions.

Buying Apps

When you find an app that you want to use, you can download it to your computer. To do this:

1. Access the app and click on the **Free (or price)** button

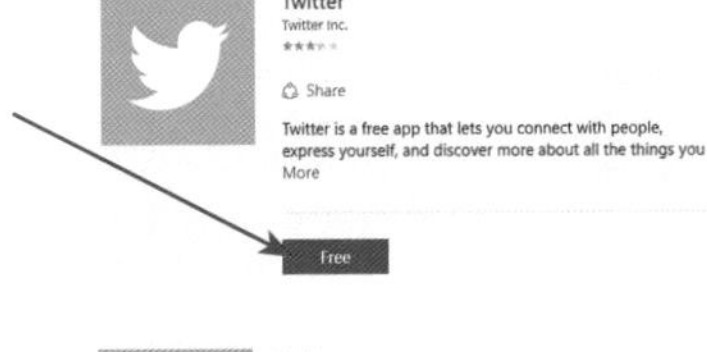

2. The app downloads from the Windows Store. Click on the **Install** button to install the downloaded app

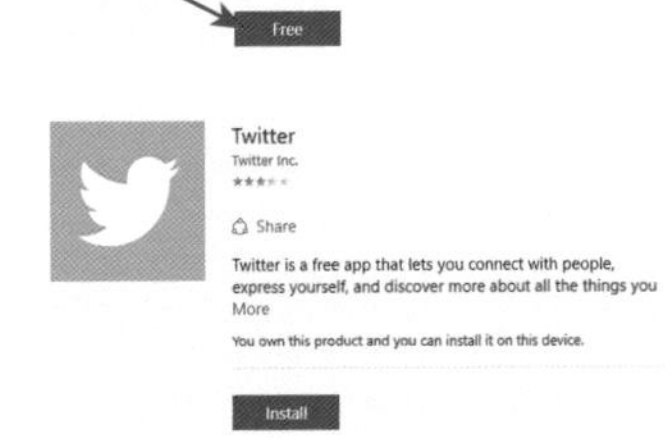

3. The app is added to the All apps page and has a **New** tag next to it. This disappears once the app has been opened

4. Click on the app to open it and use it (initially it will be available under the **Recently added** section of the Start Menu and also from the **All apps** button)

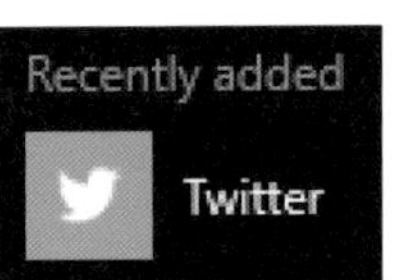

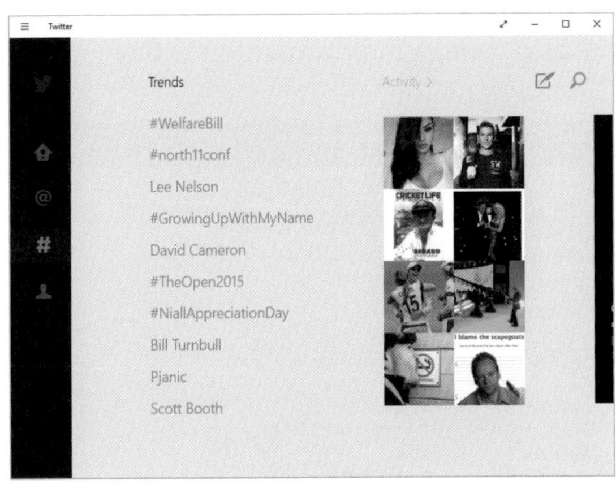

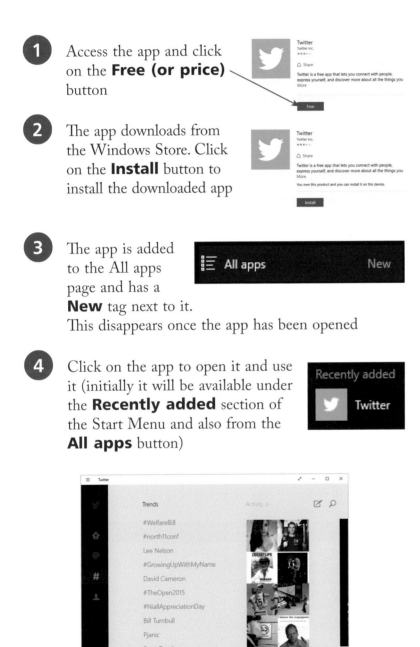

Don't forget

If there is a fee for an app, this will be displayed on, or next to, the **Install** button.

Once apps have been downloaded they can be reorganized and moved into different groups on the Start Menu, or dragged away from their default group to start a new one.

Viewing Apps

As you download more and more apps from the Windows Store you may lose track of which ones you have obtained and when. To help with this, you can review all of the apps you have downloaded, from within the Windows Store. To do this:

1. Open the Windows Store and click on your user account photo at the top of the screen

When there are updates available for apps that you have downloaded from the Windows Store, this will be indicated in the **Downloads and updates** section, which can be accessed from the menu in Step 2.

2. Click on the **Purchased** button

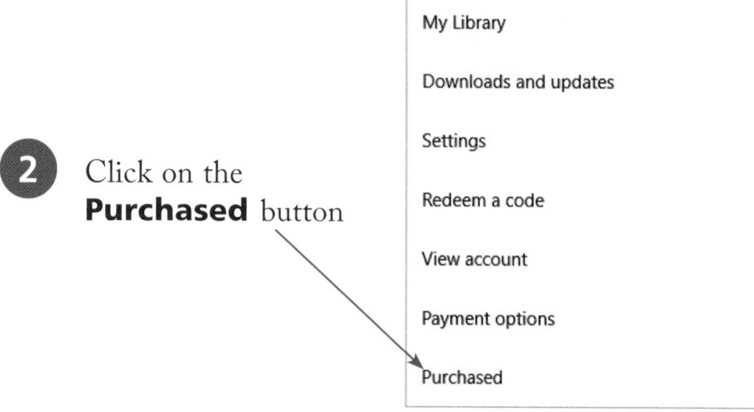

You can reinstall apps from the Downloads section, even if you have previously uninstalled them. If there was a fee for an app, you will not have to pay again to reinstall it.

3. Your Microsoft Account page opens in the Microsoft Edge browser and displays details of the apps that you have bought and downloaded

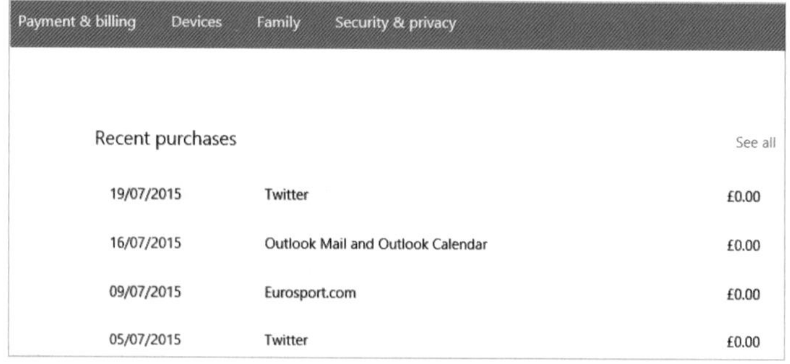

Installing and Uninstalling Apps

Installing apps from a CD or DVD

If the app you want to install is provided on a CD or DVD, you normally just insert the disc. The installation starts up automatically and you can follow the instructions to select features and complete the installation. To do this:

1. Insert the disc and click on this window

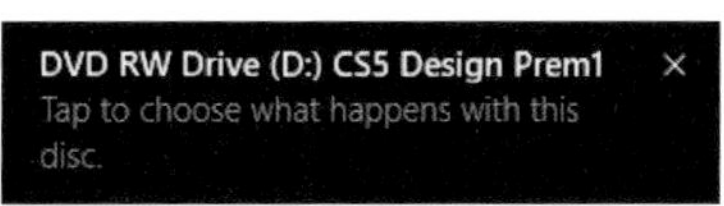

DVD RW Drive (D:) CS5 Design Prem1
Tap to choose what happens with this disc.

2. Double-click on the **Set-up.exe** file link to run it. Follow the on-screen prompts to install the app

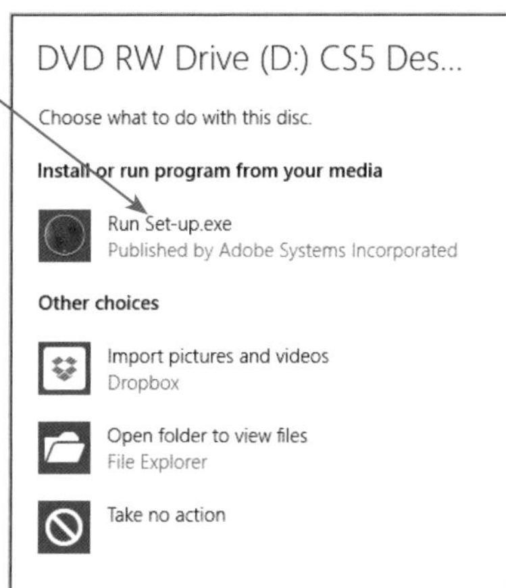

3. Apps that are installed from a CD or DVD are added within the **All apps** section on the Start Menu

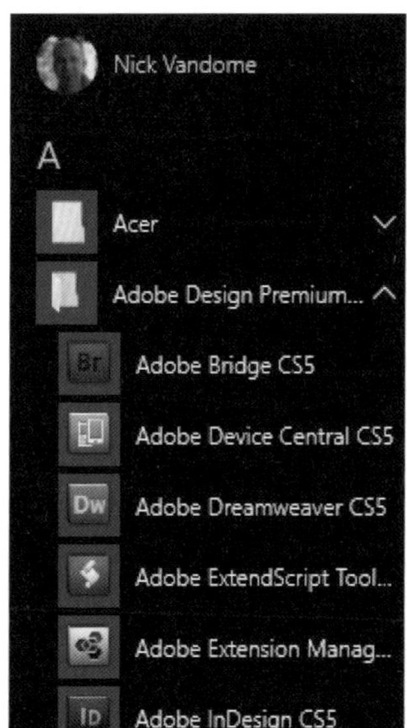

You can access the Run function in Windows 10 by right-clicking on the **Start Button** and selecting **Run** from the contextual menu.

Apps can also be installed from discs from within the File Explorer. To do this, locate the Set-up.exe file and double-click on it to start the installation process in the same way as in Step 2.

...cont'd

Uninstalling apps

In some previous versions of Windows, apps were uninstalled through the Control Panel. However, in Windows 10 they can also be uninstalled directly from the Start Menu. To do this:

1. Right-click on an app to access its menu

2. Click on the **Uninstall** button

3. A window alerts you to the fact that related information will be removed if the app is uninstalled. Click on the **Uninstall** button if you want to continue

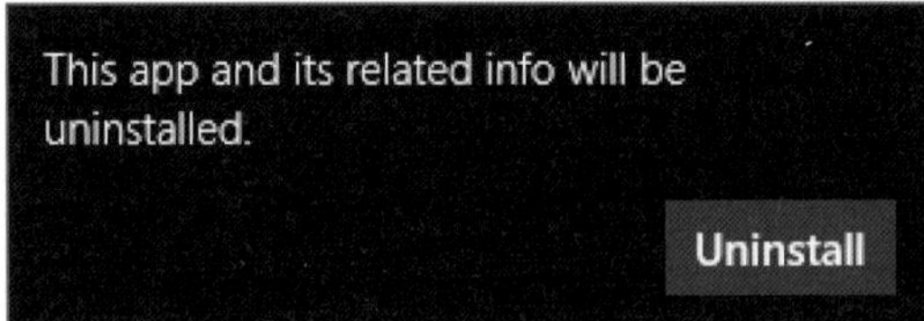

4. If the app is a new Windows 10 one, or has been pinned to the Start Menu or Taskbar, its tile will be removed from these locations. For other apps, they will no longer be available from the All apps option

If apps have been installed from a CD or DVD, they can also still be uninstalled from within the Control Panel. To do this, select the Programs options and click on the **Uninstall a Program** link. The installed apps will be displayed. Select one of the apps and click on the **Uninstall/Change** link.

Some elements of Windows 10, such as the Control Panel, still refer to apps as programs, but they are the same thing.

5 Internet and Email

Microsoft Edge is the first new web browser that Microsoft has produced in a generation. This chapter looks at how to use the Edge browser to open web pages, use tabs and bookmarks and add notes and graphics to pages. It also covers online activities such as shopping and using email.

Internet Connection

Before you can use the internet and browse the web, your computer needs to be set up for connection to the internet. To do this you will require:

- An Internet Service Provider (ISP), to provide an account that gives you access to the internet.
- A transmission network – cable, telephone or wireless.
- Some hardware to link into that transmission network.
- For a broadband connection, such as Digital Subscriber Line (DSL) or cable, you need a DSL or Cable modem or router, usually provided by the ISP.
- For dial-up connection, you need a dial-up modem, which is usually pre-installed on your computer.

Your ISP may provide software to help you set up your hardware, configure your system and register your ISP account details. However, if you are required to install the connection, or if you are configuring a second connection, you can use the Set Up a Connection or Network wizard.

Most ISPs also provide additional services such as email accounts, web servers and storage space on their internet servers, for you to create your own website.

1. Access the **Control Panel** and open the **Network and Internet** section, then select the **View network status and tasks** link, under the **Network and Sharing Center** heading

Network and Sharing Center
View network status and tasks | Connect to a network
View network computers and devices

2. Click on **Set up a new connection or network** link to display the connection options supported

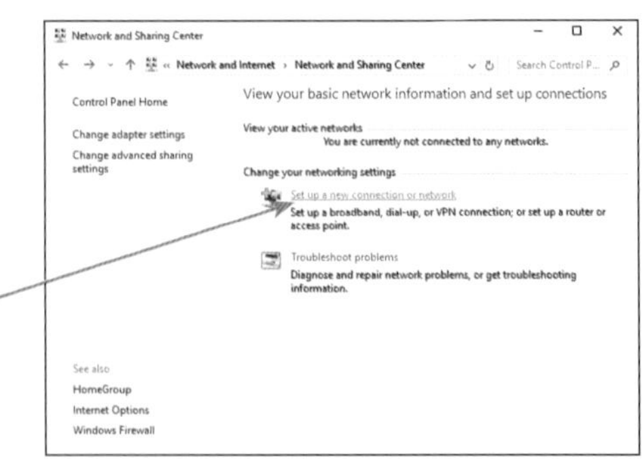

3. Select **Connect to the Internet** and click **Next**

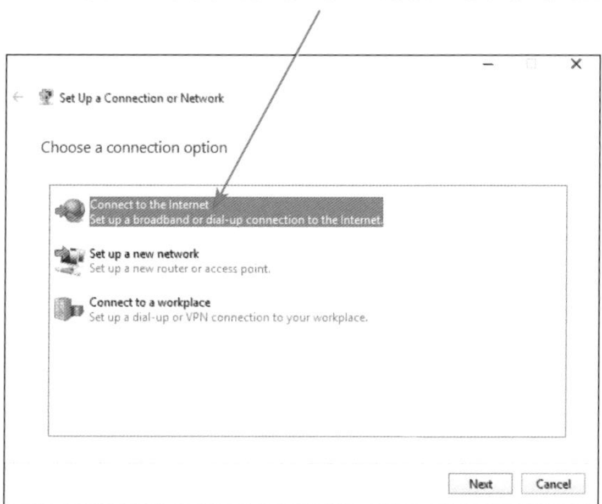

4. The **Connect to the Internet** wizard launches. Select the appropriate connection method from those offered

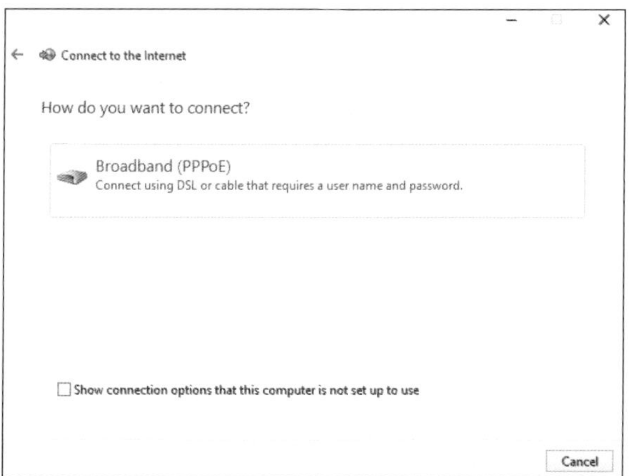

Windows identifies all of the possible connection methods based on the hardware configuration of your computer. If you have a wireless router or network, you may have an option for Wireless connection. If there is no dial-up modem installed, then the Dial-up connection method will not be offered.

If Windows has already recognized your connection, it detects this. You can select **Browse the Internet now** or **Set up a second connection** (e.g. as a backup).

Continue through the wizard to complete the definition of your internet connection, ready to start browsing the internet.

Introducing the Edge Browser

The web browser Internet Explorer (IE) has been synonymous with Microsoft for almost as long as the Windows operating system. Introduced in 1995, shortly after Windows 95, it has been the default browser for a generation of web users. However, as with most technologies, the relentless march of time has caught up with IE and, although it is still included with Windows 10, the preferred browser is a new one, designed specifically for the digital mobile age. It is called Microsoft Edge and adapts easily to whichever environment it is operating in: laptop, desktop, tablet or phone.

The Microsoft Edge browser has a number of performance and speed enhancements from IE and it also recognizes that modern web users want a lot more from their browser than simply being able to look at web pages. It includes a function for drawing on and annotating web pages, which can then be sent to other people as screenshots.

Internet Explorer can still be used with Windows 10 and it will probably continue to be supported for a considerable period of time.

There is also a Hub where you can store all of your favorites, downloads and pages that you have selected to read at a later date (which can be when you are offline if required).

Click on this icon on the **Taskbar** or the **All apps** menu to open the Microsoft Edge browser at the default Start page.

Back/forward Refresh Toolbar buttons

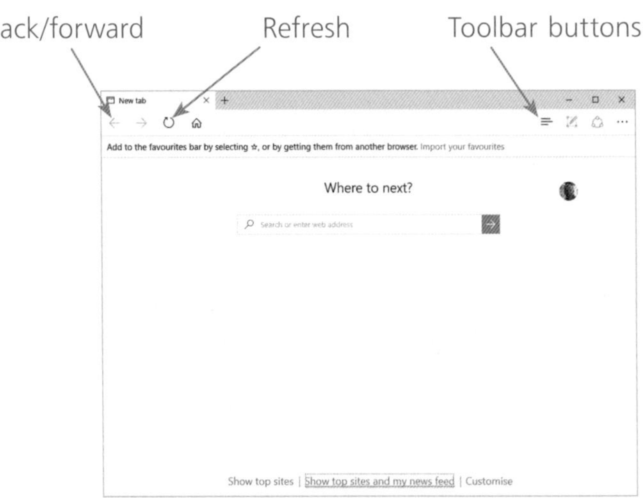

The Start page can also display news information.

The Start page can be replaced by your own specific Homepage, see page 92 for details.

Smart Address Bar

Smart address bars are now a familiar feature in a lot of modern browsers, and Microsoft Edge is no different. This can be used to enter a specific web address, to open the page, or to search for a word or phrase. To use the smart address bar:

1. Click anywhere in the Start page address box or in the address box at the top of a web page

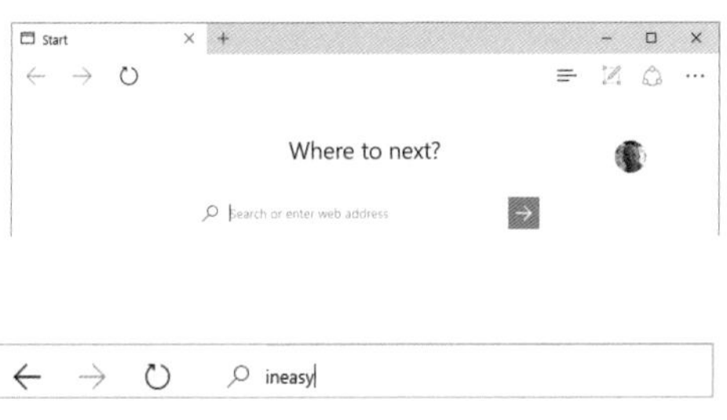

2. Start typing a word or website address. As you type, options appear below the address bar. Click on one of the options under **Sites** to go to a specific web page

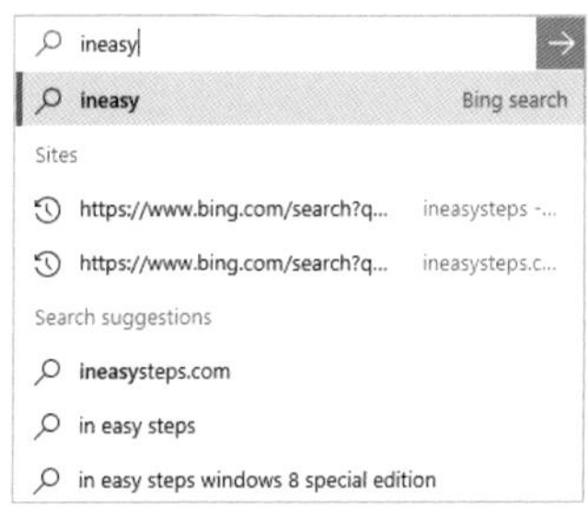

3. Click on one of the options under **Search suggestions**, to go to a page with these search results

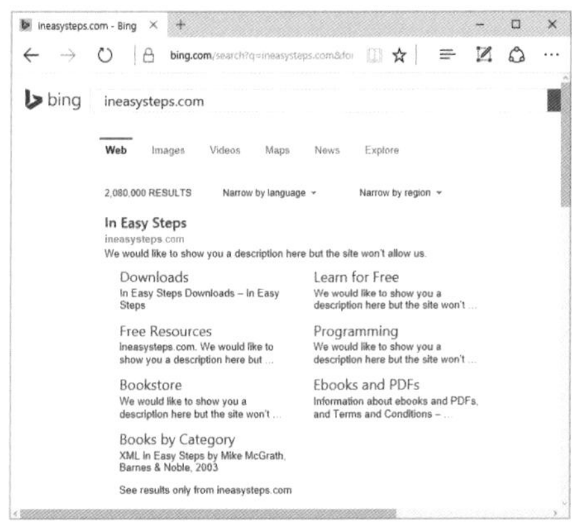

Different browsers can also be downloaded and used with Windows 10. Enter the browser name into a search engine, e.g. Firefox, select the appropriate link and follow the download instructions on the browser's Homepage.

The digital assistant, Cortana, can also be used to open web pages, by asking it to open a specific page address. The page will be opened in Microsoft Edge.

Setting a Homepage

By default, Microsoft Edge opens at its own Start page. This may not be ideal for most users, who will want to set their own Homepage to appear when Microsoft Edge is launched. To do this:

Hot tip

Within the settings for Microsoft Edge is an option for importing favorites from another web browser. To do this, click on the **Import favorites from another browser** button, select the required browser and click on the **Import** button.

1. Click on this button on the top toolbar to access the menu options
2. Click on the **Settings** button
3. By default, the Start page is selected as the opening page

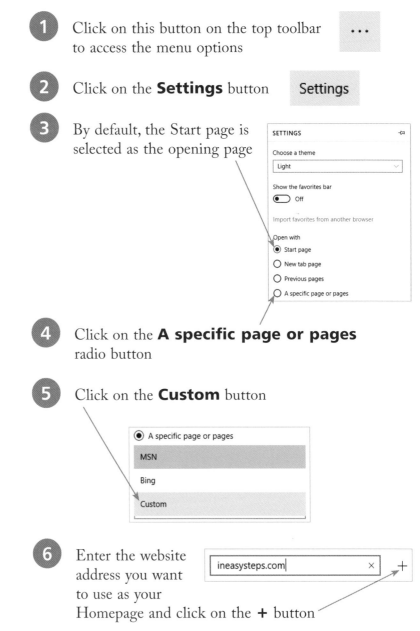

Other menu options can be accessed from the button in Step 1, including opening an InPrivate window which does not record any browsing details.

4. Click on the **A specific page or pages** radio button
5. Click on the **Custom** button

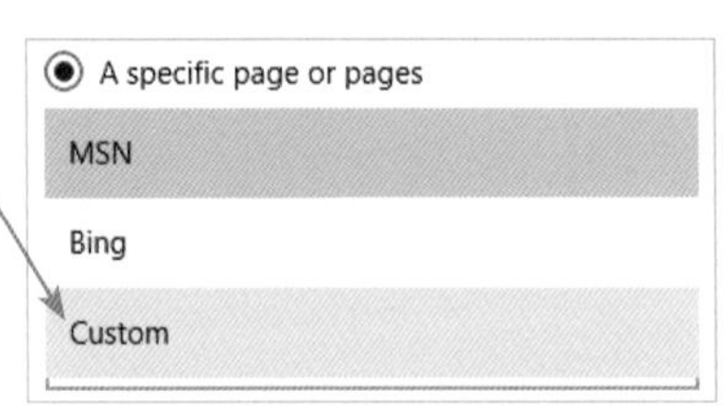

If a specific Homepage is assigned, the Start page as shown on page 90 will not be displayed.

6. Enter the website address you want to use as your Homepage and click on the **+** button

Using Tabs

Being able to open several web pages at the same time in different tabs is now a common feature of web browsers. To do this with Microsoft Edge:

1. Click on this button at the top of Microsoft Edge window

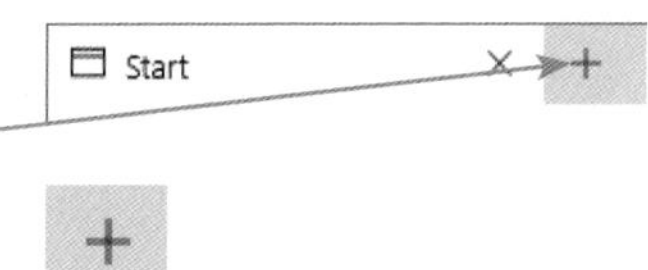

2. Pages can be opened in new tabs using the smart address bar, or via the list of **Top sites** that appears below it

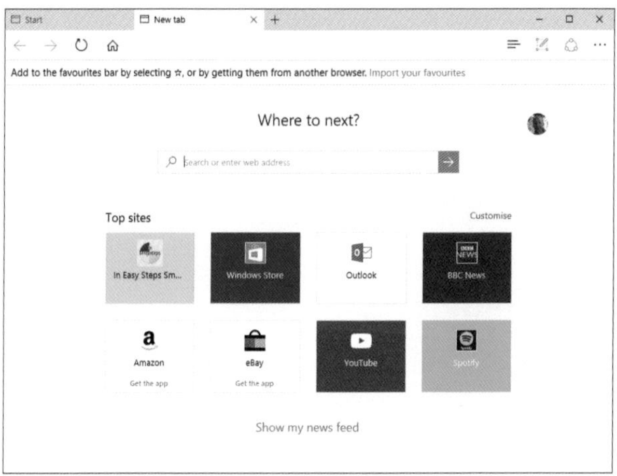

3. All open tabs are displayed at the top of the window. Click and hold on a tab to drag it into a new position

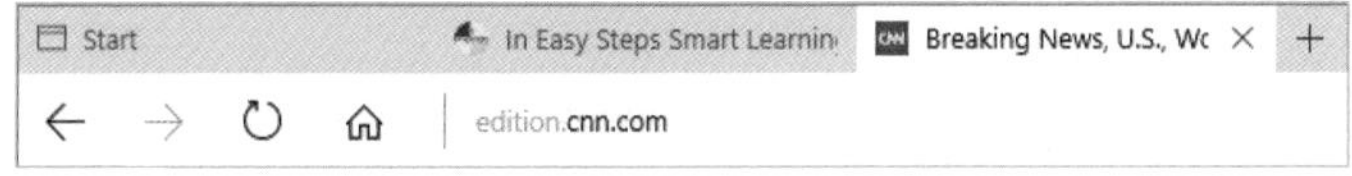

The Start page for new tabs, as displayed in Step 2, can be changed, if required. To do this, open the Microsoft Edge Settings as shown on the previous page, and change the selection under the **Open new tabs with** heading.

Move the cursor over one of the tabs at the top of the window to view a thumbnail of what the tab contains.

Bookmarking Web Pages

Your favorite web pages can be bookmarked so that you can access them with one click from the Hub area, rather than having to enter the web address each time. To do this:

1. Open the web page which you want to bookmark
2. Click on this button on the toolbar

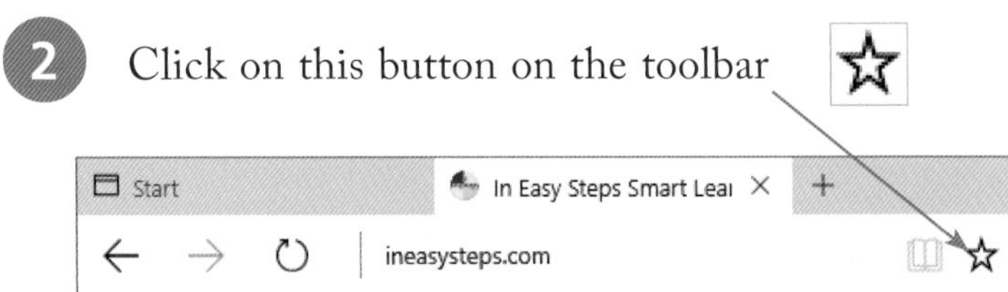

3. Click on the **Favorites** button
4. Enter a name for the favorite and where you want it to be saved to (click on the **Create new folder** link if you want to save it to a new location)
5. Click on the **Add** button
6. The star button turns yellow, indicating that the web page has been added as a favorite

7. Click on this button to access your favorites (see page 98)

The Favorites bar can be displayed underneath the address bar by opening the Microsoft Edge Settings and dragging the **Show the favorites bar** to **On**.

Adding Notes to Web Pages

One of the innovations in the Microsoft Edge browser is the ability to draw on and annotate web pages. This can be useful to highlight parts of a web page or add your own comments and views, which can then be sent to other people. To add notes:

1. Open a web page to which you want to add a note or draw on, and click on this button on the toolbar of the Microsoft Edge browser

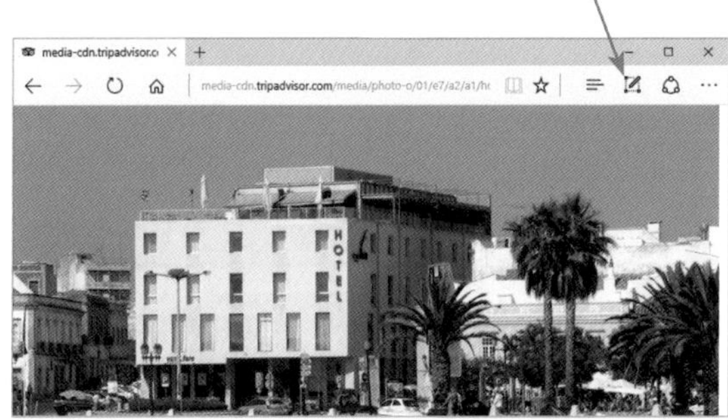

2. Click on one of the pen options

3. Select formatting and shape options for the pen

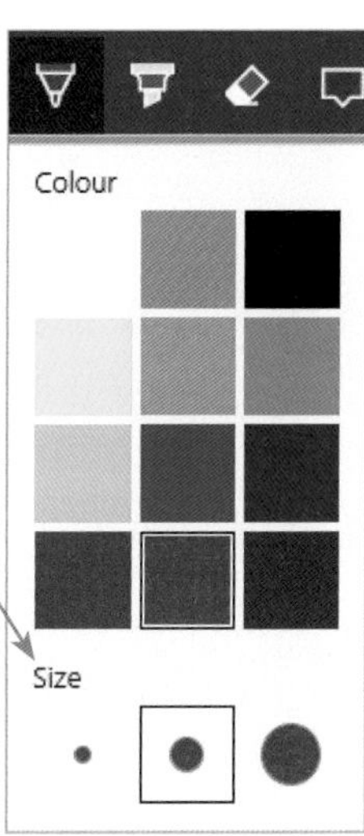

Click on this button on the Notes toolbar to create a Web clipping. This is an area of a web page that is selected by dragging over it to make the selection. Web clippings can be shared in the same way as notes.

Click on this button on the Notes toolbar to **Save** a web note or a clipping. These can then be accessed from the Favorites section of Microsoft Edge or shared (see pages 97-98).

...cont'd

4. Click and drag on the web page to draw over it

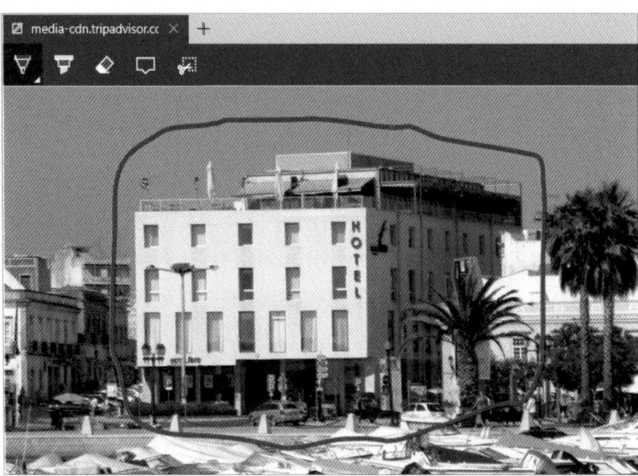

Several notes can be added to a web page, but it can begin to look a bit cluttered if there are too many.

5. Click on the eraser icon and drag over any items that you have drawn to remove them, or part of them

6. Click on the text icon to add your own text

7. Drag over the web page to create a text box

8. Type the text that you want displayed on the web page

This is the one I mentioned.

Click the recycle bin icon in Step 8 to delete a text box.

9. Click and drag here on a text box to move its position

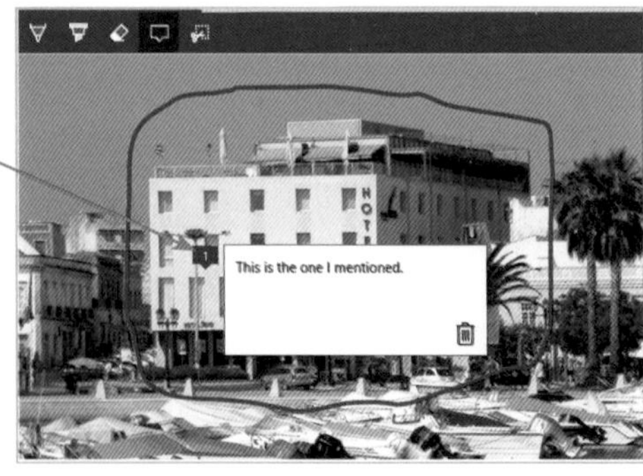

Sharing Notes and Clippings

Once you have created a web note, this can be saved or shared with other people. There is also an option for selecting part of a web page and sharing this too.

Sharing a web note

To share a web note with other people:

1. Once the web note is finished, click on this button on the toolbar to share the web note

2. Select an app with which you want to share the web note

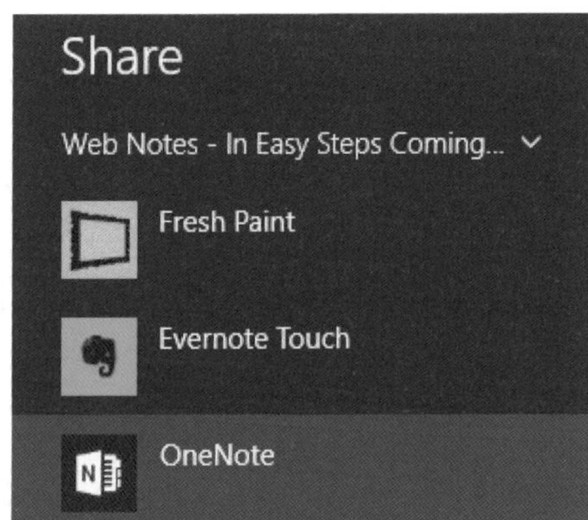

The process for sharing a web clipping is the same as for a web note.

3. The web note is displayed in the selected app

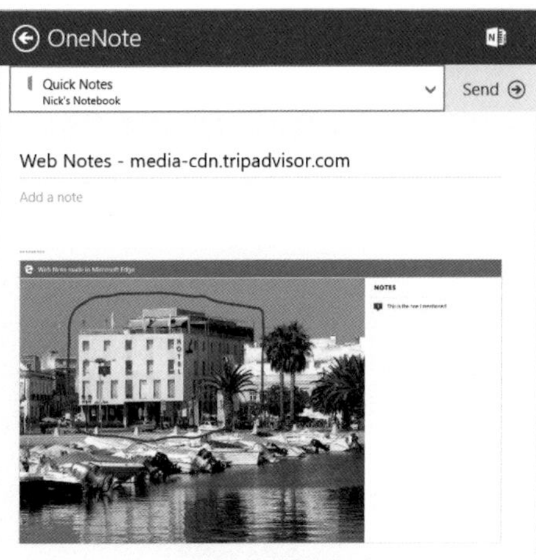

4. Click on the **Send** button to send the web note to the app

Organizing with the Hub

The Hub is the area where you can store a variety of items for the Microsoft Edge browser: from your favorite web pages, to pages that you want to read offline at a later date. To use the Hub:

The Favorites window also has an option for importing favorites from other web browsers. Click on the **Import favorites** link, select the required browser and click on the **Import** button.

1. Click on this button to open the Hub

2. Click on this button to view your favorites. Click on one to go to that page

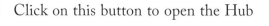

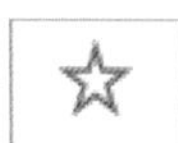

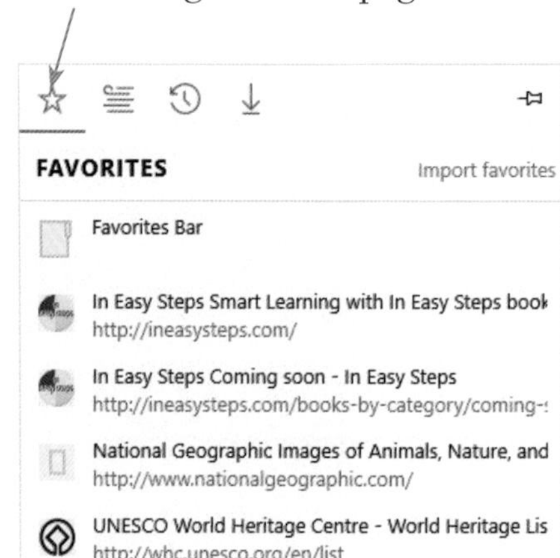

3. Click on this button to view your Reading List, for pages you have saved to read offline

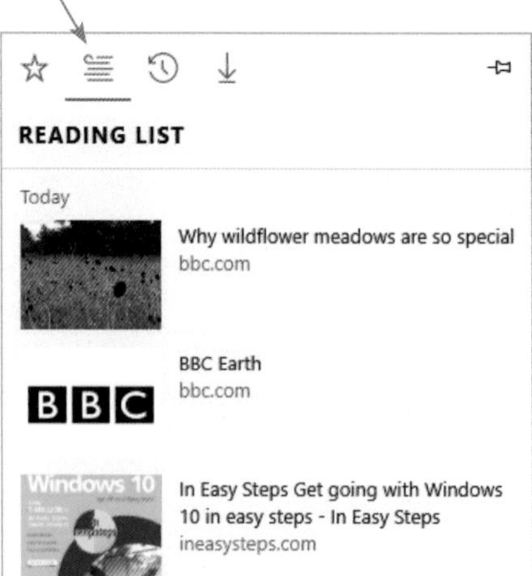

4. Click on this button to view your web browsing history

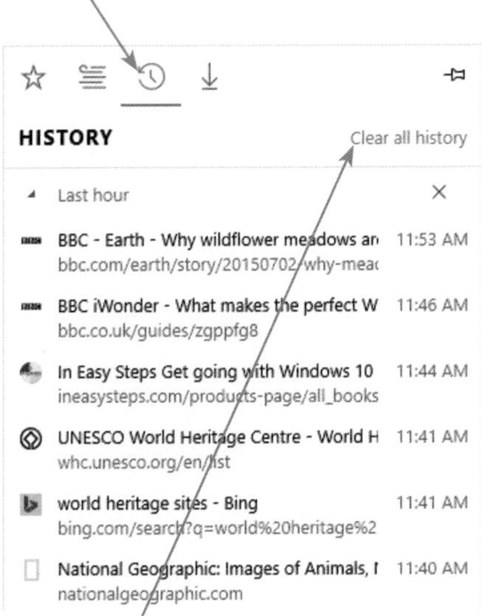

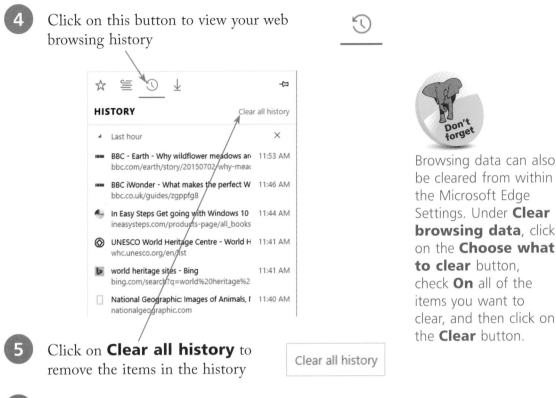

5. Click on **Clear all history** to remove the items in the history

6. Click on this button to view items that you have downloaded from the web, such as PDF documents or apps to install (although not those from the Windows Store)

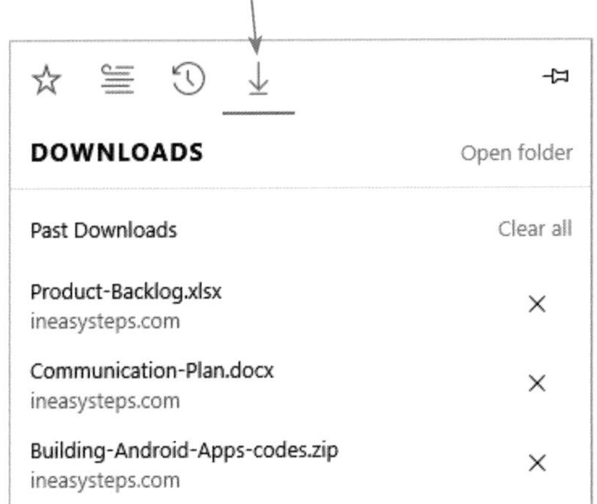

Browsing data can also be cleared from within the Microsoft Edge Settings. Under **Clear browsing data**, click on the **Choose what to clear** button, check **On** all of the items you want to clear, and then click on the **Clear** button.

Shopping Online

Some people love physically looking around shops, while for others it is a chore. For the latter group, online shopping is one of the great innovations of the web. With a laptop, it is possible to do your shopping in the comfort of your own home, while also avoiding the crowds.

When you are shopping online there are some guidelines that you should follow, to try to ensure you are in a safe online environment and do not spend too much money:

A lot of online shopping sites list recommendations for you based on what you have already looked at or bought on the site. This is done by using "cookies", which are small programs that are downloaded from the site, and then track the items that you look at on the site (see the next page for further information on cookies).

- Make a note of what you want to buy and stick to this once you have found it. Online shopping sites are adept at displaying a lot of enticing offers and it is a lot easier to buy something by clicking a button than it is to physically take it to a checkout.
- Never buy anything that is promoted to you via an email, unless it is from a company who you have asked to send you promotional information.
- When paying for items, make sure that the online site has a secure area for accepting payment and credit card details. A lot of sites display information about this within their payment area, and another way to ascertain this is to check in the address bar of the payment page. If it is within a secure area, the address of the page will start with "https" rather than the standard "http".

Using online shopping

The majority of online shopping sites are similar in their operation:

- Goods are identified.
- Goods are placed in a shopping basket.

- Once the shopping is completed you proceed to the checkout.

- For some sites you have to register before you can complete your purchase, while with others you do not.

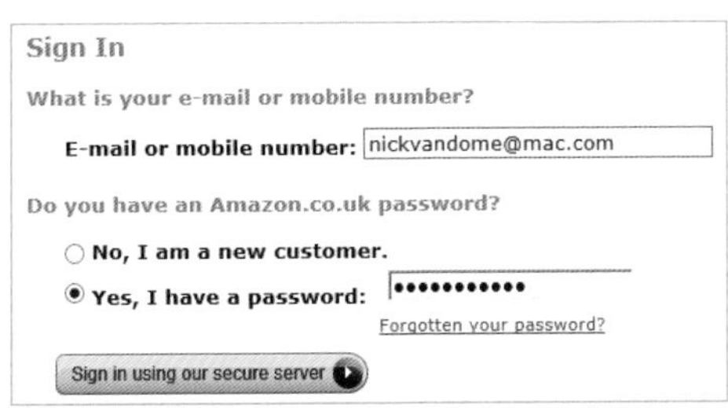

- You enter your shipping details and pay for the goods, usually with a credit or debit card.

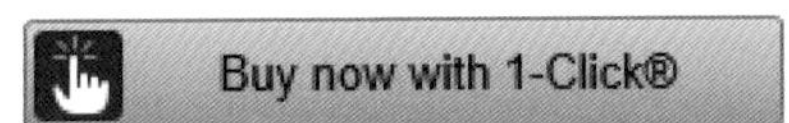

In some cases, if you are registered on a site, you can complete your shopping by using a 1-click system. This means that all of your billing, delivery and payment details are already stored on the site and you can buy goods simply by clicking one button without having to re-enter your details. One of the most prominent sites to use this method is Amazon.

Using cookies

A lot of online shopping sites use cookies, which are small programs that store information about your browsing habits on the site. Sites have to tell you if they are using cookies and they can be a good way to receive targeted information about products in which you are interested. This can be done on the sites when you are logged in, or via email.

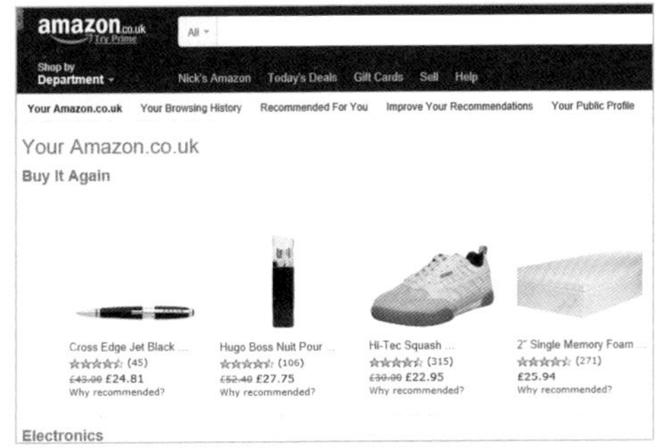

One-click shopping is an effective way to spend money very quickly. However, you usually have a period of time in which you can cancel your purchases after you have bought them in this way.

Booking a Vacation

Just as many retailers have created an online presence, the same is also true for vacation companies and travel agents. It is now possible to book almost any type of vacation on the web, from cruises to city breaks.

Several sites offer full travel services where they can deal with flights, hotels, insurance, car hire and excursions. These sites include:

- **www.expedia.com**
- **www.kayak.com**
- **www.orbitz.com**
- **www.travelocity.com**

These sites usually list special offers and last-minute deals on their Homepages, or if you sign up to an email newsletter. There is also a facility for specifying your precise requirements. To do this:

It is always worth searching different sites to get the best possible prices. In some cases, it is cheapest to buy different elements of a vacation from different sites, e.g. flights from one and accommodation from another.

1. Select your vacation requirements. This can include flight or hotel only, or a combination of both, with or without car hire options

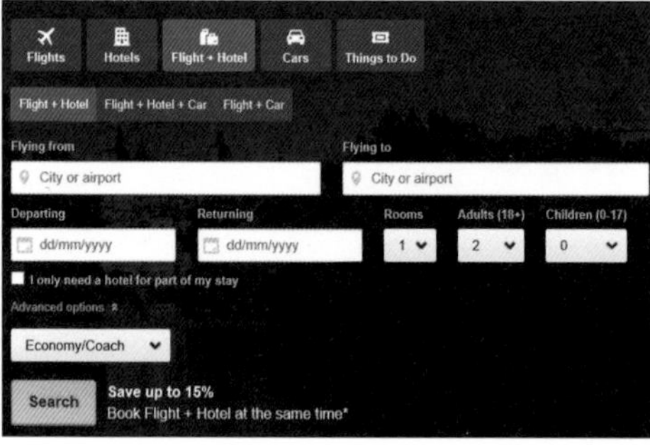

2. Enter flight details
3. Enter dates for your vacation
4. Click on the **Search** button

TripAdvisor

One of the best resources for travelers is TripAdvisor. Not only does the site provide a full range of opportunities for booking flights and hotels, it also has an extensive network of reviews from people who have visited the countries, hotels and restaurants on the site. These are independent and usually very fair and honest. In a lot of cases, if there are issues with a hotel or restaurant, the proprietor posts a reply to explain what is being done to address any problems.

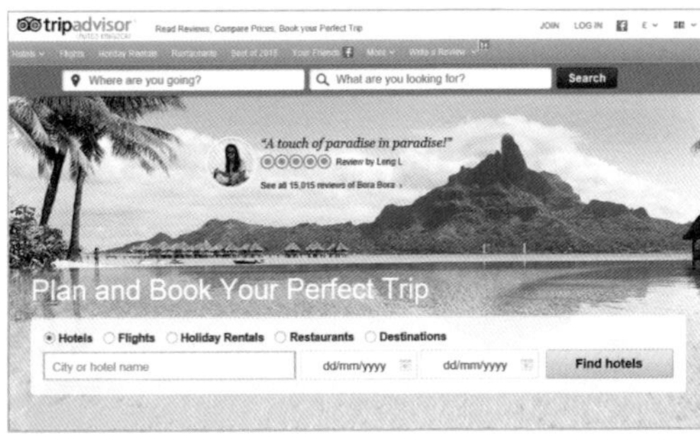

Vacation and hotel websites usually have versions that are specific to your geographical location.

Cruises

There are also websites dedicated specifically to cruises:

- **www.carnival.com**
- **www.cruises.com**
- **www.princess.com**

The web is also excellent for researching family history and genealogy. Some sites to try are Ancestry, Genealogy, FamilySearch and RootsWeb.Ancestry.

Hotels

There are a range of websites that specialize in hotel bookings, a lot of them at short notice to get the best price:

- **www.choicehotels.com**
- **www.hotels.com**
- **www.laterooms.com**
- **www.trivago.com**

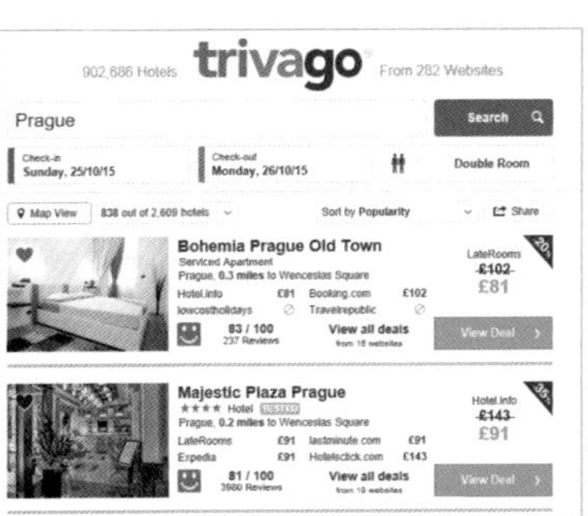

Setting Up Mail

Email has become an essential part of everyday life, both socially and in the business world. Windows 10 accommodates this with the Mail app. This can be used to link to online services such as Gmail and Outlook (the renamed version of Hotmail), and also other email accounts. To set up an email account with Mail:

You will also be prompted to add an account when you first access **Mail**, if you do not already have an account set up.

1. Click on the **Mail** app on the Start Menu

2. Click on the **Get started** button

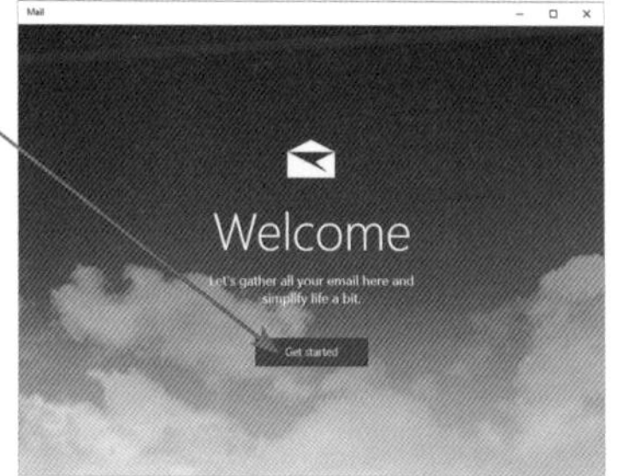

The **Other account** option in Step 4 can be used to add a non-web-mail account. This is usually a POP3 account and you will need your email address, username, password, and usually the incoming and outgoing email servers. If you do not know these, they should be supplied by your email provider. They should also be available in the Accounts settings of the email app you want to add to the Mail app.

3. Click on the **Add account** button

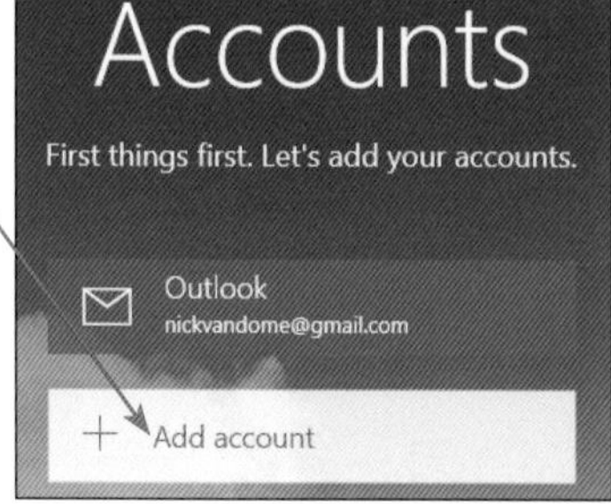

4. Select the type of account to which you want to link, via the Mail app. This can be an online email account that you have already set up

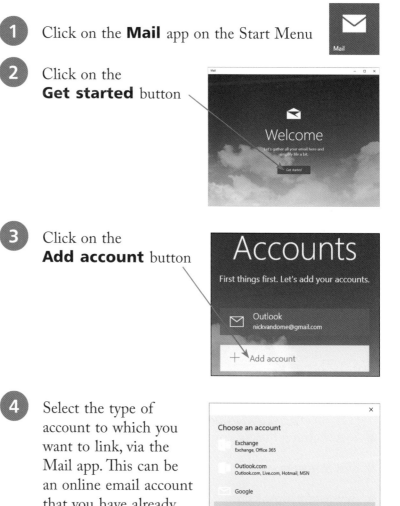

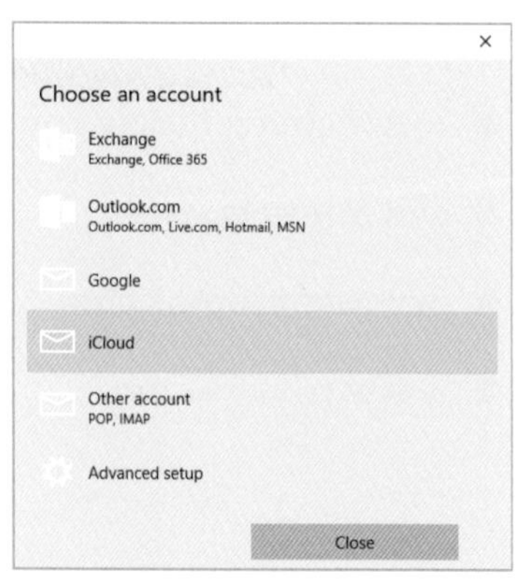

5 Enter your current login details for the selected email account and click on the **Sign-in** button

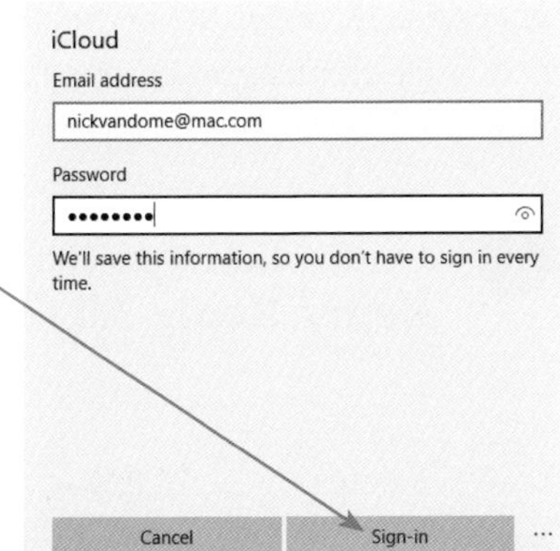

6 Once it has been connected, the details of the account are shown under the Accounts heading, including the mailboxes within the account. Click on the **Inbox** to view the emails within it

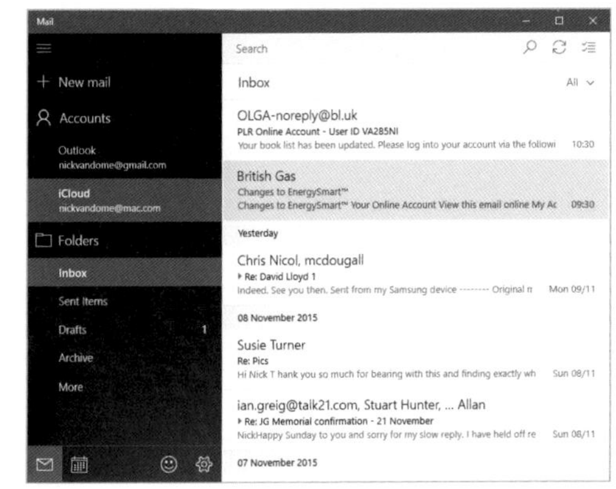

7 The list of emails appears in the left-hand pane. Double-click on an email to view it at full size

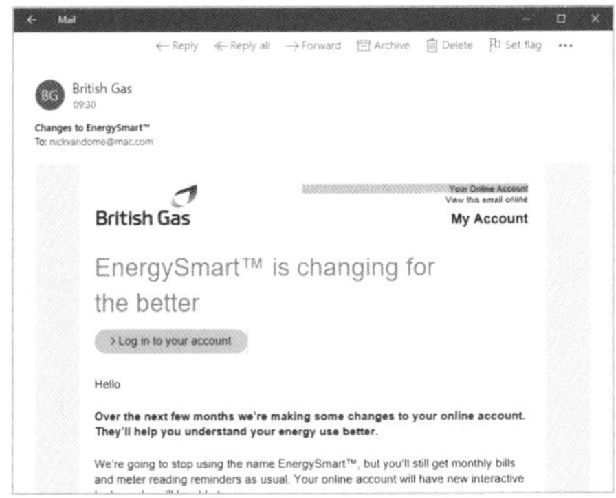

You can add more than one account to the Mail app. If you do this you will be able to select the different accounts to view them within Mail.

By default, the main window displays the item that was most recently selected in your Inbox.

Working with Mail

Once you have set up an account in the Mail app, you can then start creating and managing your emails with it.

1. On the Inbox page, open an email and click on the **Reply**, **Reply All** or **Forward** buttons to respond

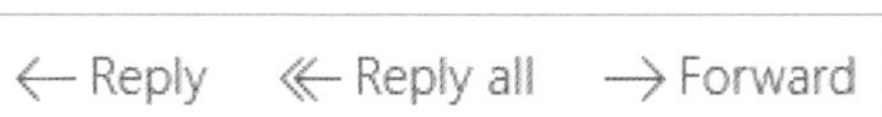

2. Open an email and click on the **Delete** button to remove it

Contacts that are added automatically as email recipients are taken from the People app, providing there is an email address connected to their entry.

Composing email

To compose and send an email message:

1. Click on this button to create a new message

2. Click in the **To** field and enter an email address

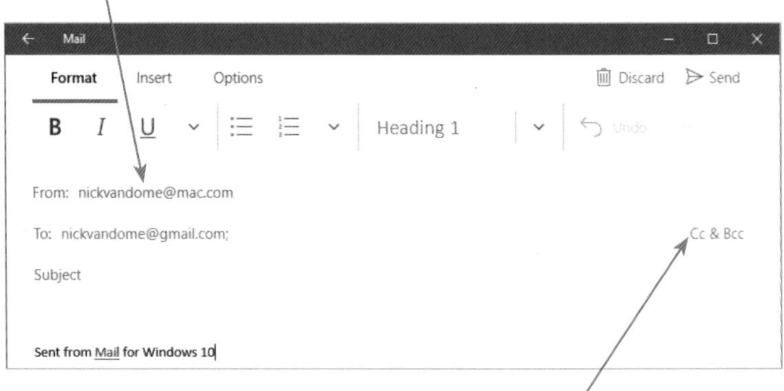

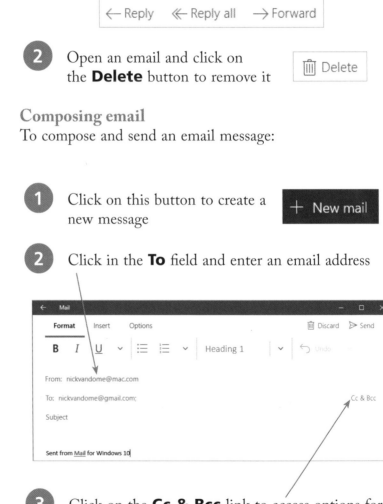

3. Click on the **Cc & Bcc** link to access options for blind copying and priority level

4. The email address can be in the format of myname@provider.com or enter the name of one of your contacts in the People app, and the email address will be entered automatically

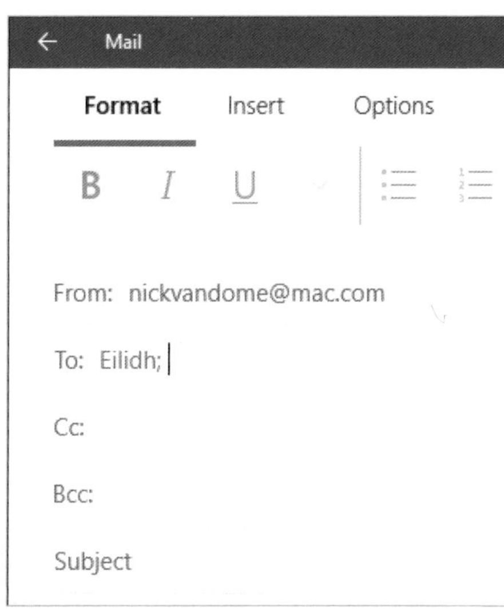

5. Enter a subject heading and body text to the email

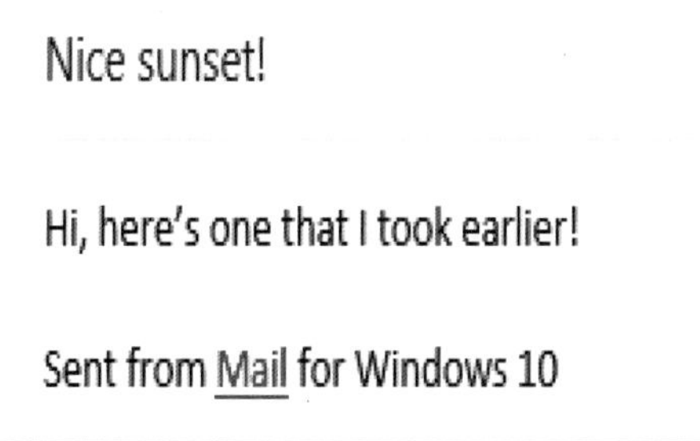

Nice sunset!
Hi, here's one that I took earlier!
Sent from Mail for Windows 10

6. Highlight an item of text and select the text formatting options from the top toolbar

Several recipients can be added to a single email, as long as you are happy for them to receive the same message and for them to see each others' email addresses. If not, use the Bcc (blind copy) option to hide recipients from one another.

...cont'd

7. Click on the **Insert** button on the top toolbar in the new email window and select one of the options, such as **Pictures**

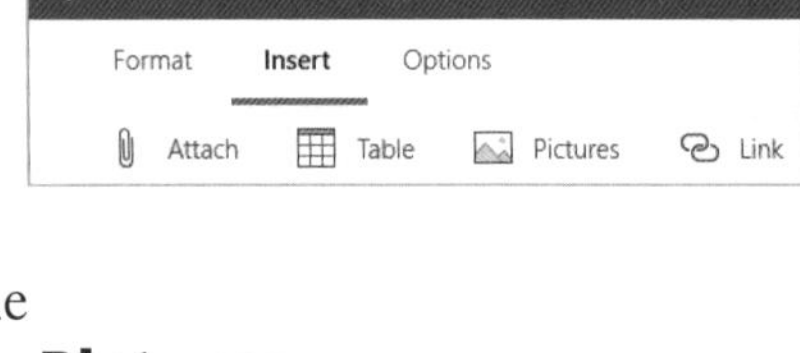

8. Click on a folder to locate the file, select the file, then click on the **Insert** button

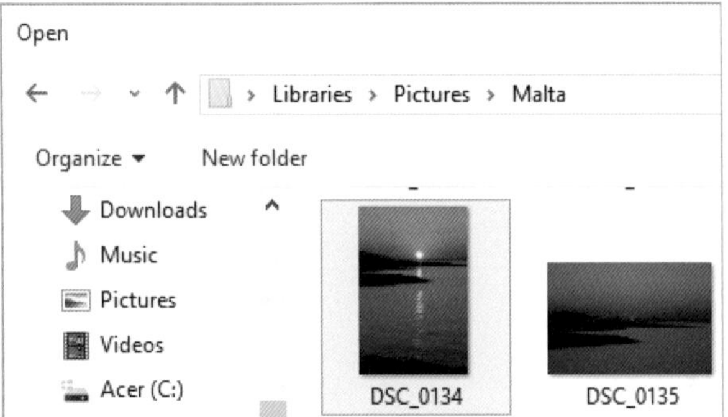

9. The file is shown in the body of the email

10. Click on this button to send the email

6 It's a Digital World

This chapter shows how to work with a range of apps that can be used for entertainment and organization, so that you can fully immerse yourself in the digital world with your laptop.

Viewing Photos

The Photos app can be used to manage and edit your photos, including those stored in your **Pictures** Library. To do this:

1. Click on the **Photos** app on the **Start Menu**

2. Click here to expand and contract the Photos app's menu

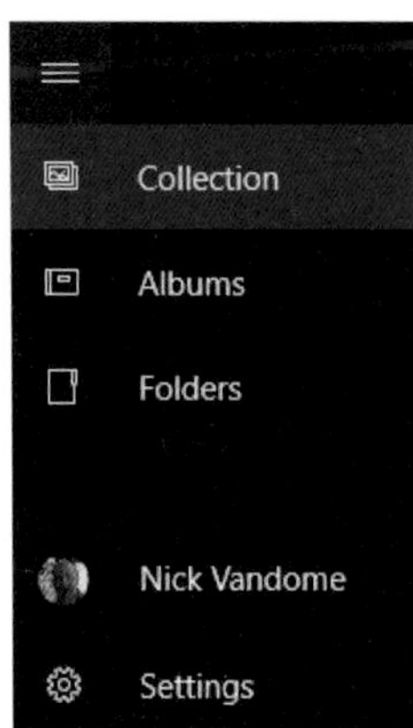

3. Click on the **Collection** button to view all of the photos in the Photos app, arranged by date. Scroll up and down to view the photos

Hot tip

To import photos into the Photos app, click on this button on the top toolbar and select the location from where you want to import the photos. This can be a folder on your own computer; a camera or pen drive attached with a USB cable; or a memory card from a camera inserted into a card reader.

4. Click on the **Albums** button to view photos from specific albums. This includes the Camera roll

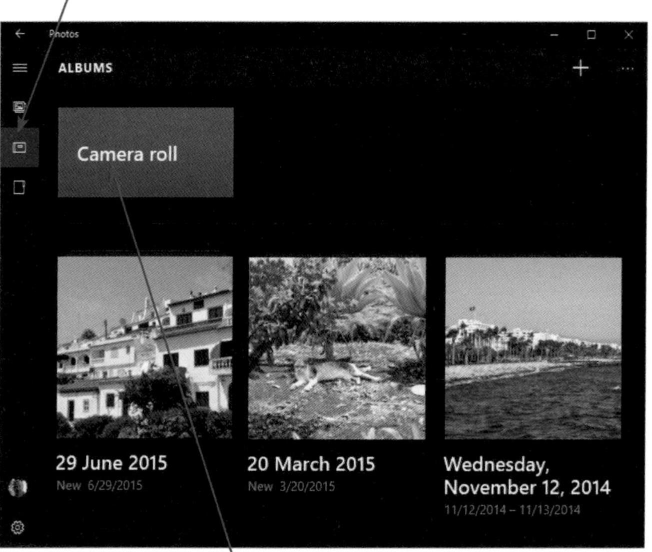

5. Click on the **Camera roll** button to view photos that have been taken with your computer's camera (or copied into this folder from another location)

The albums displayed are taken from those stored in the specific folders in File Explorer (by default the Pictures library). However, the Photos app displays what it thinks are the best photos in the folder, thus creating its own albums.

To include an existing folder in the Camera roll, right-click on it in File Explorer and click on **Include in library > Camera Roll** from the menu.

...cont'd

6. Within the Albums section, double-click on an album to view its contents. The first photo is also displayed as a banner at the top of the album

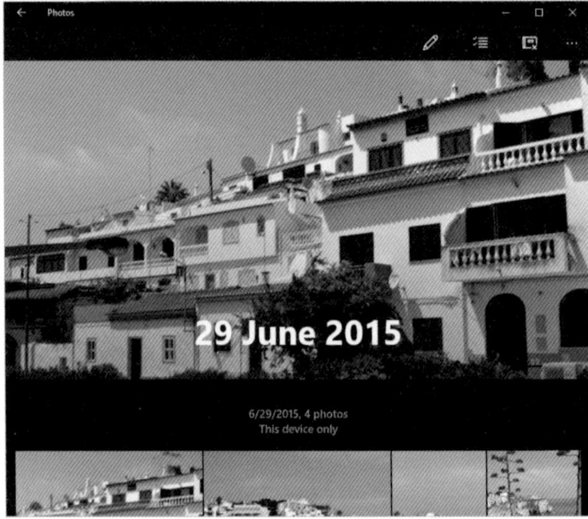

The options from where photos are displayed in the Albums section can be specified from the **Settings** button on the Photos left-hand toolbar. The default album is **Pictures**, but new ones can be added using the **Add a folder** button. There is also an option for showing photos and videos from your OneDrive folder.

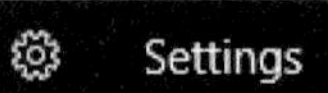

7. Double-click on a photo within an album, or collection, to view it at full size. Move the cursor over the photo and click on the left and right arrows (if available) to move through an album or collection

8. Move the cursor over the bottom, right-hand corner and click on the **+** or - symbols to zoom in or out on a photo

Selecting Photos

Photos within either a collection or an album in the Photos app can be selected and then shared with other people in various ways, or deleted. To do this:

1. In Collections, or an open album, click on this button at the top of the Photos toolbar

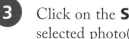

2. Click here to select a photo or photos

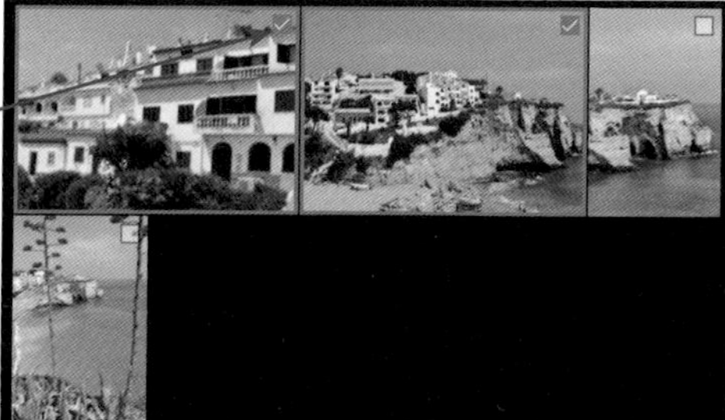

3. Click on the **Share** button to share the selected photo(s)

4. Click on one of the options for sharing the selected photo(s)

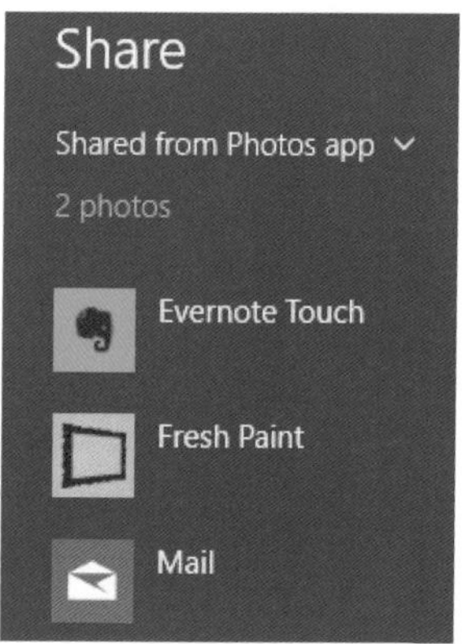

5. Click on the **Copy** button in Step 3 so that they can be pasted into another app

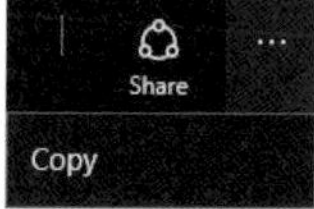

Editing Photos

In Windows 10, the Photos app now has a range of editing functions so that you can improve and enhance your photos. To use these:

NEW

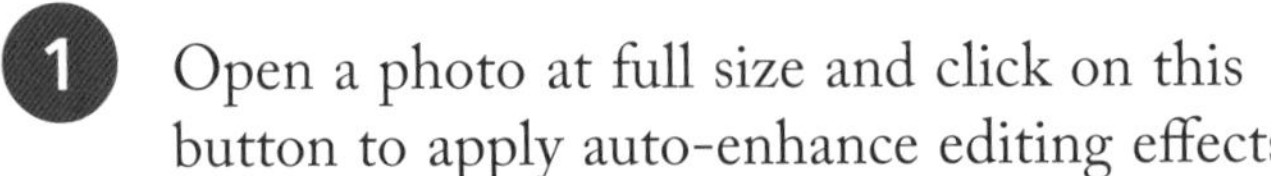

1. Open a photo at full size and click on this button to apply auto-enhance editing effects

2. Click on the **Edit** button on the top toolbar to access additional editing options. Click on one of the buttons on the left-hand side to view the options on the right-hand side

3. For the **Basic fixes** option, click on one of the buttons at the right-hand side of the screen to apply that effect to the photo, including Enhance, Rotate, Crop, Straighten, Red eye and Retouch

4. For the **Crop** option in Step 3, drag the resizing handles at the corner of the photo to select the area that you want to keep. The area outside of the crop area will be removed

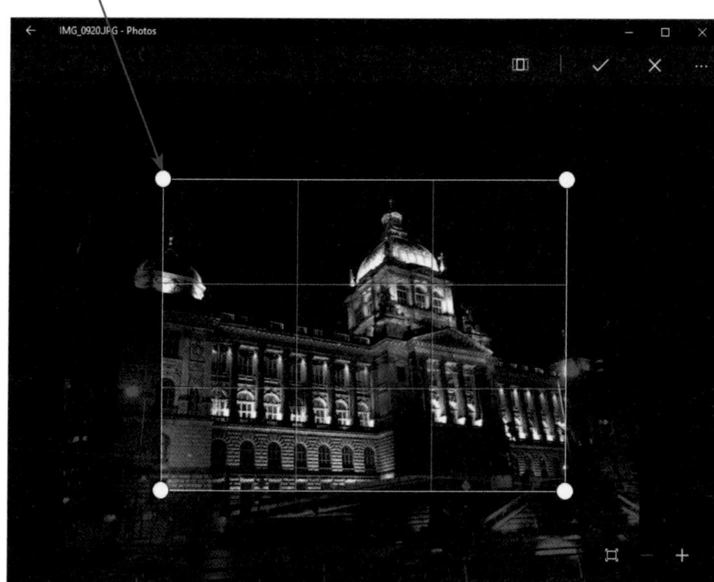

Most photos benefit from some degree of cropping, so that the main subject is given greater prominence by removing unwanted items in the background.

...cont'd

5. For the **Filters** option, click on one of the filter effects to apply that to the current photo

It is always worth editing the brightness and contrast of a photo, if only to see if you like the effect. If not, you can undo the action (see Step 11 on the next page).

6. For the **Light** option, click on one of the options at the right-hand side to edit the Brightness, Contrast, Highlights and Shadows of the photo

7. For the **Color** option, click on one of the options at the right-hand side to edit the Temperature, Tint, Saturation and apply a Color boost to the color in the photo

8. For the **Effects** option, click on one of the options at the right-hand side to create a Vignette or a Selective focus effect

9. For the **Vignette** effect, a circular drop-shadow border is created around the photo, to give it an artistic effect

10. For the **Light, Color** and **Effects** options, drag around this circle to apply the effect

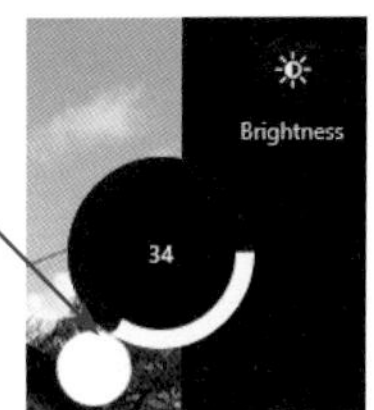

11. Click on the **Undo** button to go back one step in the editing process

12. Click on these buttons to, from left to right, save a copy of the edited photo, apply the changes to the original or cancel the editing changes

Selective focus enables areas of a photo to be blurred, to create an artistic effect and highlight the main subject. In traditional photography, this is known as "depth of field".

Groove Music App

The Groove Music app is used to access music that you have added to your computer and also the Music section of the Windows Store. From there, you can preview, buy and download more music. To do this:

1. Click on the **Groove Music** app on the Start Menu

2. Click on the **Menu** button to expand the menu so that the titles are visible, not just the icons

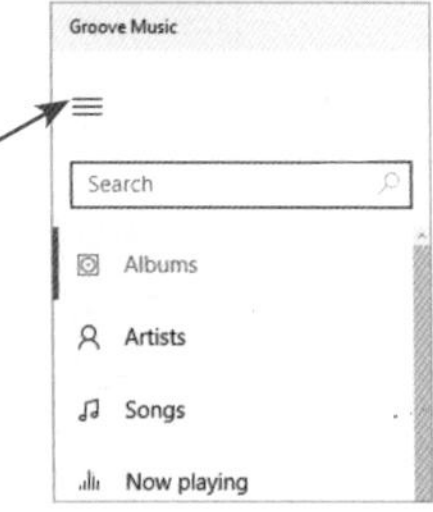

3. Click on a category to view those items

4. Click on the **Get music in Store** button to access the Music section of the Windows Store

5. Browse through the store using the categories in the main window. Click on an item to preview it

6. Once you have selected an item, you can preview individual tracks, view information about the artist and buy albums or specific tracks

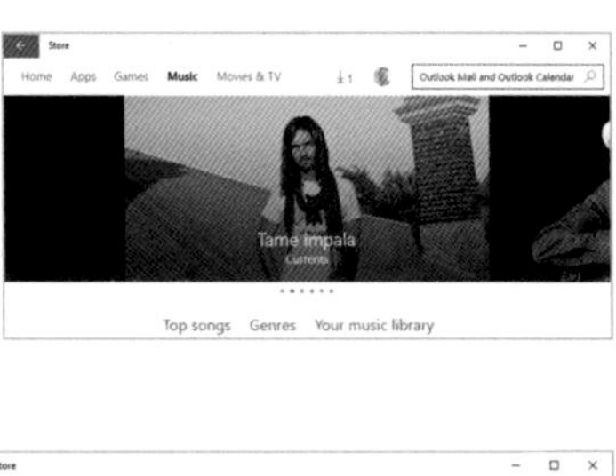

Don't forget

Scroll up and down to view the rest of the available content in the Music section of the Windows Store.

Hot tip

Use the Search box in the top right-hand corner to search for artists, albums or tracks.

Don't forget

Music that has been bought in the Music section of the Windows Store is then available to be played within the Groove Music app.

Playing Music

Playing your own music

Music that has been added to your computer can be played through the Groove Music app, and you can specify more music to be included as and when it is added. To do this:

1. Open the Groove Music app and click on either the **Albums**, **Artists**, or **Songs** buttons

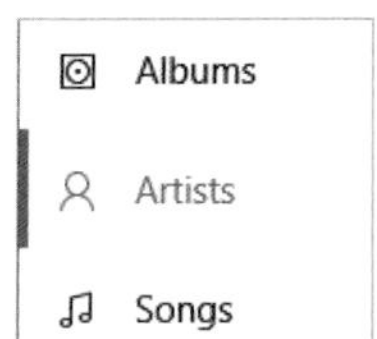

You can also add music that you have stored in your OneDrive folder.

2. Click on the **Change where we look** link to edit where the Groove Music app looks for music on your computer

All done! We've added the music from this PC.
Change where we look

3. Click on this button to add a new location from where music can be added to the Groove Music app

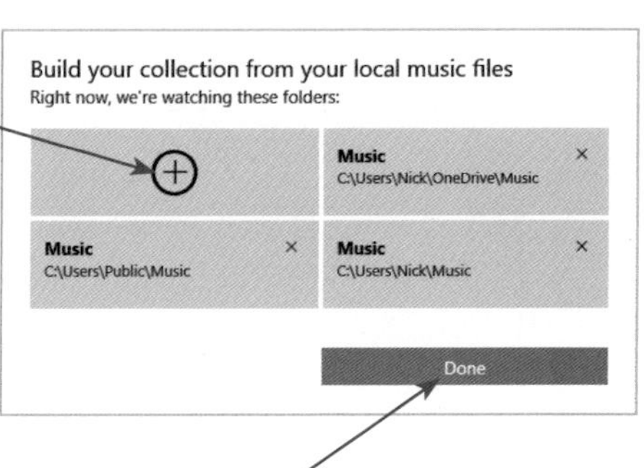

Hot tip

When a folder is added to the Music library, any music that is copied here will be displayed by the Groove Music app.

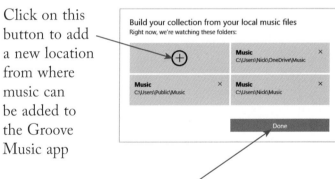

4. Click on the **Done** button

5. Items from the locations selected in Step 3 are displayed under the categories buttons. For albums, click on an item to view all of its tracks

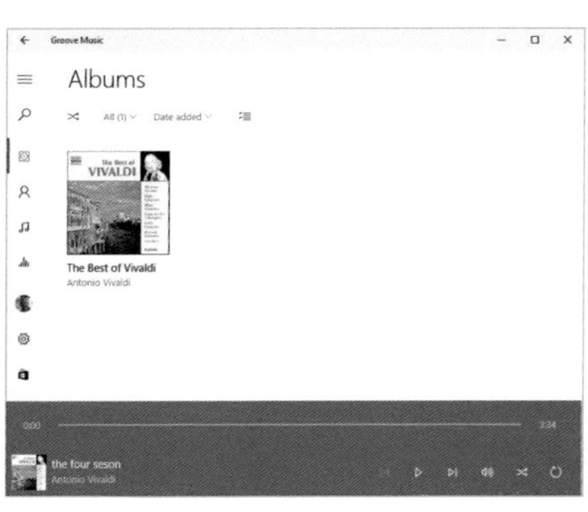

...cont'd

6. Double-click on an individual track to play it or click on the **Play** button to play a whole album

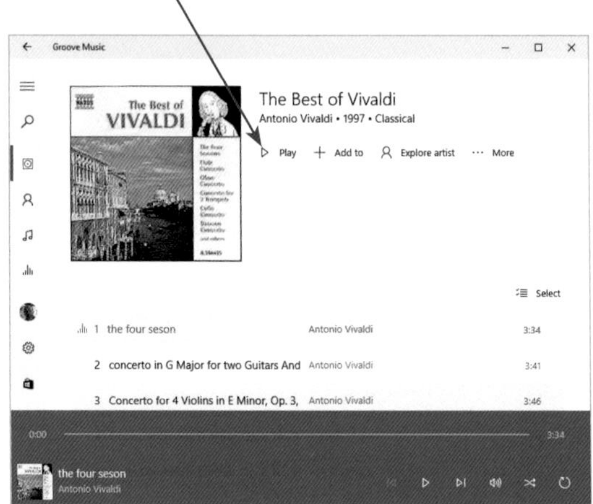

7. This button is displayed next to the currently playing track and its details are displayed at the bottom of the Groove Music app's window

8. Drag this button to move through the current track

9. Use these buttons to, from left to right: go to the start of a track; pause/play a track; go to the end of a track; change, or mute, the volume; shuffle the available tracks; or repeat a track

Do not copy any music and use it for commercial purposes, as this will infringe the copyright of the artist.

Viewing Movies and TV

For movie and TV lovers, the Movies & TV app performs a similar function to the Groove Music app. It connects to the Windows Store from where you can preview and buy your favorite movies and TV shows.

By default, DVDs cannot be played on Windows 10 computers. To do this you have to download and buy an enhanced version of the Windows Media Player from the Microsoft website.

1. Click on the **Movies & TV** app on the Start Menu

2. Click on the Menu button to view the titles for each category (in the same way as for the Groove Music app)

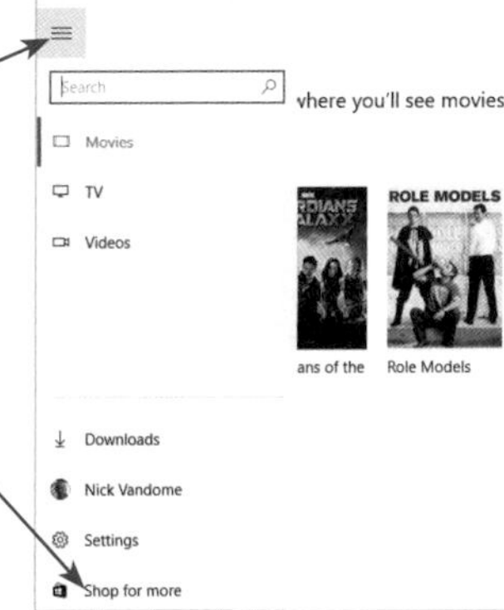

3. Click on the **Shop for more** button to access the **Movies & TV** section of the Windows Store

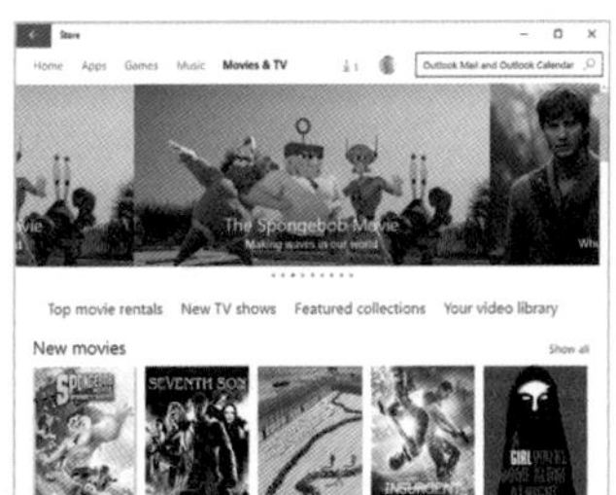

You can add your own video clips to the Movies & TV app, from the Videos library in File Explorer, in the same way as adding your own music to the Groove Music app.

4. Click on an item to see more information, view a preview clip and rent or buy and download the movie

Finding People

An electronic address book is always a good feature to have on a computer, and with Windows 10 this function is provided by the People app. This not only allows you to add your own contacts manually, you can also link to any of your online accounts, such as Facebook and LinkedIn, and import the contacts that you have there. To do this:

1. Click on the **People** app on the Start Menu

2. The current contacts are displayed. (By default, these will be linked to your Microsoft Account, if you have created one)

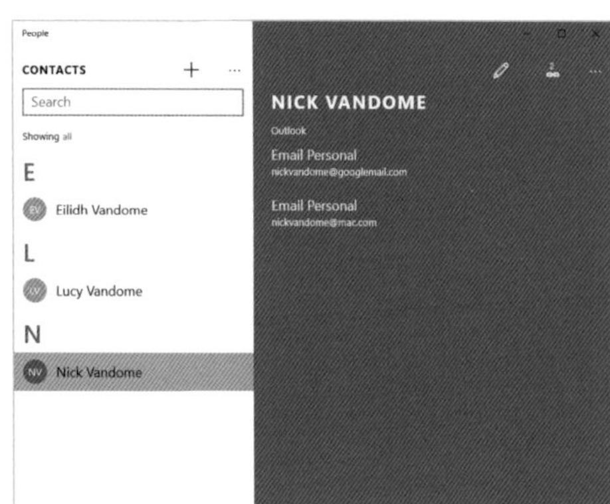

3. Click on this button and click on the **Settings** button to add new accounts from which you can import contacts

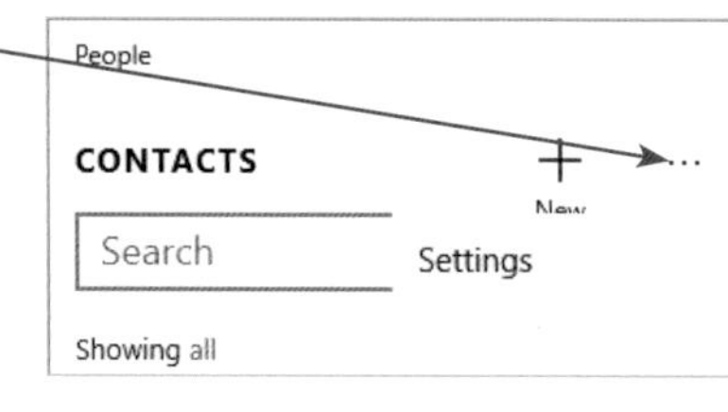

4. Click on the **Add an account** button

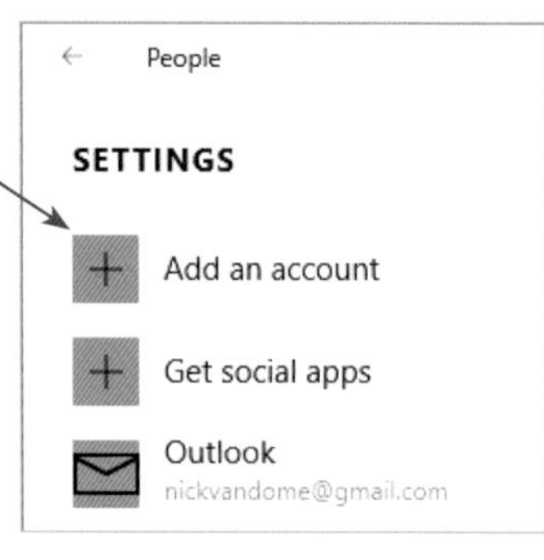

You can also select accounts to add to the People app from the Homepage when you first open it.

Click on the **Get social apps** button in Step 4 to download apps such as LinkedIn and Facebook, which can then be used to link to your contacts in these apps.

5. Select the account or service from which you would like to import your contacts

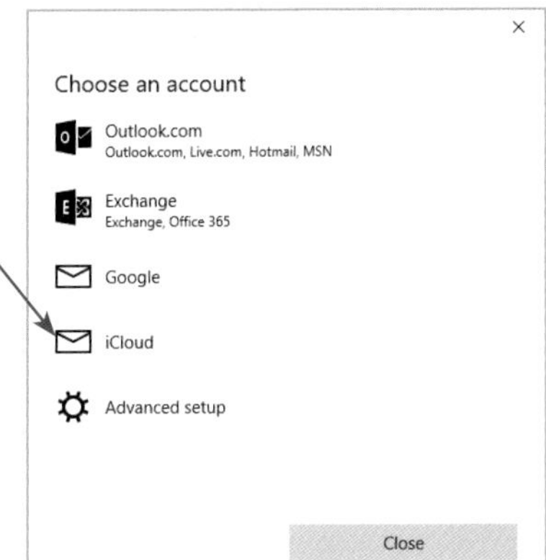

6. Enter your sign-in details for the selected account and click on the **Sign-in** button

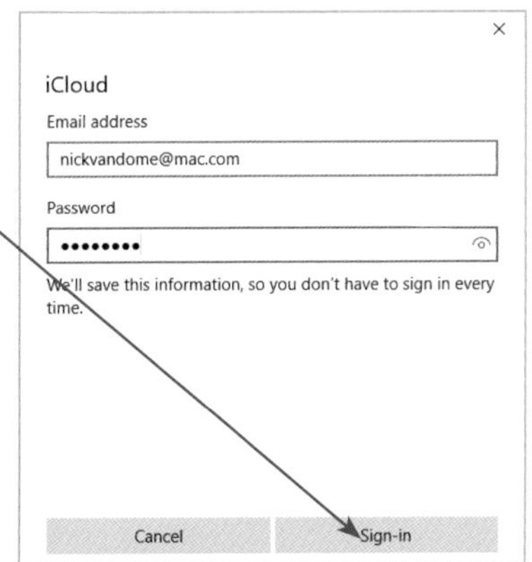

7. A confirmation window informs you that the account has been set up and linked to the People app. Click on the **Done** button

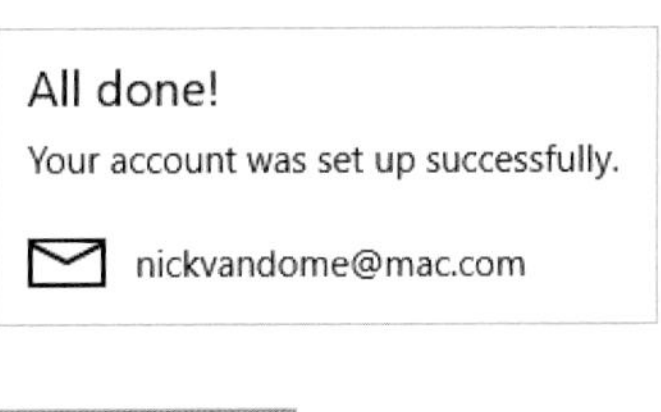

8. The contacts from the linked account are imported and added under the **Contacts** heading. Click on a contact to view the details

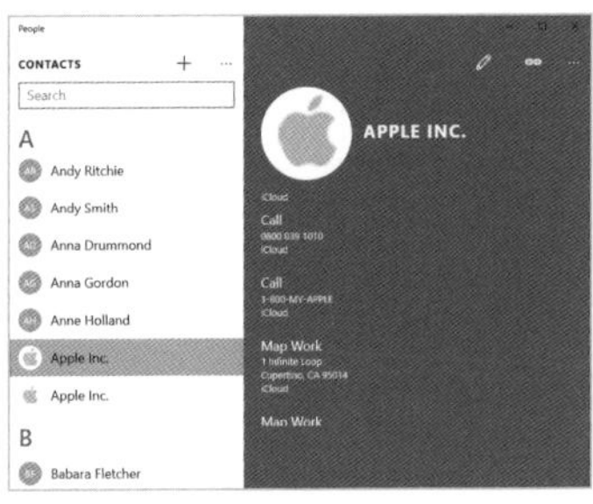

Using the Calendar

The Calendar app can be used to include important events and reminders. To view the calendar:

Accounts can be added to the Calendar app in the same way as for the Mail and People apps.

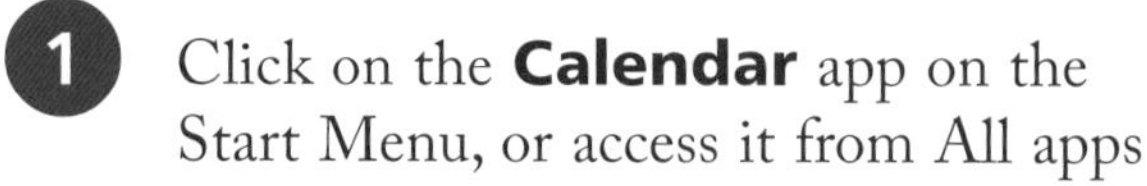

1. Click on the **Calendar** app on the Start Menu, or access it from All apps

2. Click on the **Get started** button

3. Select an account to link with your calendar (or add a new one) and click on the **Ready to go** button

4. Click here to view specific months and click on the top toolbar to view by **Day**, **Work week**, **Week**, **Month** or **Today**

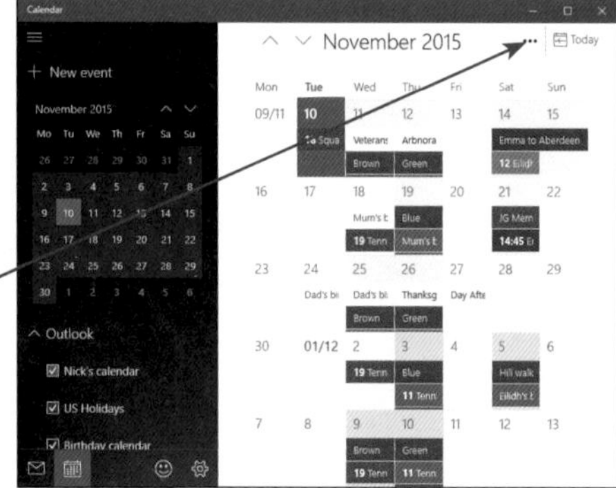

5. Click on these buttons to move between months (or swipe left or right on a touchpad)

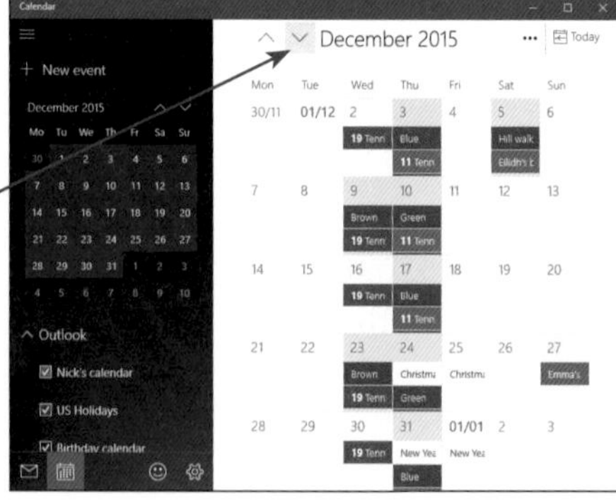

Adding events

Events can be added to the calendar and various settings can be applied to them such as recurrences and reminders.

1. Click on a date to create a new event or click on the **New event** button

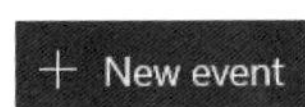

2. The Event window opens so that you can add details about your event, including name, location and date

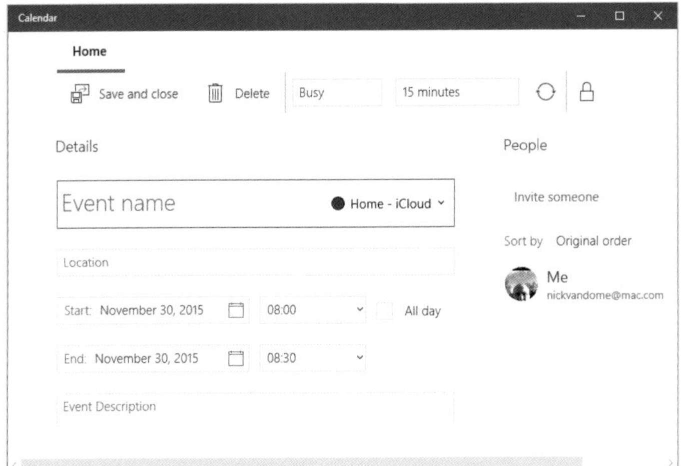

3. Click on the **Start** field and enter a time

4. If **All day** is selected, the time in the **Start** and **End** fields will be grayed-out

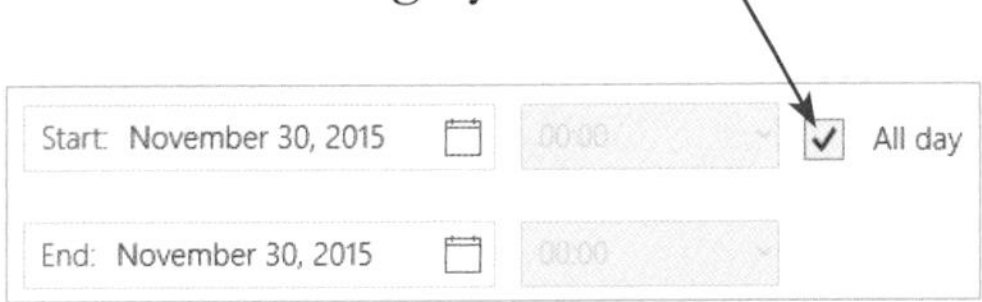

Reminders can be set for calendar events and these appear in the **Notifications** section. Click on this box at the top of the event window to set a time period for a reminder.

Playing Games

The Xbox app can be used to play games, join friends for multi-player games, watch TV shows and movies and listen to music. It links into a number of services so that you can access content from websites such as YouTube and Netflix. To use the Xbox app:

You can also play games with the Xbox app without signing in with your Microsoft Account.

1. Click on the **Xbox** app on the Start Menu

2. You have to log in with your Microsoft Account details in order to play Xbox games and interact with other users. Click on the **Click here to sign in** link

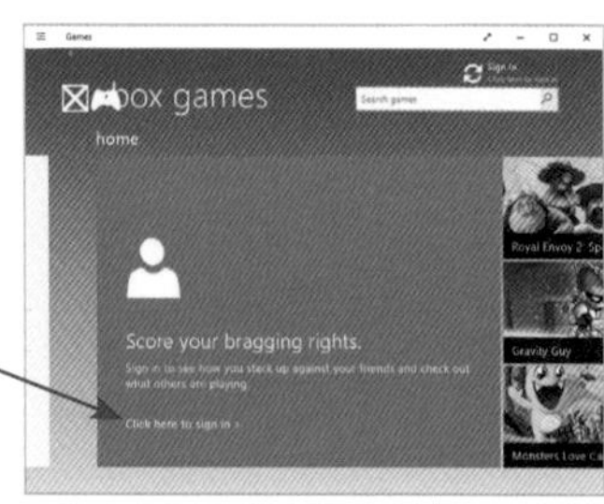

3. Enter your Microsoft Account details and click on the **Sign in** button

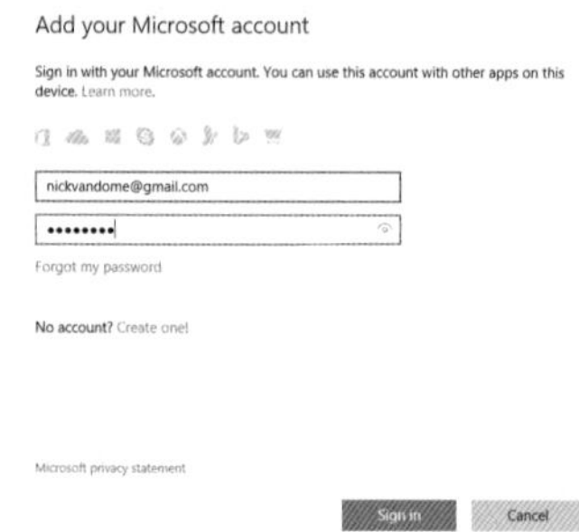

You can also log in to the Xbox site at **www.xbox.com** to download games and find other people with whom to play games.

4. Click on games to play them and click on these buttons to view your scores and interact with other players

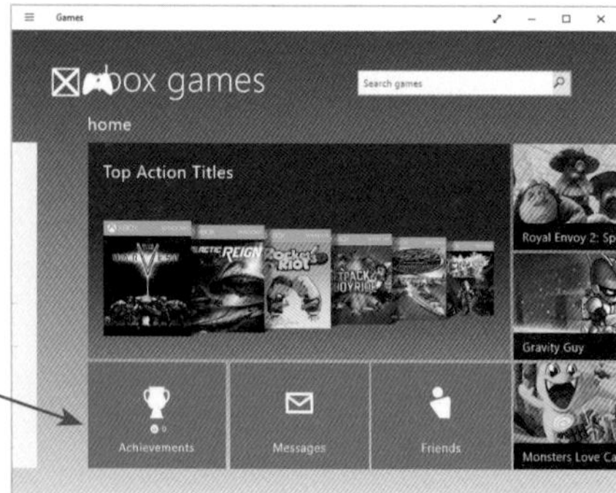

Backing Up with OneDrive

Cloud computing is now a mainstream part of our online experience. This involves saving content to an online server connected to the service that you are using, i.e. through your Microsoft Account. You can then access this content from any computer, using your account login details, and also share it with other people by giving them access to your cloud service. It can also be used to backup your files, in case they are corrupted or damaged on your PC.

The cloud service with Windows 10 is known as OneDrive and you can use it providing that you have a Microsoft Account:

1. Click on the **OneDrive** app on the Start Menu

2. Click on the **Sign in** button

3. Sign in with your Microsoft Account details and click on the **Sign in** button (or the **Sign up now** button to create a Microsoft Account)

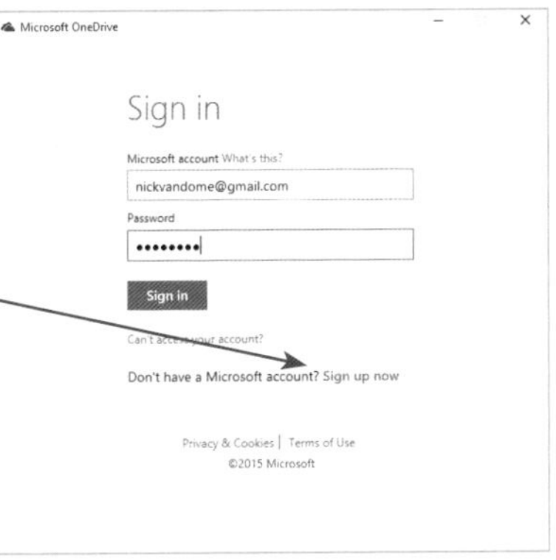

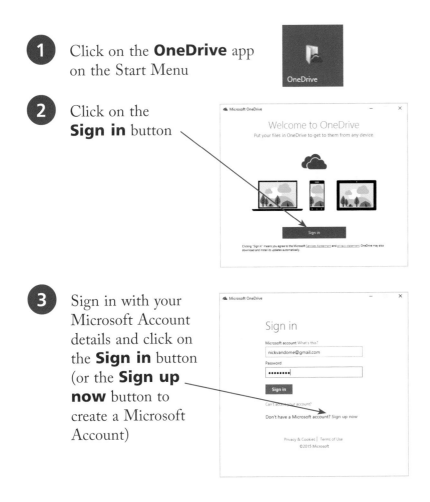

By default, you get 5GB of free OneDrive storage space with Windows 10 (*correct at the time of printing*). This is an excellent way to back up your important documents since they are stored away from your computer.

...cont'd

4. Select the folder that you want to sync with OneDrive and click on the **Next** button (the synced folders will appear in File Explorer and your online OneDrive account)

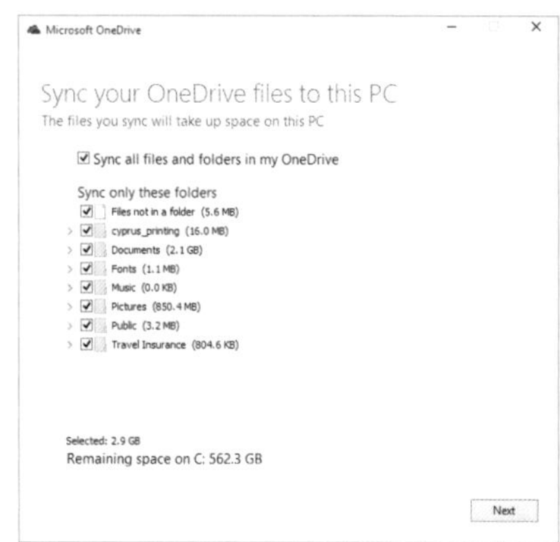

5. If you want to use OneDrive to access files from other devices (such as a smartphone using Windows 10) check on this checkbox and click on the **Done** button

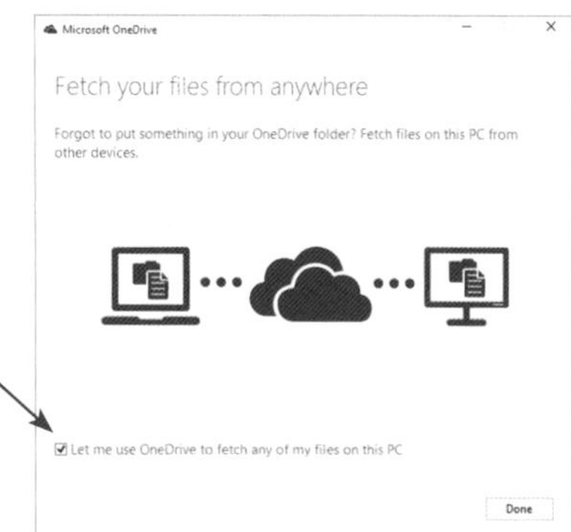

6. Open File Explorer and click on the **OneDrive** folder. Click on one of the folders to view its contents

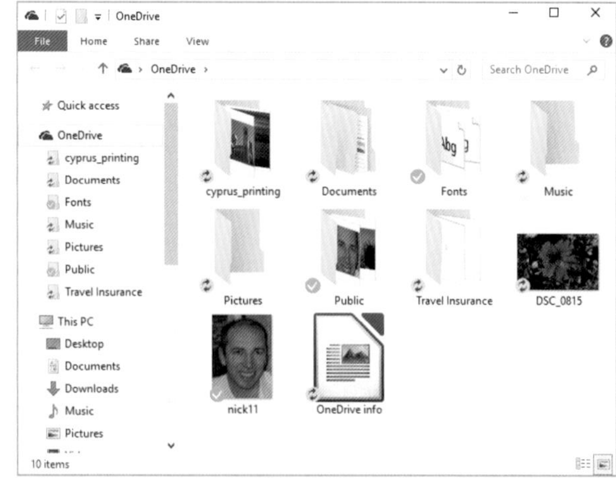

Files can be saved into the OneDrive folder on your laptop in the same way as saving any other files, e.g. by copying and pasting them from within File Explorer or by selecting the OneDrive folder as the location when you save them in the app in which they are created. Once files have been saved into the OneDrive folder they will be available on other OneDrive-enabled devices and through your online OneDrive service, at **OneDrive.live.com** (You will need to sign in with your Microsoft Account details.)

7 On Vacation

Due to their portability, laptops are ideal for taking on vacation. This chapter looks at the issues of taking your laptop with you and keeping it safe.

Transporting Your Laptop

When you are going on vacation, your laptop can be a valuable companion. It can be used to download vacation photographs from a digital camera, download home movies from a digital video camera, keep a diary of your vacation, and keep a record of your itinerary and important documents. In many parts of the world, it can access the internet via wireless hotspots so that you can view the web and send emails. However, when you are traveling with your laptop it is sensible to transport this valuable asset as safely and securely as possible. Some of the options include:

A backpack for carrying a laptop can be more comfortable than a shoulder bag as it distributes the weight more evenly.

Laptop case

A standard laptop case is a good option for when you are on vacation; it is compact, lightweight and designed to accommodate your laptop and its accessories.

Metal case

If you are concerned that your laptop may be in danger of physical damage on your vacation, you may want to consider a more robust metal case. These are similar to those used by photographers and, depending on its size and design, you may also be able to include your photographic equipment.

Backpacks

A serious option for transporting your laptop on vacation is a small backpack. This can either be a standard backpack or a backpack specifically designed for a laptop. The latter is clearly a better option as the laptop will fit more securely and there are also pockets designed for accessories:

Keeping Your Laptop Safe

By most measures, laptops are valuable items. However, in a lot of countries around the world their relative value can be a lot more than it is to their owners: in some countries the value of a laptop could easily equate to a month's, or even a year's wages. Even in countries where their relative value is not so high, they can still be seen as a lucrative opportunity for thieves. Therefore, it is important to try to keep your laptop as safe as possible when you are on vacation. Some points to consider in relation to this are:

- If possible, try to keep your laptop with you at all times, i.e. transport it in a piece of luggage that you can carry rather than having to put it into a large case.
- Never hand over your laptop, or any other items of your belongings, to any local who promises to look after them.
- If you do have to detach yourself from your laptop, try to put it somewhere secure, such as a hotel safe.
- When you are traveling, try to keep your laptop as unobtrusive as possible. This is where a backpack carrying case can prove useful as it is not immediately apparent that you are carrying a laptop.
- Do not use your laptop in areas where you think it may attract undue interest from the locals, particularly in obviously poor areas. For instance, if you are in a local café, the appearance of a laptop may create unwanted attention for you. If in doubt, wait until you get back to your hotel.
- If you are accosted by criminals who demand your laptop then hand it over. No piece of equipment is worth suffering physical injury for.
- Make sure your laptop is covered by your vacation insurance. If not, get separate insurance for it.
- Trust your instincts with your laptop. If something doesn't feel right then don't do it.

Save your important documents, such as vacation photos, onto a pen drive or CD/DVD on a daily basis when on vacation, and keep this away from your laptop. This way, you will still have these items if your laptop is lost or stolen.

Temperature Extremes

Traveling includes seeing different places and cultures, but it also invariably involves different extremes of temperature: a visit to the pyramids of Egypt can see the mercury in the upper reaches of the thermometer, while a cruise to Alaska would present much colder conditions. Whether it is hot or cold, looking after your laptop is an important consideration in extremes of temperature.

If a laptop gets too hot it could buckle the plastic casing, making it difficult to close.

Heat

When traveling in hot countries, the best way of avoiding damage to your laptop is to prevent it from getting too hot in the first place:

- Do not place your laptop in direct sunlight.
- Keep your laptop insulated from the heat.
- Do not leave your laptop in an enclosed space, such as a car. Not only can this get very hot, but the sun's power can be increased by the vehicle's glass.

Try wrapping your laptop in something white, such as a t-shirt or a towel, to insulate it against the heat.

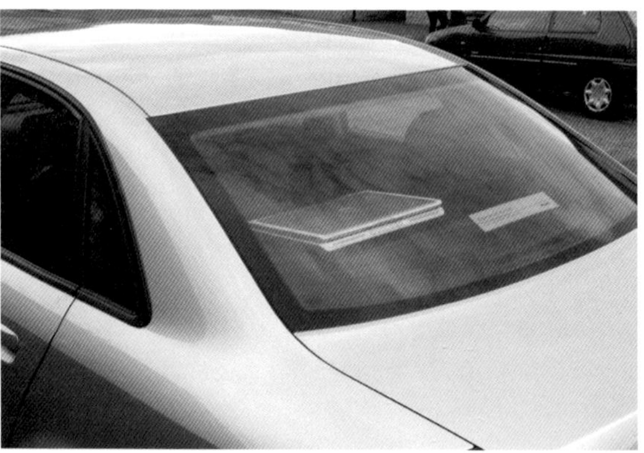

Cold

Again, it is best to try to avoid your laptop getting too cold in the first place and this can be done by following similar precautions as for heat. However, if your laptop does suffer from extremes of cold, allow it to warm up to normal room temperature again before you try to use it. This may take a couple of hours, but it will be worth the wait, rather than risking damaging the delicate computing elements inside.

Laptops at Sea

Water is the greatest enemy of any electrical device, and laptops are no different. This is of particular relevance to anyone who is taking their laptop on vacation near water, such as on a cruise. This not only has the obvious element of water in the sea, but also the proliferation of swimming pools that are a feature of cruise ships. If you are going on vacation near water then bear in mind the following:

- **Avoid water**. The best way to keep your laptop dry is to keep it away from water whenever possible. For instance, if you want to update your diary or download some photographs, then it would be best to do this in an indoor environment, rather than sitting around the pool.
- **Keeping dry**. If you think you will be transporting your laptop near water then it is a good precaution to protect it with some form of waterproof bag. There is a range of "dry-bags" that are excellent for this type of occasion as they remain waterproof even if fully immersed in water. These can be bought from a number of outdoor suppliers.

- **Drying out**. If the worst does occur and your laptop does get a good soaking, then all is not lost. However, you will have to ensure that it is fully dried out before you try to use it again.

Power Sockets

Different countries and regions around the world use different types of power sockets, and this is an issue when you are on vacation with your laptop. Wherever you are going in the world, it is vital to have an adapter that will fit the sockets in the countries you intend to visit, otherwise you will not be able to charge your laptop.

There are over a dozen different types of plugs and sockets used around the world, with the four most popular being:

North America, Japan

This is a two-point plug and socket. The pins on the plug are flat and parallel.

Hot tip

Power adapters can be bought for all regions around the world. There are also kits that provide all of the adapters together. These provide connections for anywhere worldwide.

Continental Europe

This is a two-point plug and socket. The pins are rounded.

Hot tip

Check before you travel which type of power socket your ship has and get the right adapter.

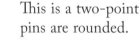

Australasia, China, Argentina

This is a three-point socket that can accommodate either a two- or a three-pin plug. In a two-pin plug, the pins are angled in a V shape.

UK

This is a three-point plug. The pins are rectangular.

Airport Security

Because of the increased global security following terrorist attacks, the levels of airport security have been greatly increased around the world. This has implications for all travelers, and if you are traveling with a laptop this will add to the security scrutiny which you will face. When dealing with airport security when traveling with a laptop, there are some issues that you should always keep in mind:

- Keep your laptop with you at all times. Unguarded baggage at airports immediately raises suspicion and it can make life very easy for thieves.
- Carry your laptop in a small bag so that you can take it on board as hand luggage. On no account should it be put in with your luggage that goes in the hold.
- X-ray machines at airports will not harm your laptop. However, if anyone tries to scan it with a metal detector, ask them if they can inspect it by hand instead.
- Keep a careful eye on your laptop when it goes through the X-ray conveyor belt and try to be there at the other side as soon as it emerges. There have been some stories of people causing a commotion at the security gate just after someone has placed their laptop on the conveyor belt. While everyone's attention (including yours) is distracted, an accomplice takes the laptop from the conveyor belt. If you are worried about this, you can ask for the security guard to hand-check your laptop rather than putting it on the conveyor belt.
- Make sure the battery of your laptop is fully charged. This is because you may be asked to turn on your laptop to verify that it is just that, and not some other device disguised as a laptop.
- When you are on the plane, keep the laptop in the storage area under your seat, rather than in the overhead locker, so that you know where it is at all times.

If there is any kind of distraction when you are going through security checks at an airport, it could be because someone is trying to divert your attention in order to steal your laptop.

When traveling through airport security, leave your laptop in Sleep mode so that it can be powered up quickly if anyone needs to check that it works properly.

Keeping in Touch

Skype has become established as one of the premier services for free voice and video calls (to other Skype users) and instant messaging for text messages. It can now be incorporated into your Windows 10 experience and used to keep in touch with family, friends and work colleagues, at home and around the world. To use Skype:

When you create a text conversation with one of your contacts in Skype, it will continue down the page as you respond to each other.

When you add someone as a contact you have to send them a contact request, which they must accept to become one of your contacts.

1. Skype can be downloaded, for free, from the Windows Store, if it is not already installed on your computer. Click on the **Install** button

2. Click on the **Get Skype** button on the Start Menu or in the **All apps** section

3. If you already have a Skype account, sign in with these details, or you can also sign in with your Microsoft Account details (or create a new account)

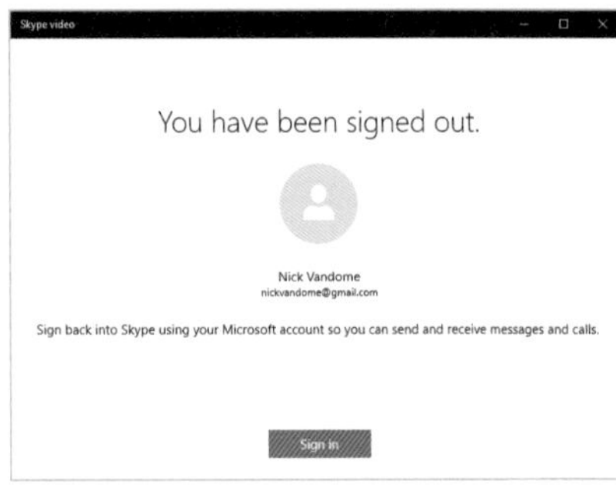

4. Once you have entered your login details click on the **Continue** button to contact other Skype users and start conversations with them

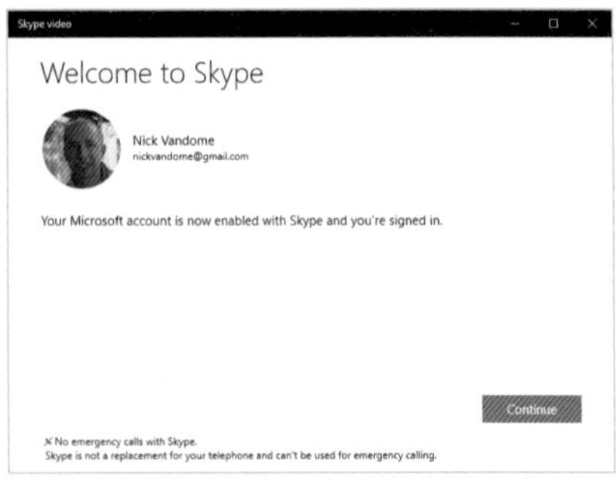

8 Sharing with Your Family

This chapter deals with sharing your laptop.

About Multiple Users

Because of the power and flexibility that is available in a laptop computer, it seems a waste to restrict it to a single user. Thankfully, it is possible for multiple users to use the same laptop. One way to do this is simply to let different people use the laptop whenever they have access to it. However, since everyone creates their own files and documents, and different people use different types of apps, it makes much more sense to allow people to set up their own user accounts. This creates their own personal computing area that is protected from anyone else accessing it. User accounts create a sense of personalization, and also security as each account can be protected by a password.

Without user accounts, the laptop will display the default account automatically. However, if different user accounts have been set up on the laptop, a list of these accounts will be displayed at the top of the Start Menu.

If no other user accounts have been set up, yours will be the only one, and you will be the administrator. This means that you can set up new accounts and alter a variety of settings on the laptop.

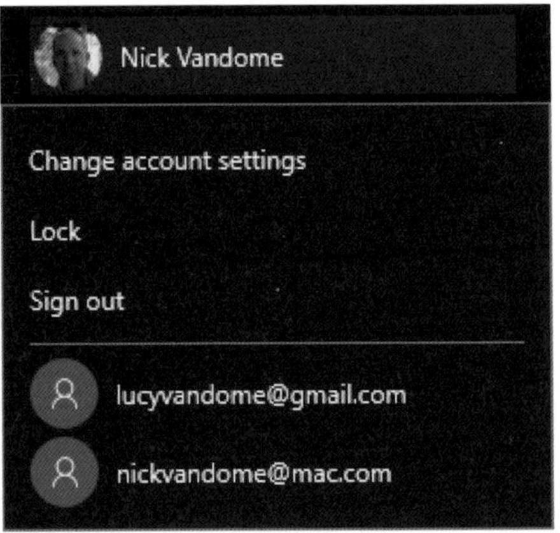

The relevant user can then click on their own account to access it. At this point they will have to enter the correct password to gain access to their account. A user can have a Local Account or a Microsoft Account. If it is the latter, the user will have access to a selection of Microsoft services, through the Windows 10 apps. A password is required for either a Local Account or a Microsoft one. To see how to add new user accounts, see pages 140-141.

Customization

Once individual user accounts have been set up, it is possible for each user to customize their account, i.e. to set the way in which their account appears and operates. This means that each user can set their own preferences, such as for the way the Start Menu and Desktop background appear, and also the items on the Taskbar:

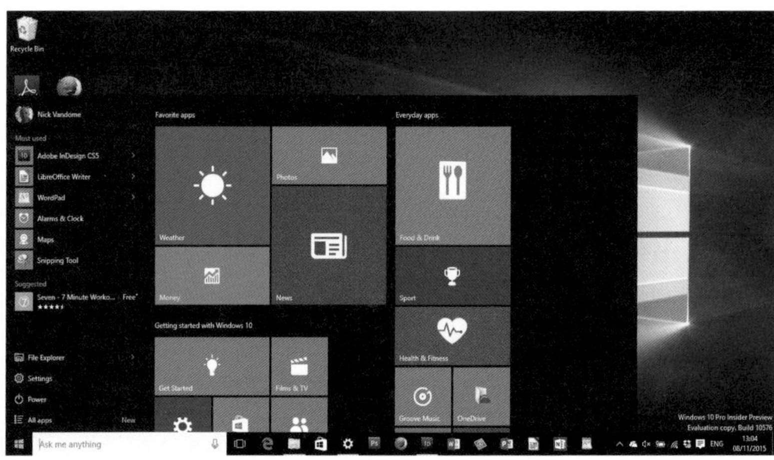

The whole Desktop environment can be customized. This is done within the **Personalization** section of the **Settings** app.

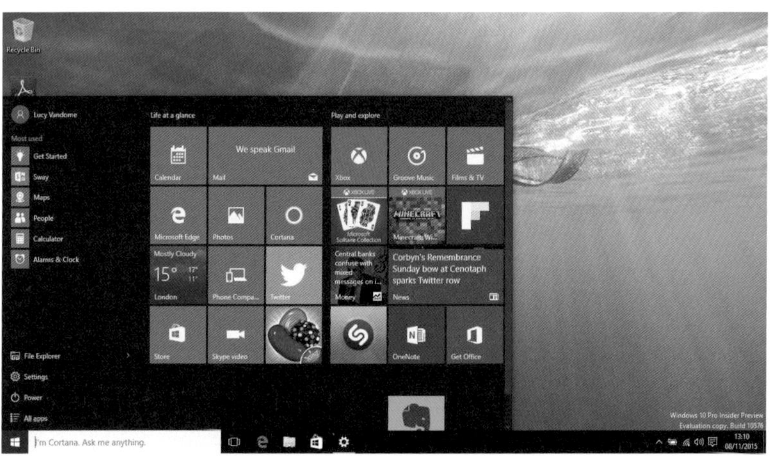

This shows two different user accounts and the changes in Settings, Live, Tiles, Background and Taskbar apps.

Adding Users

If more than one person uses the computer, each person can have a user account defined with a username and a password. To create a new user account:

1. Access the **Settings** app and click on the **Family & other users** button under **Accounts**

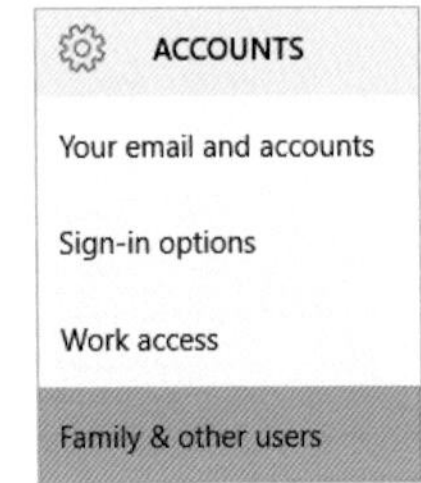

2. Click on the **Add a family member** button

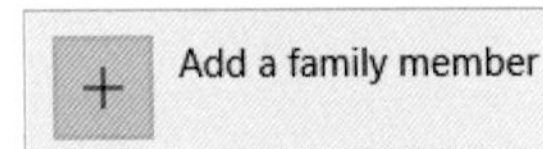

3. Select whether you want to create an account for a child or an adult, and enter their email address

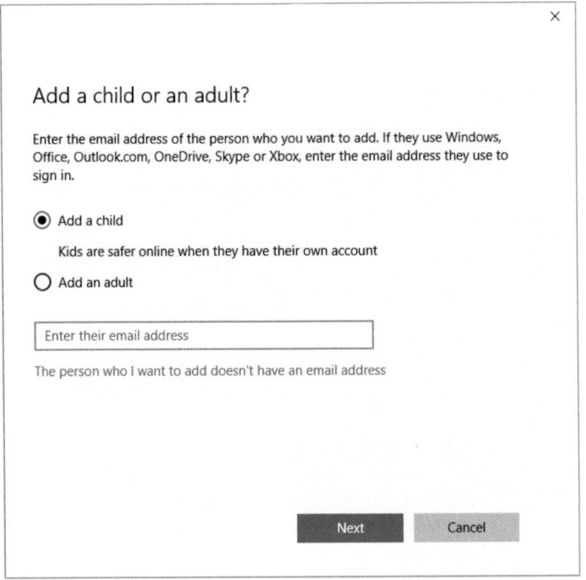

4. Click on the **Next** button

The email address is a required field when creating a new user with a Microsoft Account.

5. Click on the **Confirm** button to confirm that you want to add the selected person to your laptop

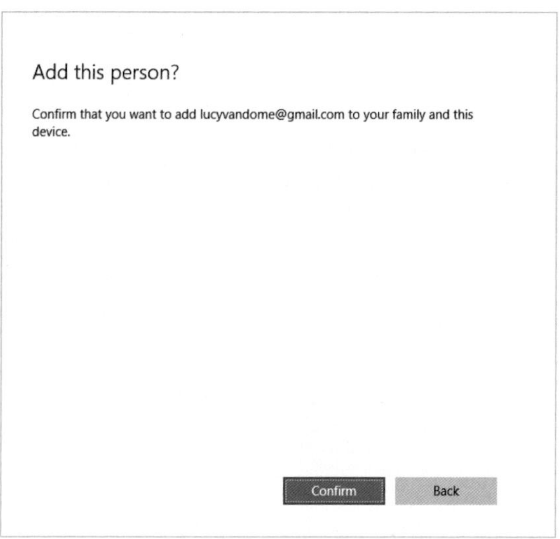

Add this person?

Confirm that you want to add lucyvandome@gmail.com to your family and this device.

Confirm Back

6. An invitation is sent to the user's email address. The new user has to accept the invitation before they are added as a user on your laptop. Click on the **Close** button to complete the process

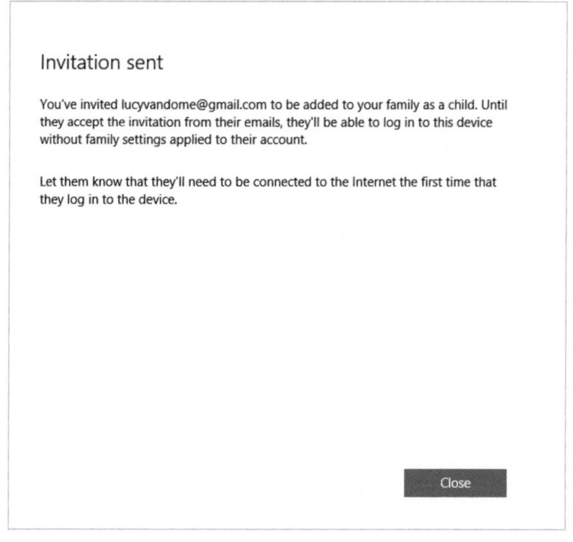

Invitation sent

You've invited lucyvandome@gmail.com to be added to your family as a child. Until they accept the invitation from their emails, they'll be able to log in to this device without family settings applied to their account.

Let them know that they'll need to be connected to the Internet the first time that they log in to the device.

Close

Non-family users can also be added to your laptop, using the **Add someone else to this PC** link under **Settings > Accounts > Family & other users**. To remove them, click on their name and click on the **Remove** button.

Family Safety

Once multiple user accounts have been set up, it is possible to apply separate online security settings to different accounts. This can be useful if you are going to be setting up an account for grandchildren and you want to have a certain amount of control over how they use the laptop. To do this:

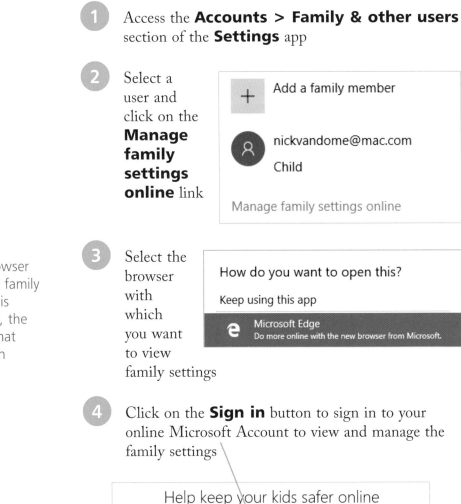

1. Access the **Accounts > Family & other users** section of the **Settings** app

2. Select a user and click on the **Manage family settings online** link

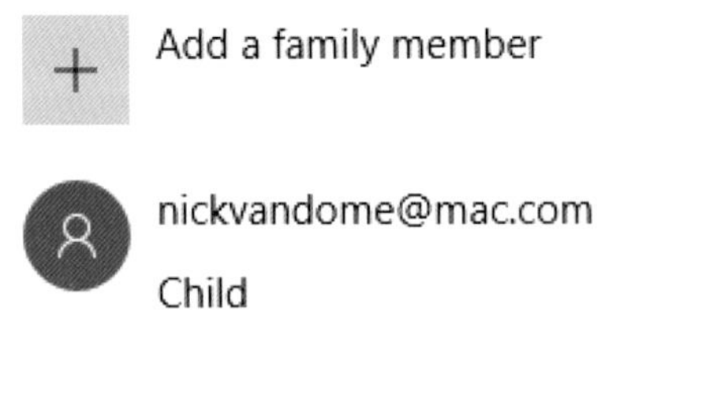

3. Select the browser with which you want to view family settings

How do you want to open this?

Keep using this app

Microsoft Edge
Do more online with the new browser from Microsoft.

4. Click on the **Sign in** button to sign in to your online Microsoft Account to view and manage the family settings

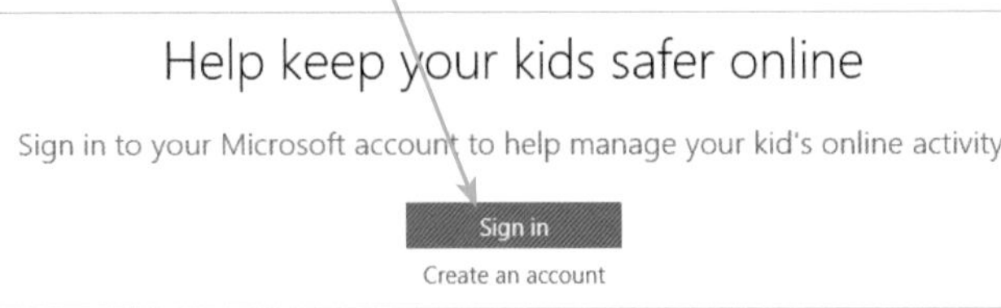

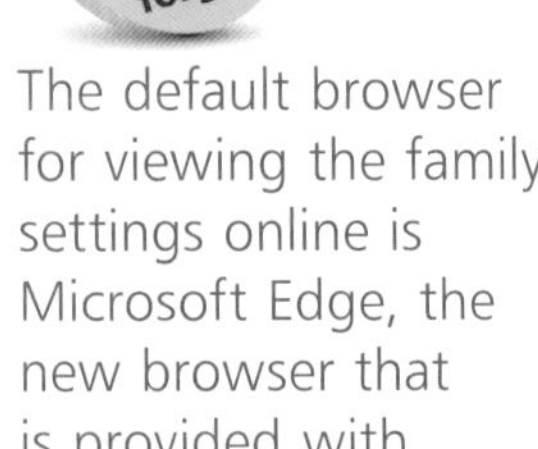

Don't forget

The default browser for viewing the family settings online is Microsoft Edge, the new browser that is provided with Windows 10.

Recent activity controls

One of the options within the family safety controls is to view recent activity by a user. To view this:

1. In the Manage family settings online section, underneath Your family, select the required user

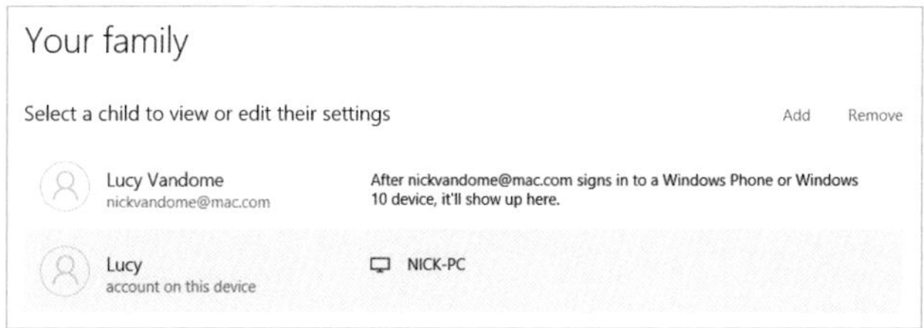

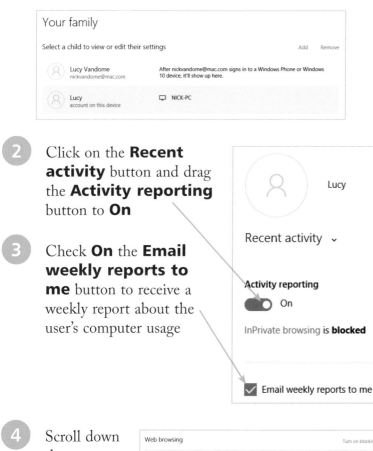

2. Click on the **Recent activity** button and drag the **Activity reporting** button to **On**

3. Check **On** the **Email weekly reports to me** button to receive a weekly report about the user's computer usage

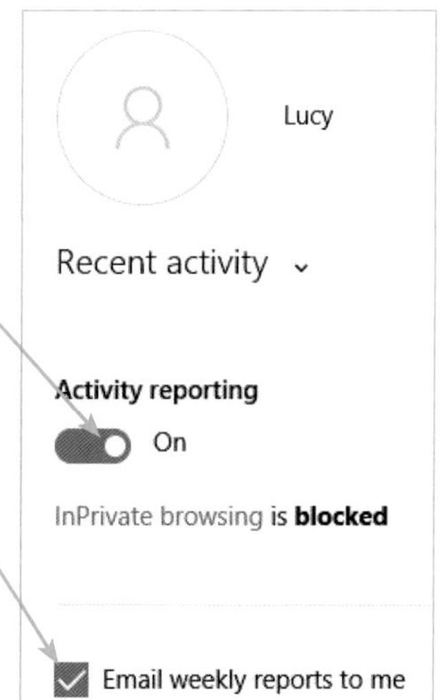

4. Scroll down the page to view and edit the other family safety options

Web browsing — Turn on blocking
When your child browses websites they'll appear here.
Apps & games — Turn on blocking
When your child uses apps or games, they'll appear here.
Screen time — Set allowed times
When your child uses their device, it will show here.

If you are setting family safety for young people, such as grandchildren, make sure you tell them what you have done, so that they understand the reasons behind your actions.

Web browsing controls

The websites accessed by a specific user can also be controlled through family safety:

1. Click on the **Web browsing** button

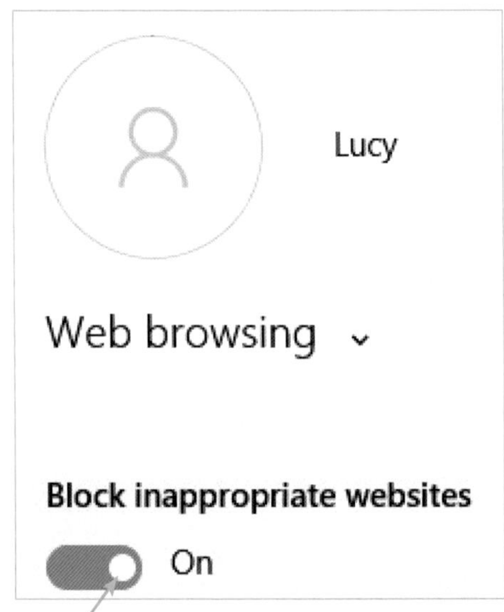

2. Drag the **Block inappropriate websites** button to **On**

3. Enter the web addresses of any websites you want to include and click on the **Allow** button

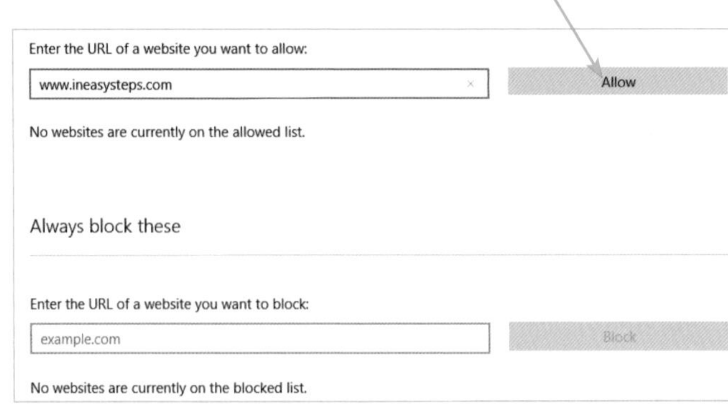

To block specific websites, add them in the **Always block these** section and click on the **Block** button.

Apps and games controls

Computer games and apps are another very popular pastime for young people. These include games that are downloaded from the web, and also those that are bought on CDs or DVDs. However, just as with movies, some games and apps are unsuitable for younger children and should have ratings to specify the age groups for which they are suitable. It is then possible to control which games are played. To do this:

1. From the Manage family settings online link (shown in the image in Step 2 on page 142), click on the **Apps, games & media** link to restrict the type of content the user can access

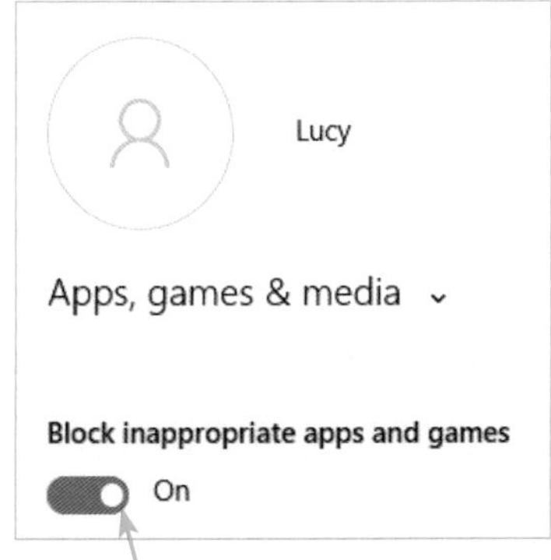

2. Drag the **Block inappropriate apps and games** button to **On**

3. Click here to select the appropriate age group, and rating, for which you want restrictions to apply

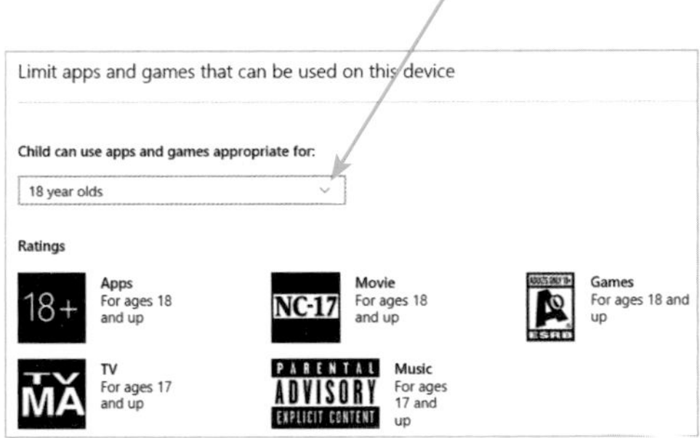

The age ratings in Step 3 will be applicable to your geographic location.

...cont'd

Screen time controls

A familiar worry when young people are using computers is the amount of time that they are spending on them. However, this can also be controlled in the Screen time controls for a selected user. To do this:

1. From the Manage family settings online link (shown in the image in Step 2 on page 142), click on the **Screen time** button to specify times at which a user can use the computer

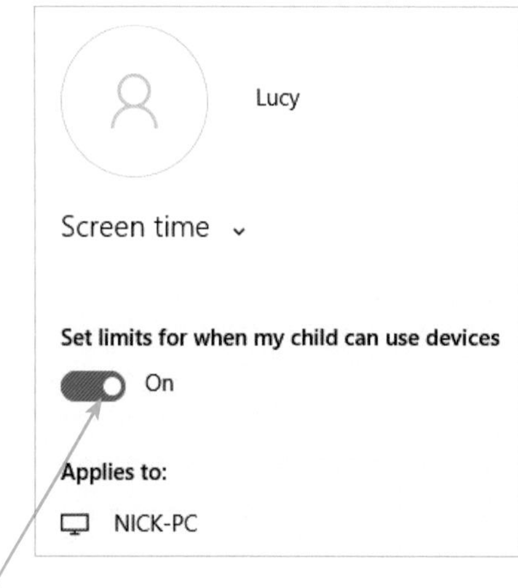

2. Drag the **Set limits for when my child can use devices** button to **On**

3. Select the times for using the laptop on specific days (each day can have its own times and also an overall limit per day)

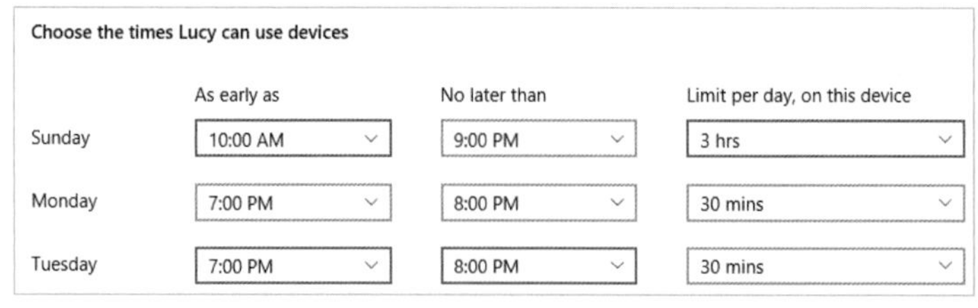

Choose the times Lucy can use devices
As early as
No later than
Limit per day, on this device
Sunday
10:00 AM
9:00 PM
3 hrs
Monday
7:00 PM
8:00 PM
30 mins
Tuesday
7:00 PM
8:00 PM
30 mins

If time controls have been set, the affected user will not be able to access their account outside the times that have been specified.

9 Networking and Wireless

This chapter shows how to use the networking functions in Windows 10, allowing you to share files and folders and use the HomeGroup file sharing feature.

Setting up a Network

In computing terms, a network is a when a computer is connected to one, or more computers, or it is connected to the internet. This means that content and files can be shared between computers.

To set up a network you must first get all of the required hardware in place. For this, you will require a router, which is the device through which all of the elements of the network will communicate. To set up your network:

1. Plug in your router to the mains electricity

2. Connect your router to your internet connection, via either a phone line or an Ethernet cable. This plugs into the back of the router

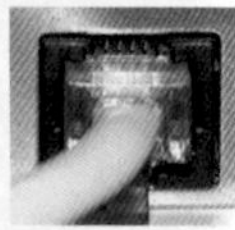

3. For a Ethernet connection, attach one end of the cable to the computer and the other to the router

4. If you have a laptop with wireless connectivity, the laptop will communicate with the router wirelessly when the network software creates the network

5. Connect any other items of hardware that you want to include in the network, such as a printer. This can be done wirelessly, if the printer is equipped with a wireless card, or more commonly, with a USB or an Ethernet connection

If your network uses a wireless router, this means that anyone within the range of the router could connect to the network, even if they are outside your house. To avoid this, you have to set a password for your router, which can be done when you initially connect it.

Going Wireless

For networking, "wireless" means connecting your computer to other devices using radio waves rather than cables. These can include a router for connecting to a network, a printer, keyboard, mouse or speakers (as long as these devices also have a wireless capability). For the laptop user in particular, this gives you the ultimate freedom; you can take your laptop wherever you want and still be able to access the internet and use a variety of peripherals.

Wireless standards

As with everything in the world of computers, there are industry standards for wireless connections: for networking devices the standard is known as IEEE 802.11. The purpose of standards is to ensure that all of the connected devices can communicate with each other.

Very few new devices use the 802.11a version of the standard, although newer devices will usually be backwards-compatible with it.

The IEEE 802.11 standard (or just 802.11) used for networks has a number of different variations (known as protocols) of the original standard. These variations have been developed since the introduction of 802.11 in 1997 with a view to making it work faster and cover a greater range. Early wireless devices used the 802.11a and 802.11b protocols, while the most widely used protocol at the time of printing is 802.11n, with 802.11ac also beginning to be used. When you are creating a wireless network it is best to have all of the devices using the same version of 802.11. For instance, if you have a wireless card in your laptop that uses 802.11n, then it is best to have the same version in your router. However, most modern wireless cards and routers have multiple compatibility and can cater for at least the b and g versions of the standard. If two devices use different 802.11 protocols, they should still be able to communicate, but the rate of data transfer may be slower than if both of the devices used the same protocol.

Devices using the 802.11n protocol can communicate with each other via radio waves over distances of approximately 25 yards (indoors) and 75 yards (outdoors).

The Bluetooth standard is another method of connecting devices wirelessly. It does not have the same range as 802.11 and is now mainly used for connecting devices over short distances, such as a wireless mouse.

Discover Networks

To form your network, connect your computers using Ethernet cables and adapters or by setting up your wireless adapters and routers. When you start up each computer, Windows 10 will examine the current configuration and discover any new networks that have been established since the last start up. You can check this, or connect manually to a network, from within the default settings from the Settings app. To do this:

If your network is unavailable there will be a warning on the network button in Step 2.

1. Click on the **Settings** app and click on the **Network & Internet** button

2. Drag the Wi-Fi button to **On**. Under the **Wi-Fi** heading, click on one of the available networks

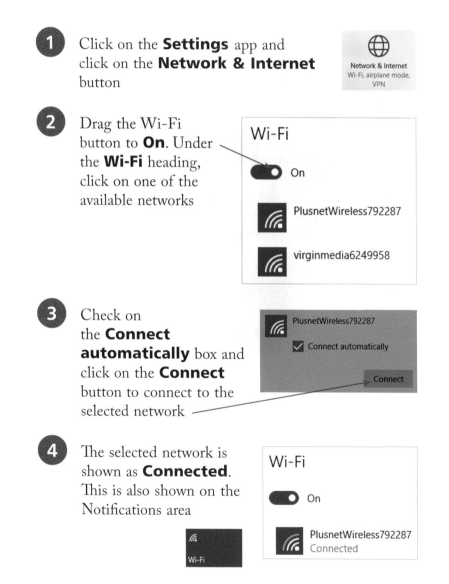

3. Check on the **Connect automatically** box and click on the **Connect** button to connect to the selected network

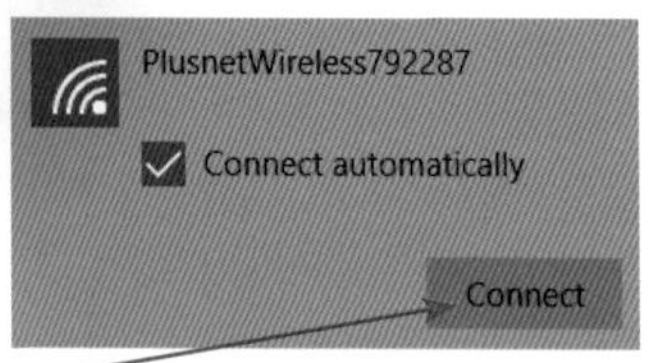

4. The selected network is shown as **Connected**. This is also shown on the Notifications area

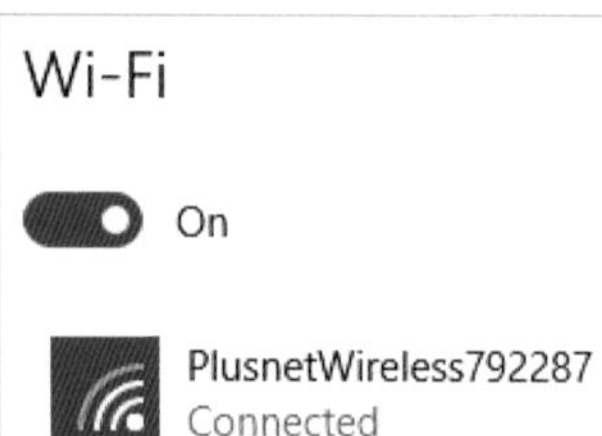

Network and Sharing Center

The Network and Sharing Center within the Control Panel is where you can view settings for your network.

The Network and Sharing Center displays network settings and provides access to networking tasks for the computer.

1. To open the Network and Sharing Center, access the Control Panel and click on the **Network and Internet** link

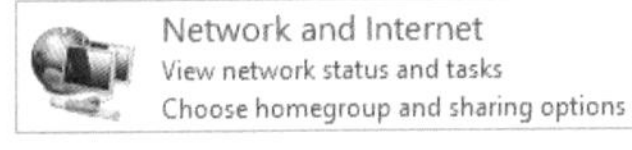

2. Click on the **Network and Sharing Center** link

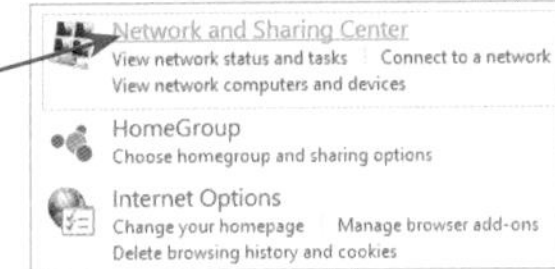

3. Details of the current network are displayed in the Network and Sharing Center

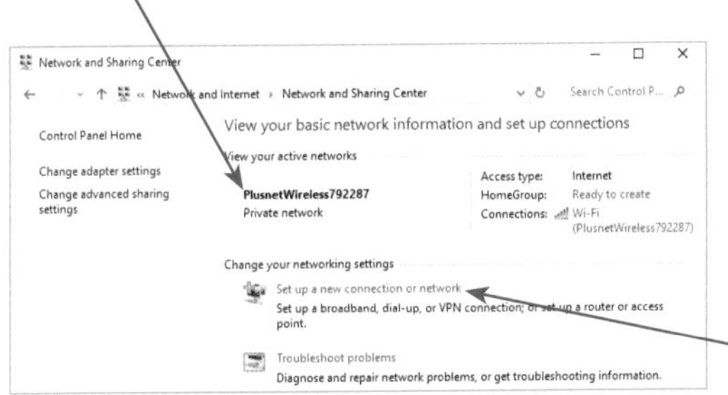

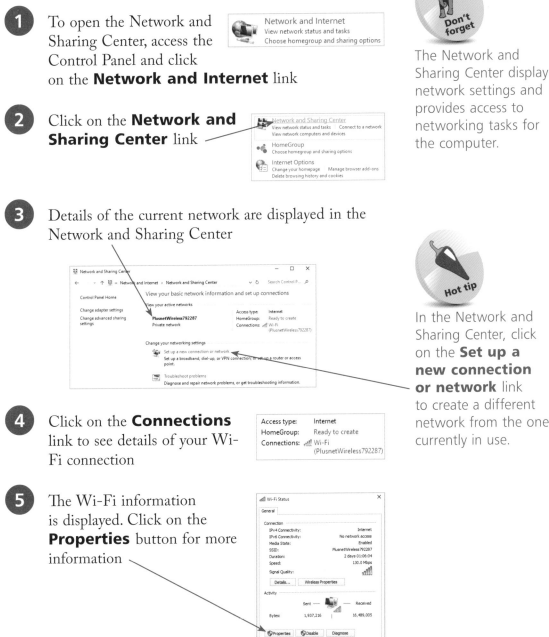

In the Network and Sharing Center, click on the **Set up a new connection or network** link to create a different network from the one currently in use.

4. Click on the **Connections** link to see details of your Wi-Fi connection

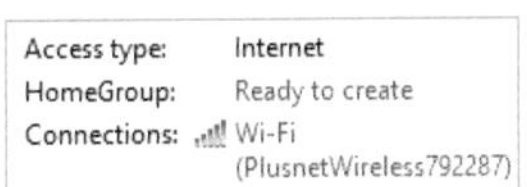

5. The Wi-Fi information is displayed. Click on the **Properties** button for more information

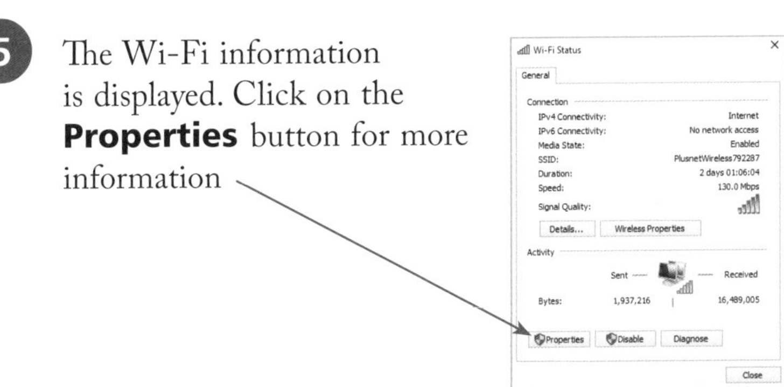

Join the HomeGroup

A HomeGroup is a network function that enables a Windows 10 computer to connect to another Windows 10 machine (or Windows 7/8/8.1) and share content. You can set up and connect to the HomeGroup through the Control Panel:

1. Access **Network and Internet** in the Control Panel and click on the **HomeGroup** link

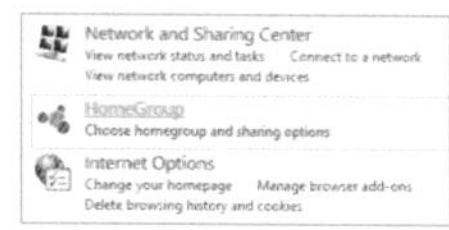

2. Click on the **Create a homegroup** button to start setting up the HomeGroup

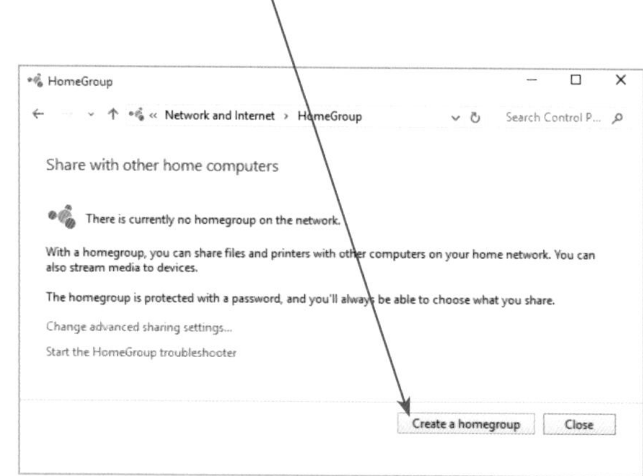

3. Click on the **Next** button

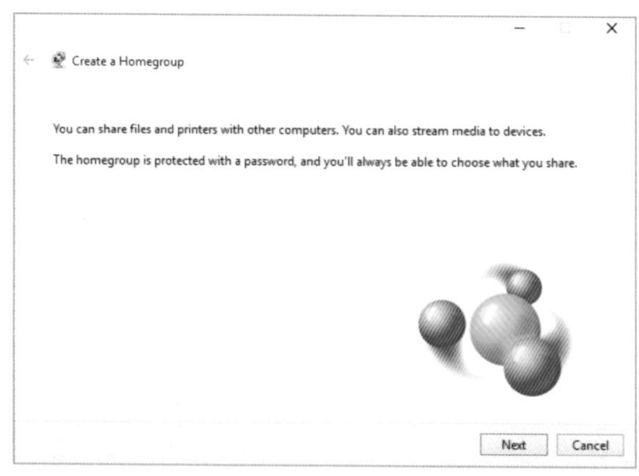

HomeGroup applies to any user with an account on the computer, so if a different user logs on, the associated files will also be accessible.

4. Select the items that you want to share in the HomeGroup and click on the **Next** button

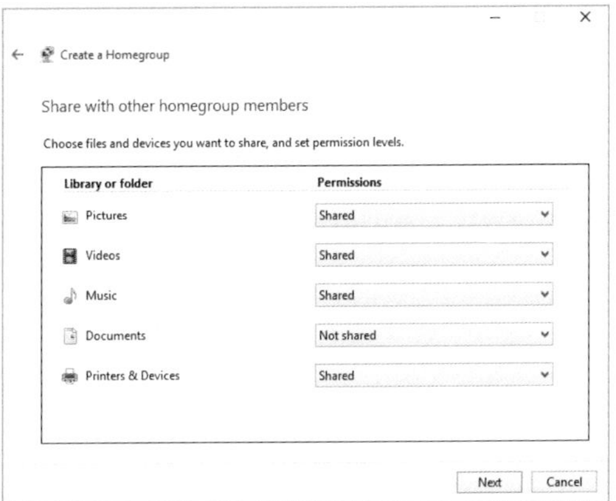
Create a Homegroup

Share with other homegroup members

Choose files and devices you want to share, and set permission levels.

Library or folder	Permissions
Pictures	Shared
Videos	Shared
Music	Shared
Documents	Not shared
Printers & Devices	Shared

Next Cancel

5. Write down the password that has to be provided from the other. Click on the **Finish** button. Once you have created the HomeGroup, and linked the necessary computers, you will be able to share your files on the other computer and vice versa

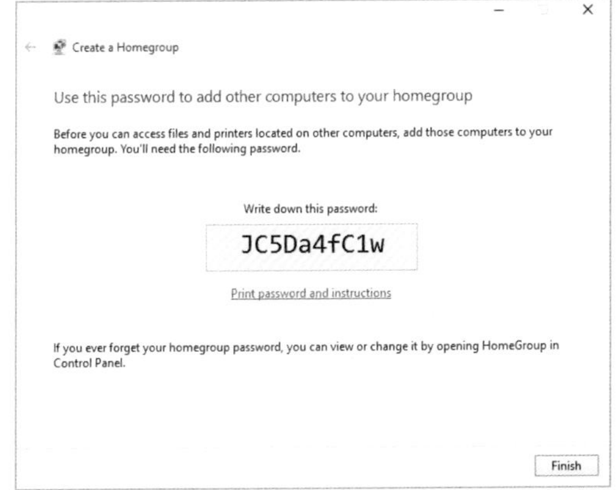
Create a Homegroup

Use this password to add other computers to your homegroup

Before you can access files and printers located on other computers, add those computers to your homegroup. You'll need the following password.

Write down this password:

JC5Da4fC1w

Print password and instructions

If you ever forget your homegroup password, you can view or change it by opening HomeGroup in Control Panel.

Finish

6. To then join the HomeGroup, access Network and Internet on the computer you wish to connect, click HomeGroup and enter the password from the original computer. You will then be able to access all items you have previously selected to share

Windows generates the password when the HomeGroup is created. If you forget the password, you can find it in the Control Panel on any computer already joined to the HomeGroup.

Sharing Files and Folders

There are different ways in which you can share items once a HomeGroup has been set up:

1. Open the File Explorer and select **HomeGroup** in the Library pane and click on the **Share libraries and devices** button in the Share section of the File Explorer

Don't forget

The Share section in File Explorer is accessed from the Scenic Ribbon.

2. Select the items that you want to share with the HomeGroup. This will be done automatically, i.e. if you share Pictures then all of the items in the Pictures Library will be shared, as will new ones that are added

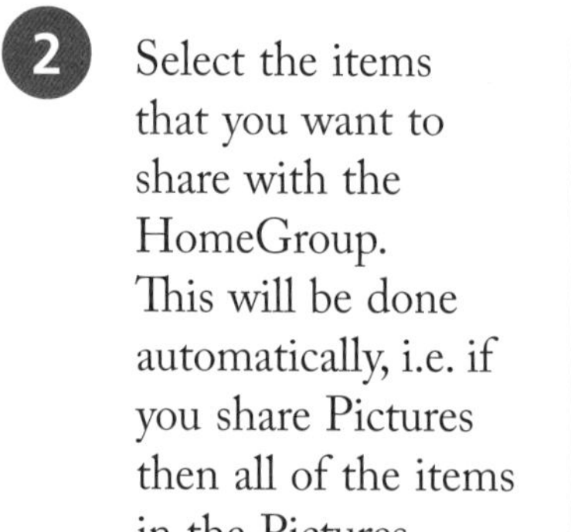

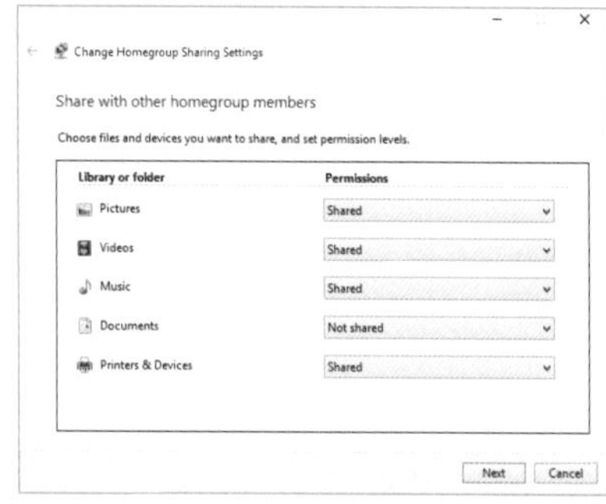

3. To share a specific item, select it in the File Explorer and click on the **HomeGroup** button in the **Share** section

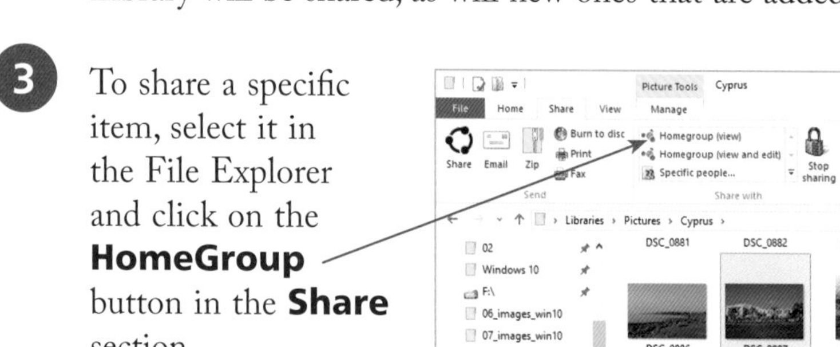

4. Select **HomeGroup** in the Navigation pane of the File Explorer Library pane to view the shared item in Step 3

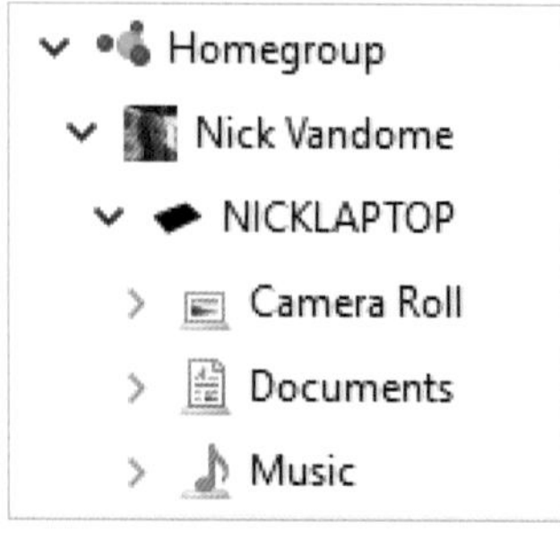

Sharing Settings

Within the Network and Sharing Center, there are also options for specifying how items are shared over the network, not just in the HomeGroup. To select these:

If you are sharing documents and files over a network you should be able to access the Public folder on another computer (providing that network discovery is turned on). If you are the administrator of the other computer you will also be able to access your own home folder, although you will need to enter the required password for this.

1. Open the Network and Sharing Center and click on the **Change advanced sharing settings** link

Change advanced sharing settings

2. Select sharing options for different networks, including private, guest or public, and all networks. Options can be selected for turning on network discovery so that your computer can see other computers on the network, and file and printer sharing

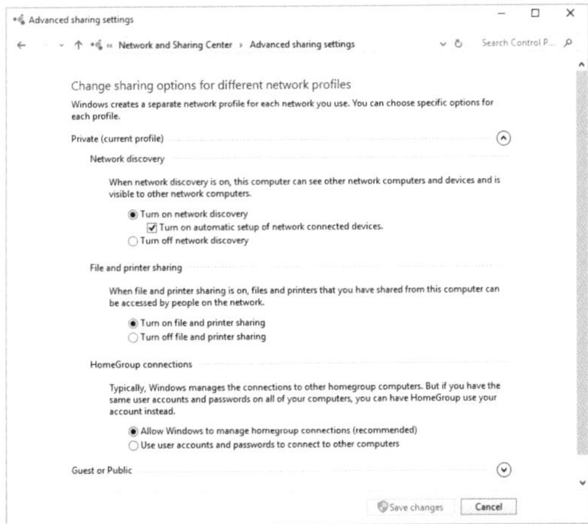

3. Click on these buttons to expand and view the options for each network category

Change sharing options for different network profiles

Windows creates a separate network profile for each network you use. You can choose specific options for each profile.

Private (current profile)

Guest or Public

All Networks

Public folder sharing

The Public folder on your own computer can be used to make items available to other users on the network.

Saving Files for Sharing

When you want to save files so that other people on your network can access them (other than with the HomeGroup), this can be done by either saving them into the Public folder on your own laptop, or saving them into the Public folder of another computer on your network. To do this:

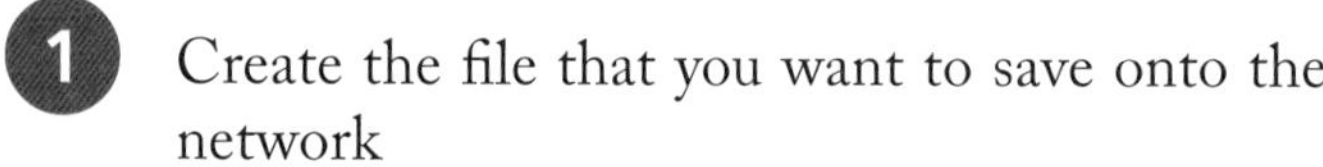

1. Create the file that you want to save onto the network

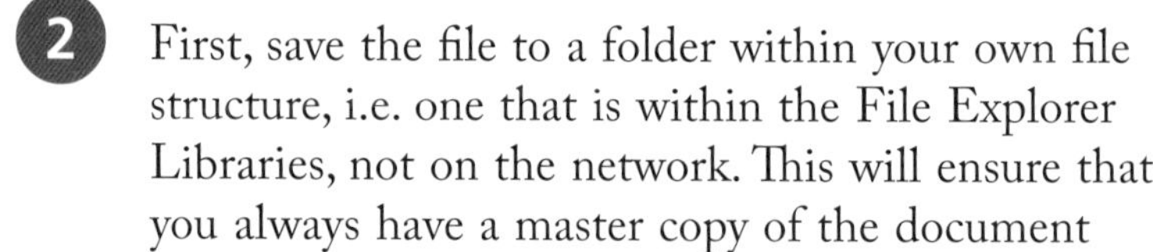

2. First, save the file to a folder within your own file structure, i.e. one that is within the File Explorer Libraries, not on the network. This will ensure that you always have a master copy of the document
3. Select **File > Save As** from the Menu bar (this is standard in most types of apps)
4. The Save As window has options for where you can save the file

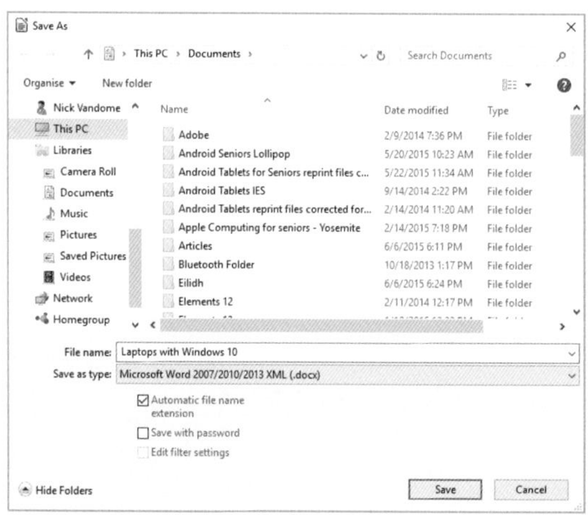

5. Click on the **Network** icon in the left-hand pane

Files can also be copied to Public folders on the network by dragging and dropping them from within your own file structure. This can be done within the File Explorer window.

6. Double-click on the Public folder on your laptop if this is where you want to save the file; or

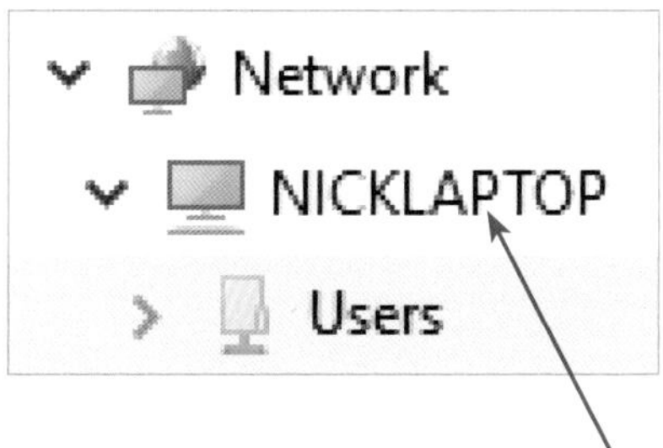

7. Double-click on another computer on the network to save the file here

8. Double-click on the **Users** folder, then the **Public** folder

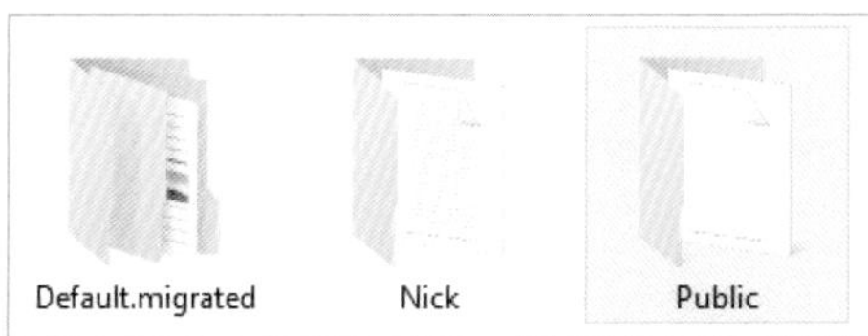

9. Double-click on the folder into which you want to save the file

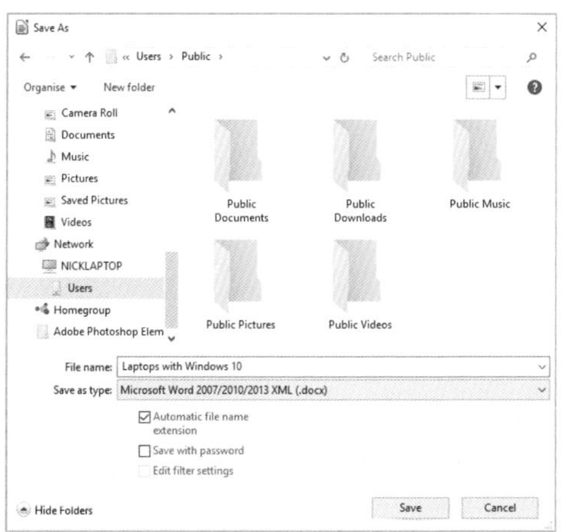

If you copy files to your own Public folder, other computers on the network will only be able to access these when your laptop is turned on.

Network Troubleshooting

1. Open the Network and Sharing Center and select **Troubleshoot problems**

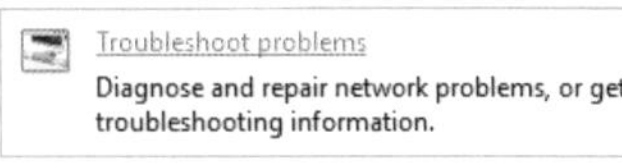
Troubleshoot problems
Diagnose and repair network problems, or get troubleshooting information.

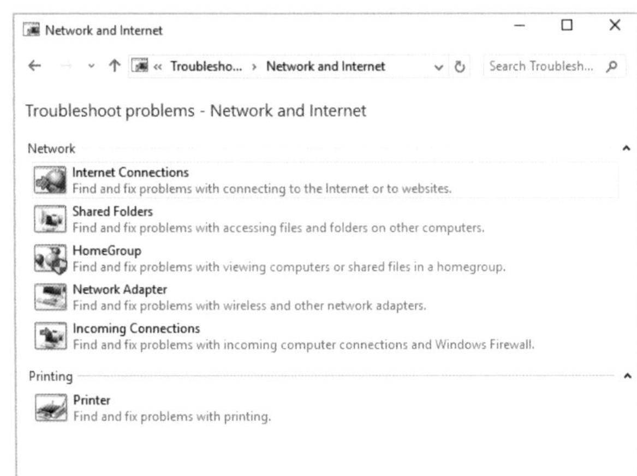
Network and Internet
Troublesho... › Network and Internet
Search Troublesh...
Troubleshoot problems - Network and Internet
Network
Internet Connections
Find and fix problems with connecting to the Internet or to websites.
Shared Folders
Find and fix problems with accessing files and folders on other computers.
HomeGroup
Find and fix problems with viewing computers or shared files in a homegroup.
Network Adapter
Find and fix problems with wireless and other network adapters.
Incoming Connections
Find and fix problems with incoming computer connections and Windows Firewall.
Printing
Printer
Find and fix problems with printing.

2. Windows searches online for troubleshooting packs

3. Select, for example, Shared Folders and follow the prompts to describe and hopefully resolve the problems

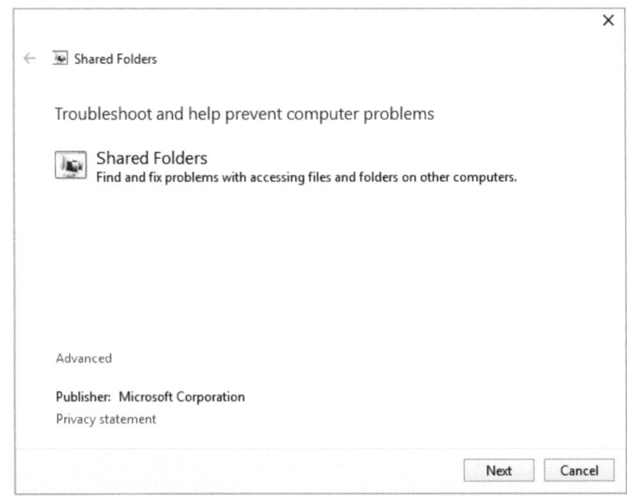
Shared Folders
Troubleshoot and help prevent computer problems
Shared Folders
Find and fix problems with accessing files and folders on other computers.
Advanced
Publisher: Microsoft Corporation
Privacy statement
Next
Cancel

Don't forget

Windows 10 provides several troubleshooters to resolve common problems with networks. They are downloaded, so you always get the most up-to-date help.

10 Battery Issues

Battery power is crucial to a laptop and this chapter shows how to get the best out of your battery and deal with any problems.

Types of Battery

A laptop's battery is one of the items that helps to define its identity: without it, the portable nature of the laptop would be very different as it would always have to be connected with a power cable. Laptops have used a variety of different types of batteries since they were first produced, and over the years these have become smaller, lighter and more powerful. However, laptop batteries are still relatively heavy and bulky and are one of the major sources of weight in the machine:

Don't forget

The type of battery provided with a laptop, and the approximate lifespan for each charge, should be displayed with the details about the machine on the manufacturer's website or in the promotional literature that comes with it.

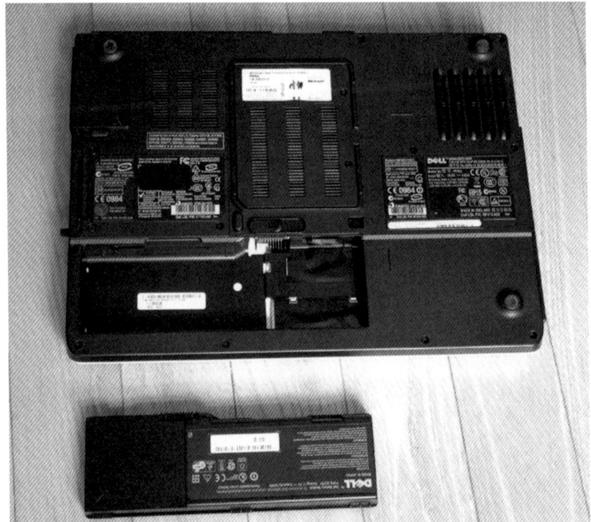

The quality of laptop batteries is improving all the time. Some models currently on the market have a battery life of up to eight or even 10 hours.

The types of batteries used in modern laptops are:

- **Lithium-ion**. This is a type of battery that has a good weight-to-power ratio and loses its charge at a relatively slow rate. However, they can be prone to overheating if they are not treated properly or are defective.
- **Lithium polymer**. This is an advanced version of the lithium-ion battery. It is generally considered to be a more stable design.

These types of batteries are rechargeable, so they can be charged and used numerous times after they initially run out. However, over time, all rechargeable batteries eventually wear out and have to be replaced.

Power Consumption

Battery life for each charge of laptop batteries is one area on which engineers have worked very hard since laptops were first introduced. For most modern laptops, the average battery life for each charge is approximately between three and five hours. However, this is dependent on the power consumption of the laptop, i.e. how much power is being used to perform particular tasks. Power-intensive tasks will reduce the battery life of each charge cycle. These types of tasks include:

- Watching a DVD (this requires the enhanced version of the Windows Media Player)
- Editing digital video
- Editing digital photographs

When you are using your laptop you can always monitor how much battery power you currently have available. This is shown by the battery icon that appears at the right-hand side of the Taskbar:

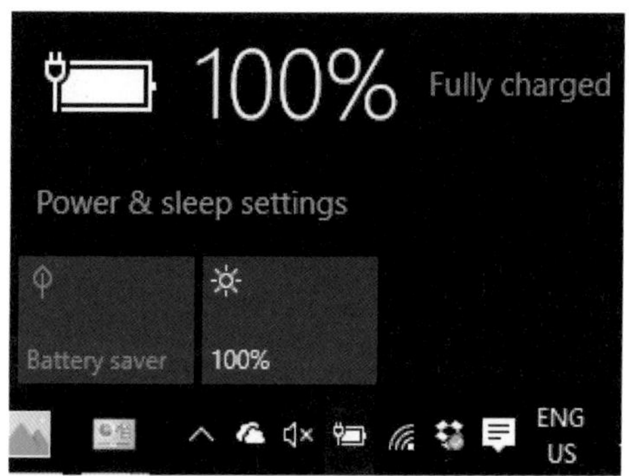

Because of the vital role that the battery plays in relation to your laptop, it is important to try to conserve its power as much as possible. To do this:

- Where possible, use the mains adapter rather than the battery when using your laptop.
- Use the Sleep function when you are not actively using your laptop.
- Use power-management functions to save battery power (see next two pages).

If you are undertaking an energy-intensive task, such as watching a DVD, try to use the external AC/DC power cable rather than the battery, otherwise the battery may drain very quickly and the laptop will close down.

Battery Management

Unlike desktop computers, laptops have options for how the battery is managed. These allow you to set things like individual power schemes for the battery and to view how much charge is left in the battery. This can be done from the Control Panel. To access the options for managing your laptop's battery:

1. Access the **Control Panel**

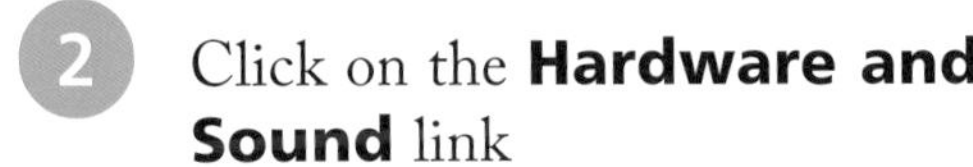

2. Click on the **Hardware and Sound** link

3. Click on the **Power Options** link

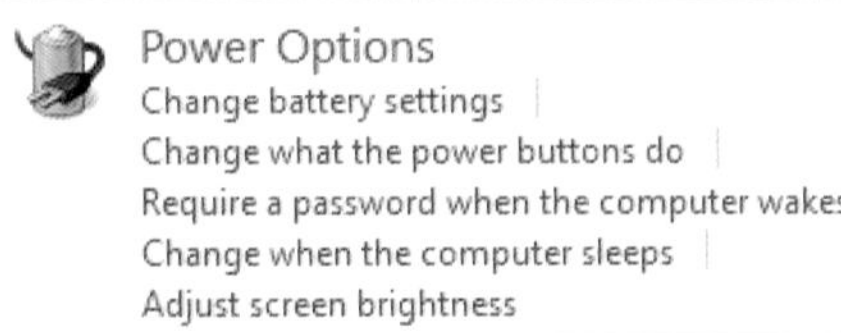

A power scheme can be set for the battery in the same way as for an external power source, and different settings can be applied.

Power Plans

The Power Options window displays the available settings for balancing battery usage and your laptop's performance. Select the buttons to change to a different power plan:

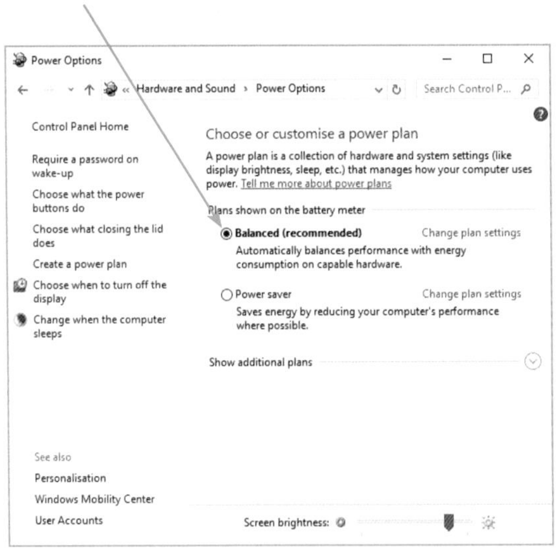

System Settings

Within the Power Options window it is possible to select settings for how the laptop operates when the Power or the Sleep button is pressed, or when the lid is closed. To do this:

1. In the Power Options window, click on one of these links to apply the settings for each item

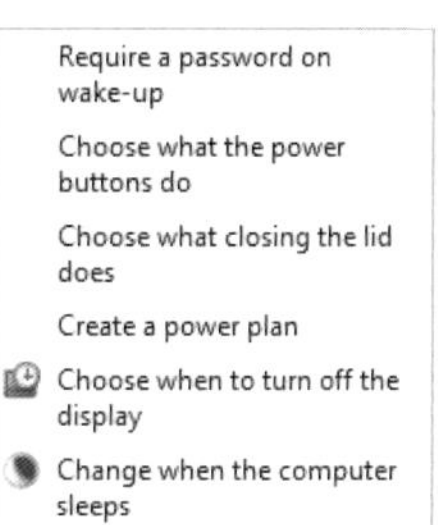

2. The options are displayed in **System Settings**

3. Click on these boxes to select an action for each item, either on battery power or when plugged in

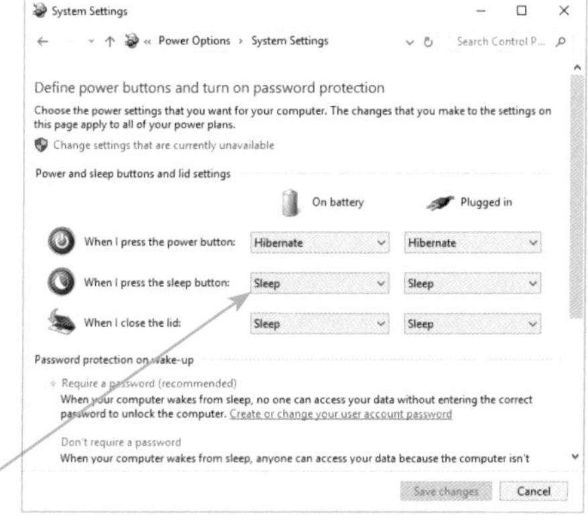

4. Click on the **Change settings that are currently unavailable** link to access more options

Change settings that are currently unavailable

5. Check on the additional options and click on the **Save changes** button at the bottom of the window to apply them

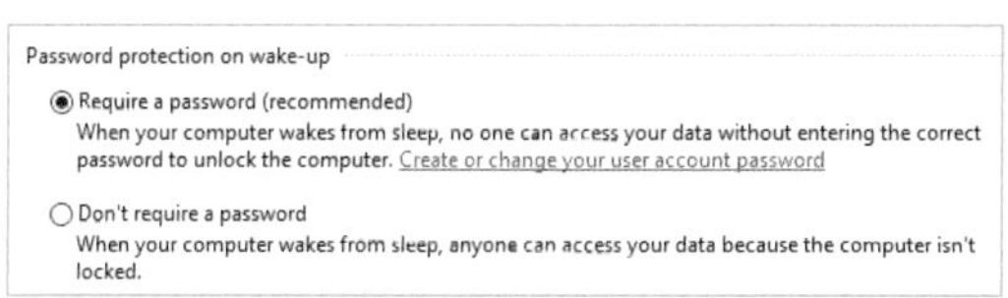

If you don't protect your laptop with a password for when it is woken from sleep, anyone could access your folders and files if they wake the laptop from sleep.

...cont'd

Editing plan settings

To edit the settings for a specific power plan:

When you are warned about a low battery, save all of your current work and either close down or switch to using an external AC/DC cable for powering your laptop.

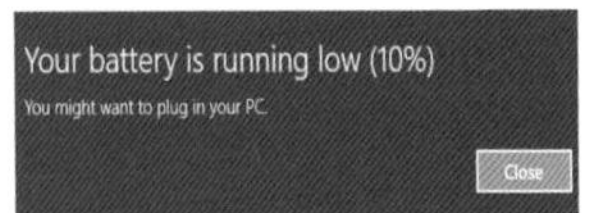

1. Click on one of the options in the Power Options window and click on the **Change plan settings** link

Balanced (recommended) Change plan settings
Automatically balances performance with energy consumption on capable hardware.

2. Select options for turning off the display when the laptop is not being used and when the computer goes to sleep, and also the display brightness, either on battery power or when the laptop is plugged in

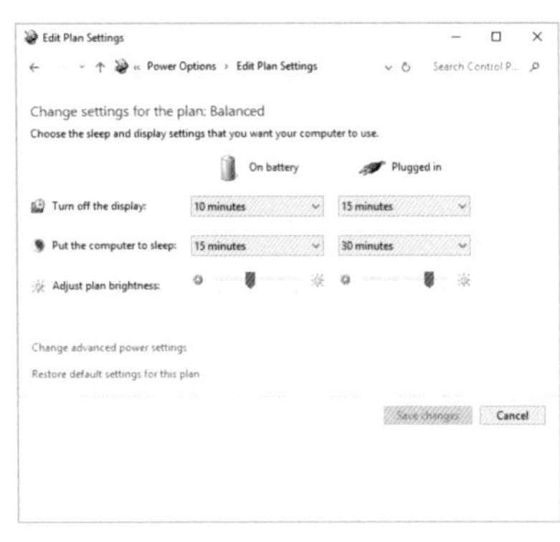

3. Click on these buttons to make selections for each item

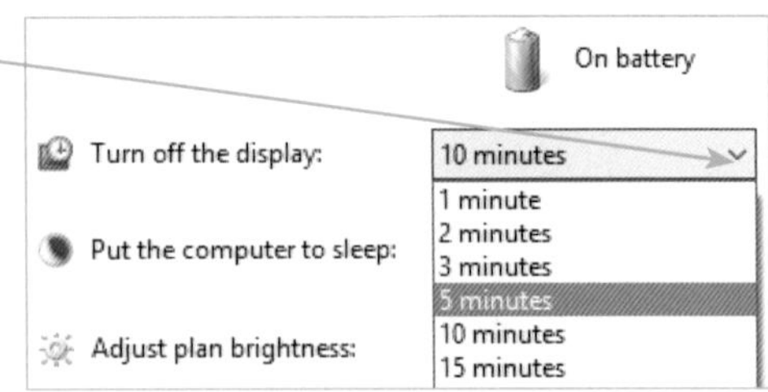

4. Click on the **Save changes** button

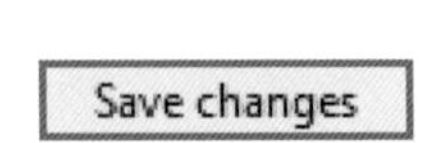

Charging the Battery

Laptop batteries are charged using an AC/DC adapter, which can also be used to power the laptop instead of the battery. If the laptop is turned on and being powered by the AC/DC adapter, the battery will be charged at the same time, although at a slower rate than if it is being charged with the laptop turned off.

The AC/DC adapter should be supplied with a new laptop and consists of a cable and a power adapter. To charge a laptop battery using an AC/DC adapter:

A laptop battery can be charged whether the laptop is turned on or off.

1. Connect the AC/DC adapter to the cable and plug it into the mains socket

2. Attach the AC/DC adapter to the laptop and turn on at the mains socket

3. When the laptop is turned on, the Power Meter icon is visible at the right-hand side of the Taskbar. Double-click on this to view the current power details

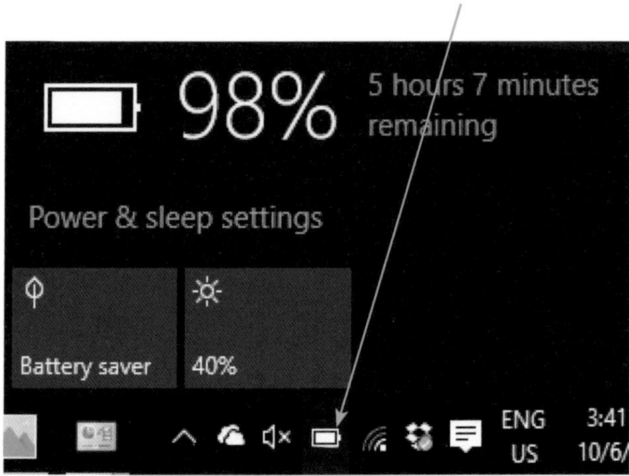

4. Click on the **Battery saver** button to activate this

Removing the Battery

Although a laptop's battery does not have to be removed on a regular basis, there may be occasions when you want to do this. These include:

- If the laptop freezes, i.e. you are unable to undertake any operations using the keyboard or mouse and you cannot turn off the laptop using the power button.
- If you are traveling, particularly in extreme temperatures. In situations such as this, you may prefer to keep the battery with you to try to avoid exposing it to either very hot or very cold temperatures.

To remove a laptop battery:

1. With the laptop turned off and the lid closed, turn the laptop upside down
2. Locate the battery compartment and either push or slide the lock that keeps the battery in place

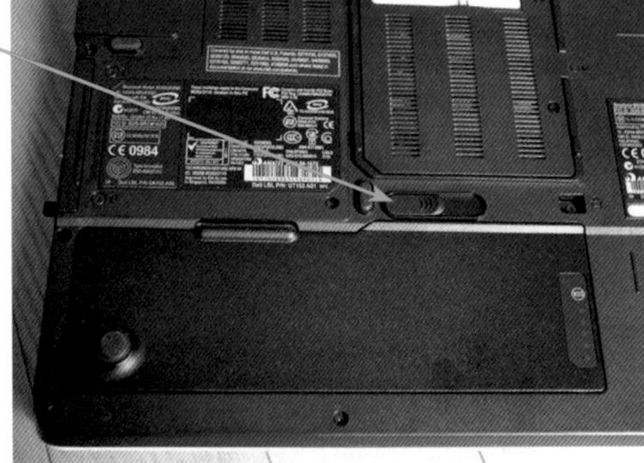

3. Slide the battery out of its compartment

To re-insert the battery, or a new battery, push it gently into the battery compartment until it clicks firmly into place.

Dead and Spare Batteries

No energy source lasts forever and laptop batteries are no exception to this rule. Over time, the battery will operate less efficiently until it will not be possible to charge the battery at all. With average usage, most laptop batteries should last approximately five years, although they will start to lose performance before this. Some signs of a dead laptop battery are:

- Nothing happens when the laptop is turned on using just battery power.
- The laptop shuts down immediately if it is being run on the AC/DC adapter and the cord is suddenly removed.
- The Battery Meter shows no movement when the AC/DC adapter is connected, i.e. the Battery Meter remains at 0% and shows as not charging at all.

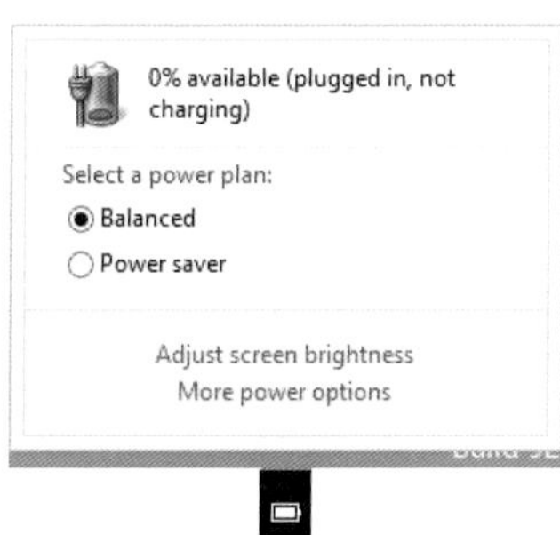

If you think that your battery may be losing its performance, make sure that you save your work at regular intervals. Although you should do this anyway, it is more important if there is a chance of your battery running out of power and abruptly turning off.

Spare battery

Because of the limited lifespan of laptop batteries it is worth considering buying a spare battery. Although these are not cheap it can be a valuable investment, particularly if you spend a lot of time traveling with your laptop and you are not always near a source of mains electricity. In situations such as this, a spare battery could enable you to keep using your laptop if your original battery runs out of power.

When buying a spare battery, check with the laptop's manufacturer that it will be compatible: in most cases the manufacturer will also be able to supply you with a spare battery for your laptop.

Battery Troubleshooting

If you look after your laptop battery well it should provide you with several years of mobile computing power. However, there are some problems which may occur with the battery:

- **It won't keep its charge even when connected to an AC/DC adapter**. The battery is probably flat and should be replaced.
- **It only charges up a limited amount**. Over time, laptop batteries become less efficient and so do not hold their charge so well. One way to try to improve this is to drain the battery completely before it is charged again.
- **It keeps its charge but runs down quickly**. This can be caused by the use of a lot of power-hungry applications on the laptop. The more work the laptop has to do to run applications, such as those involving videos or games, the more power will be required from the battery and the faster it will run down.
- **It is fully charged but does not appear to work at all when inserted**. Check that the battery has clicked into place properly in the battery compartment and that the battery and laptop terminals are clean and free from dust or moisture.
- **It is inserted correctly but still does not work**. The battery may have become damaged in some way, such as becoming very wet. If you know the battery is damaged in any way, do not insert it, as it could short-circuit the laptop. If the battery has been in contact with liquid, dry it out completely before you try inserting it into the laptop. If it is dried thoroughly, it may work again.
- **It gets very hot when in operation**. This could be caused by a faulty battery and it can be dangerous and lead to a fire. If in doubt, turn off the laptop immediately and consult the manufacturer. In some cases, faulty laptop batteries are recalled, so keep an eye on the manufacturer's website to see if there are any details of this, if you are concerned.

If there is no response from your laptop when you turn it on in battery mode, try removing the battery and re-inserting it. If there is still no response then the battery is probably flat and should be replaced.

If you are not going to be using your laptop for an extended period of time, remove the battery and store it in a safe, dry, cool place.

11 Troubleshooting

Viruses are the scourge of the computing world and this chapter shows how to best defend against any malicious software. It also covers updating your system software and backing up your data.

Protecting Against Viruses

One of the most important considerations for any computer user is to make sure that they have suitable protection to guard against malicious software which can infect their machine and compromise its operation, potentially damaging or erasing folders and files. Windows 10 comes with some built-in protection against viruses, malware and spyware (see the following pages) but it is also a good idea to have additional protection in the form of anti-virus software. There are several products on the market; three to look at are:

- McAfee at **www.mcafee.com**
- Norton at **www.norton.com**
- Kaspersky at **www.kaspersky.com**

Don't forget

When you buy an anti-virus app you will usually have to pay an annual subscription. This will enable you to keep downloading the latest virus protection files (definitions) to combat new viruses as they appear.

Using anti-virus software

Most anti-virus software works in a similar way:

New viruses are being released all the time so it is important that you scan for them on a daily basis.

1. Once downloaded and installed, open your chosen app to access its features. Click on an item to see its options

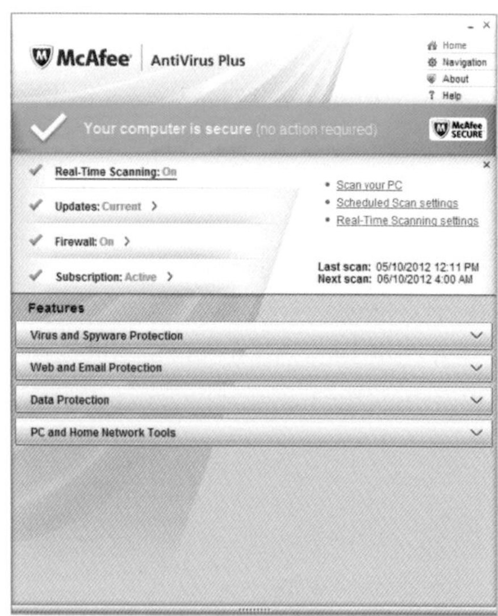

2. Click on the **Scan your PC** button to perform a scan for viruses on your laptop

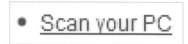

3. The progress of the scan, along with any potential problems, is displayed as it is taking place

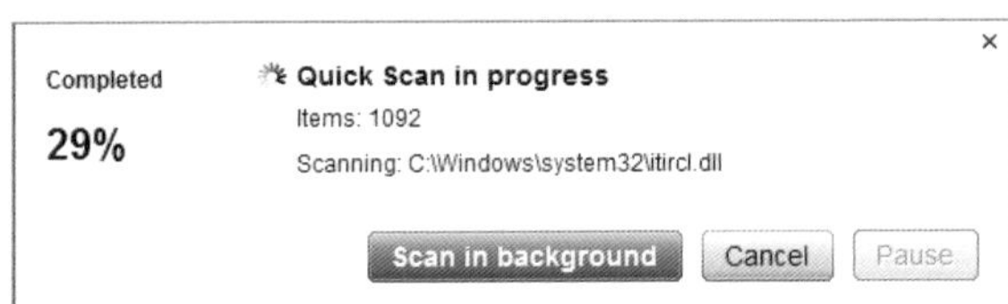

4. Once a successful scan has taken place you will be informed of issues, if any

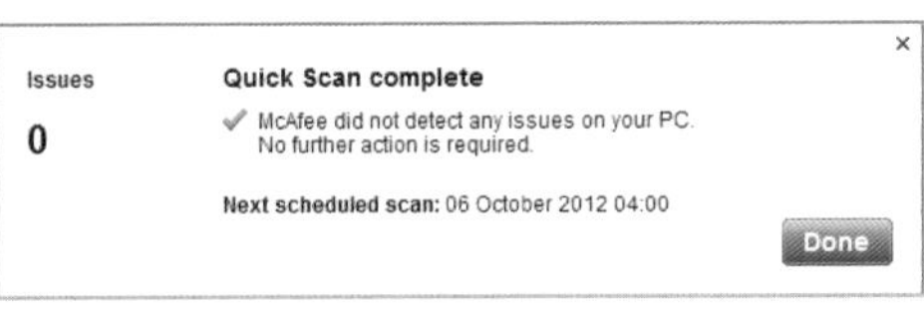

5. Click on the **Updates** button to get the latest virus definitions, i.e. the means to stop the latest viruses that have been identified. Updates can usually be set to be performed automatically

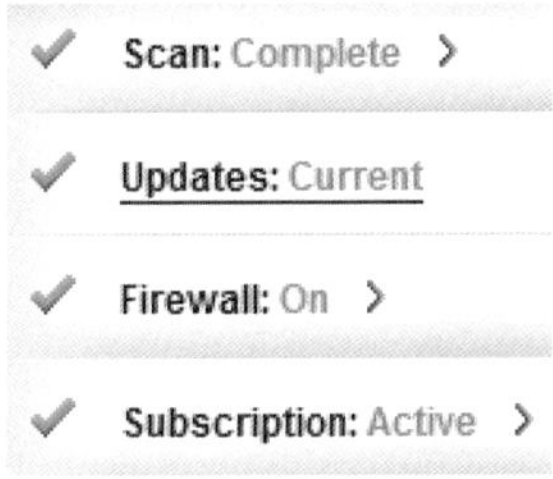

If any viruses are discovered you will be given options for how to deal with them.

Internet and networks

Anti-virus software can also warn you about potential unwanted access to your laptop from the internet or another user on the network:

1. Click on the **Web and Email Protection** option to select options for ensuring your laptop is as safe as possible when accessing the internet

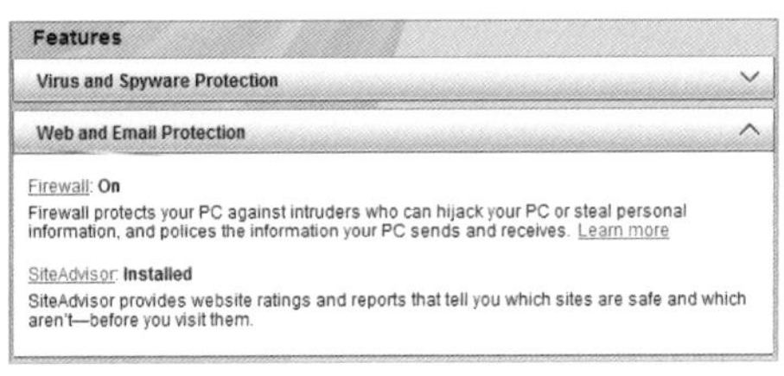

Using a Firewall

A firewall is a program that can be used to help stop malicious programs, such as viruses and spyware, from entering your laptop. It acts like a barrier around your laptop and aims to repel any items that it does not trust (these usually come from the web).

Firewalls can be purchased along with anti-virus software but there is also one that comes pre-installed with Windows 10. To use this:

Don't forget

If you have an anti-virus app it will probably also have its own firewall. This will take over from the Windows Firewall.

1. Access the **Control Panel** and click on the **System and Security** link

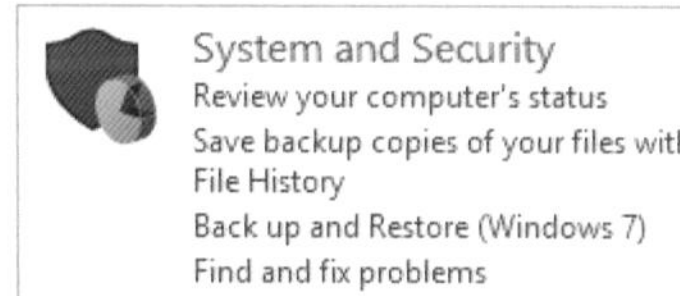

2. Click on the **Windows Firewall** link

3. By default, the firewall should be turned on, i.e. protecting your laptop

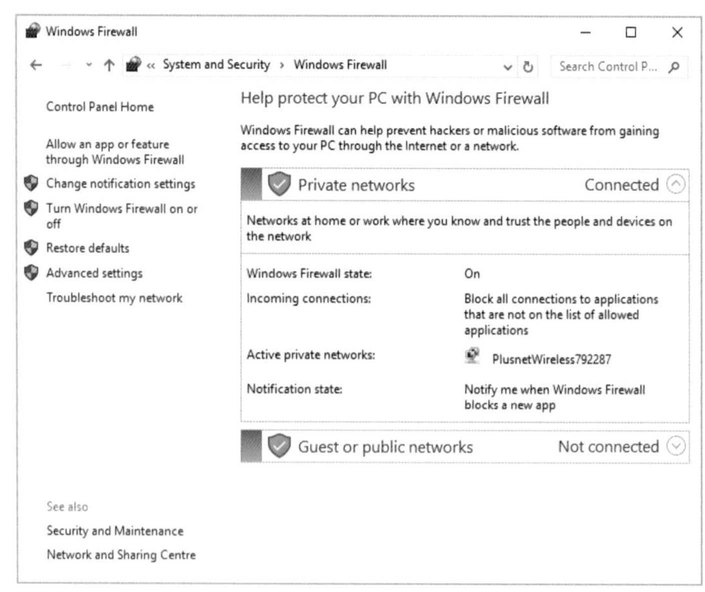

...cont'd

4. Select **Allow an app or feature through Windows Firewall,** to view the allowed apps

Allow an app or feature through Windows Firewall

5. Check on these boxes to allow specific apps and features to be allowed through the firewall

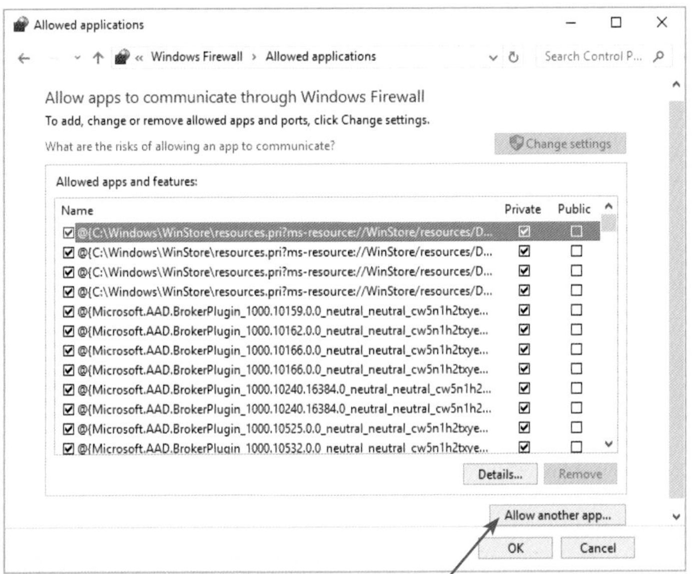

6. Select **Allow another app**, if you want to allow an app through the firewall

7. Click on an app to select it

8. Click on the **Add** button

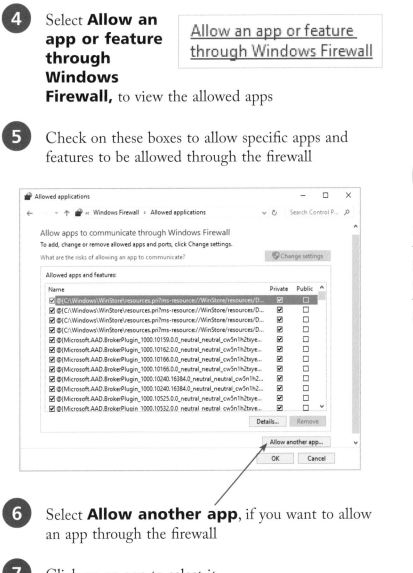

If you turn off the firewall you will keep getting system messages telling you that you should turn it back on again.

Windows Defender

Another option for stopping malicious software entering your laptop is Windows Defender, which can check for spyware and similar types of harmful programs. To use this:

Spyware is software that is downloaded (unknowingly) from the internet. It then sends information over the internet without the user's knowledge.

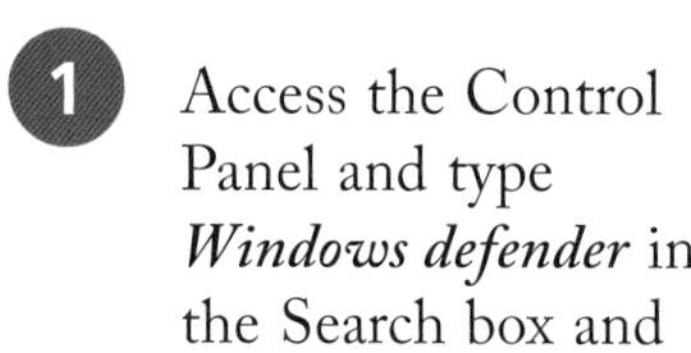

1. Access the Control Panel and type *Windows defender* in the Search box and select **Windows Defender**

2. The Windows Defender window contains details for scanning your laptop and viewing the results. If you have not performed a scan recently, the window will appear as a warning

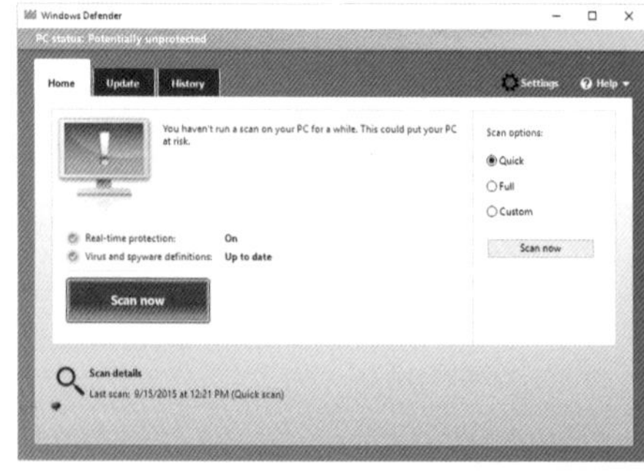

The options for scanning with Windows Defender are Quick Scan, Full Scan or Custom Scan. For a Custom Scan you can select which folders and files are looked at.

3. Click on the **Scan now** button to perform a scan on your laptop

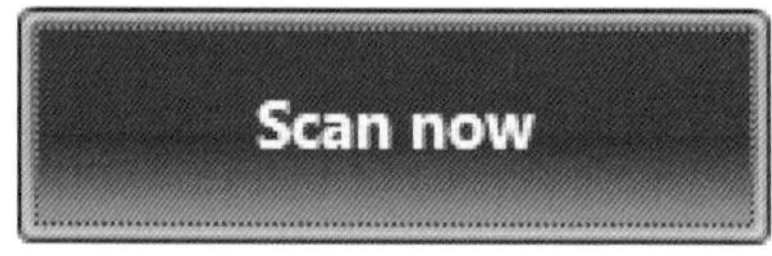

4. Once the scan is completed, the following message will appear if no malicious items are detected

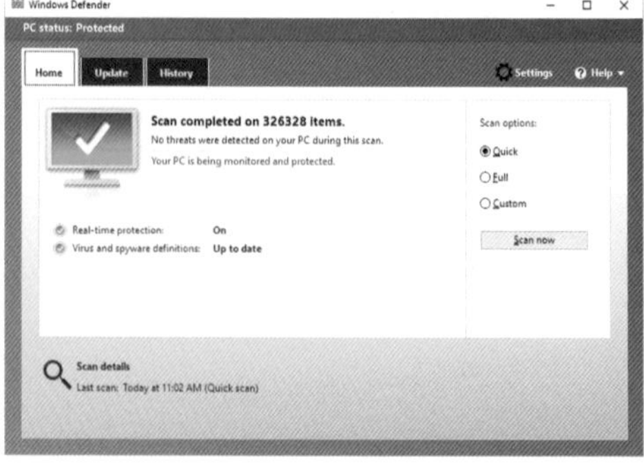

5. Click on the **Update** tab to update your virus and spyware items. This is done automatically but it can also be performed manually by clicking on the **Update** button

6. Click on the **History** tab to view the results from the previous scans that have been undertaken. Click on the **View details** button to see the scan results

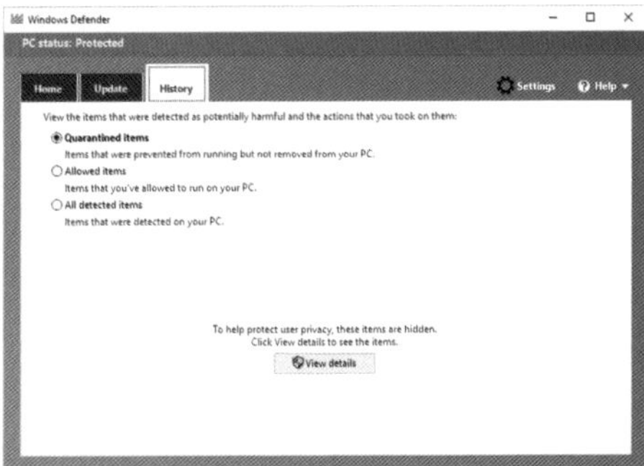

7. Click on the **Settings** button and select options for how Windows Defender operates. Select the **Real-time protection** option to activate automatic alerts if malicious software tries to access your laptop

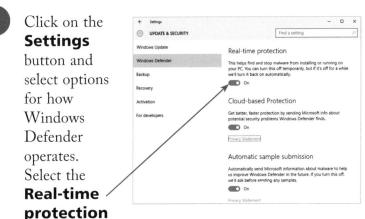

If any items are quarantined you will be given options for how to deal with them and remove them from your laptop.

User Account Controls

One of the features in Windows 10 that is aimed at stopping malicious files or apps being downloaded onto your laptop is called the User Account Controls. This produces a warning window when a variety of actions are performed, such as certain apps being run. However, after time this can become counterproductive: the window can appear so frequently that it is accepted without thinking, just to get rid of it. If this becomes too annoying, it is possible to disable the User Account Controls so that the warning windows do not appear. To do this:

1. Access the **Control Panel** and click on the **System and Security** link

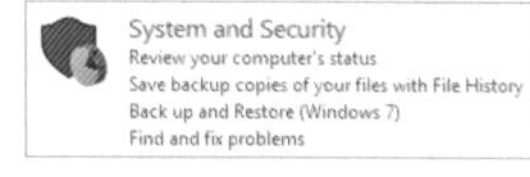

2. Click on **Change User Account Control settings** under **Security and Maintenance**

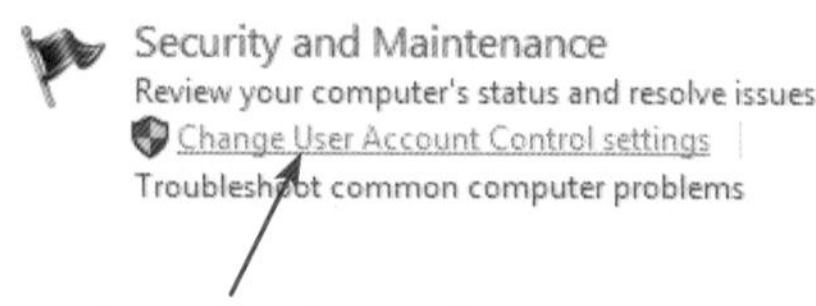

3. Drag this slider to specify the level at which you want the user controls set. The higher the setting, the more security warnings will appear while you are using your laptop

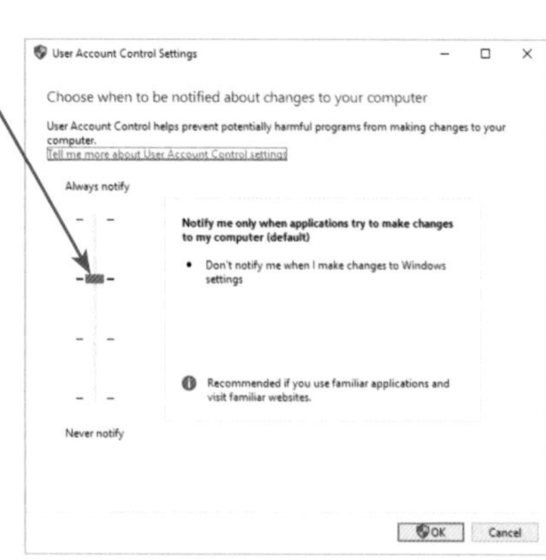

If you turn off the User Account Controls, your computer may be more vulnerable to infection from unauthorized apps. However, if you have anti-virus software running, this should pick up any of these problems.

System Maintenance

For all of the security settings on your laptop it is useful to be able to see them in one location. This can be done with the System and Maintenance settings, which also enables you to alter these settings if required. To use these:

1. Access the **Control Panel** and click on the **Review your computer's status** link under **System and Security**

System and Security
Review your computer's status
Save backup copies of your files with File History
Back up and Restore (Windows 7)
Find and fix problems

2. All of the current essential security settings are displayed. Click on an item to view more details about it and rectify any possible problems

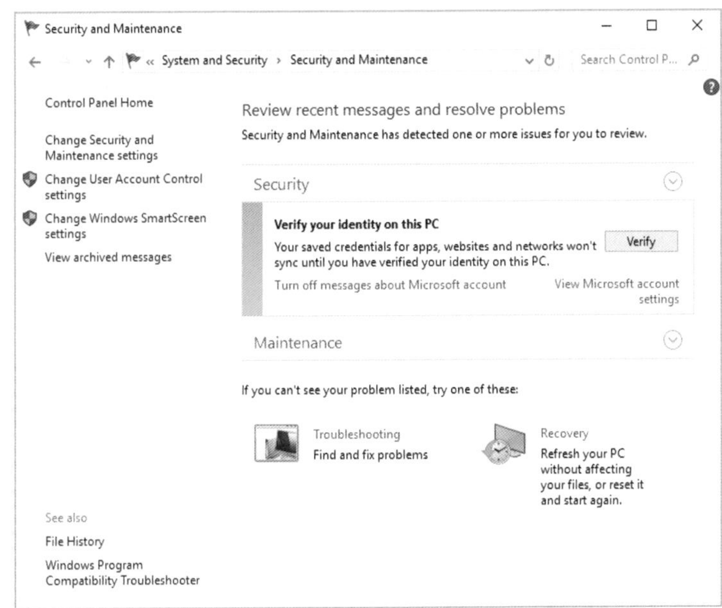

An item with a green banner is fully protected and up-to-date. An amber banner means that there are some issues relating to this item. A red banner means that the required settings are not in place and your laptop could be at risk.

The Security and Maintenance options can also be accessed from the Action Center, by clicking on this button on the Taskbar.

Updating Software

In Windows 10, updates can also be installed from the Settings app in the Windows 10 interface. To do this:

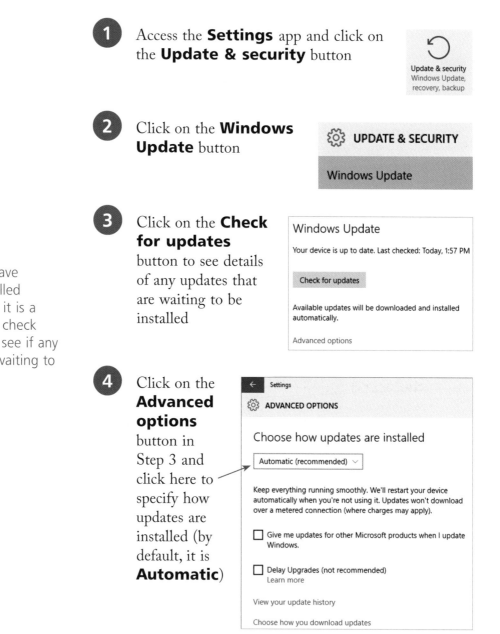

1. Access the **Settings** app and click on the **Update & security** button

2. Click on the **Windows Update** button

3. Click on the **Check for updates** button to see details of any updates that are waiting to be installed

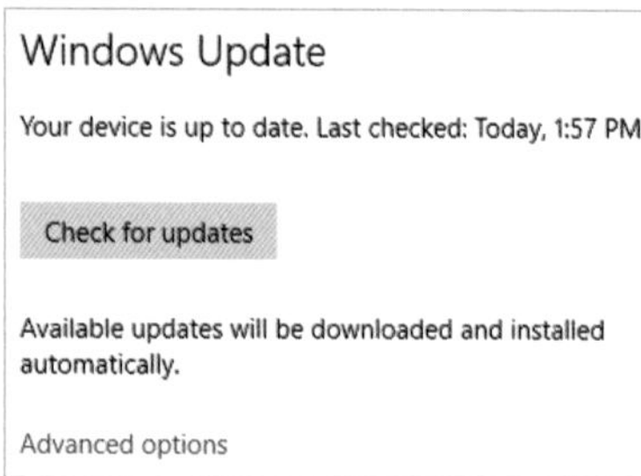

4. Click on the **Advanced options** button in Step 3 and click here to specify how updates are installed (by default, it is **Automatic**)

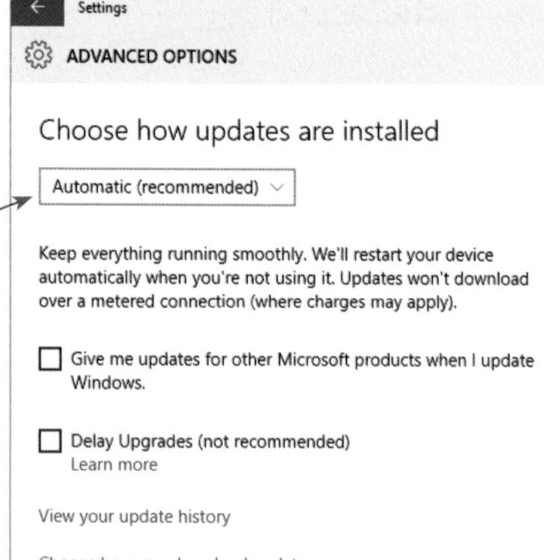

Even if you have updates installed automatically it is a good idea to check frequently to see if any updates are waiting to be installed.

5. Click on the **View your update history** button to see what has been installed

View your update history

Choose how updates are delivered

6. If you think any of the updates are not working properly click on one of the **Uninstall** buttons at the top of the window

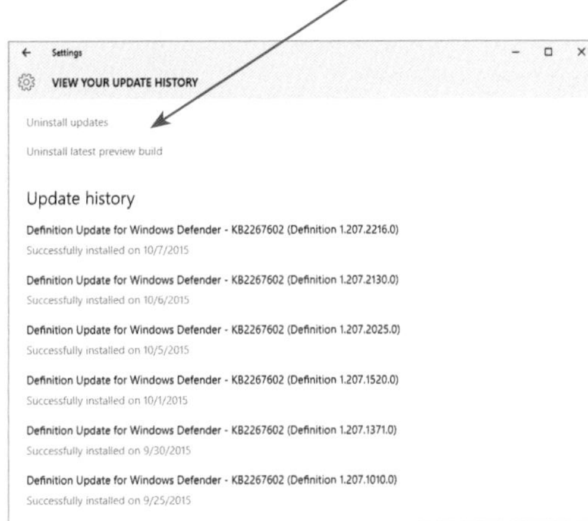

7. Click on the **Choose how updates are delivered** button in Step 5 and select whether you want to allow updates to come from more than one location, e.g. other PCs, in addition to Microsoft

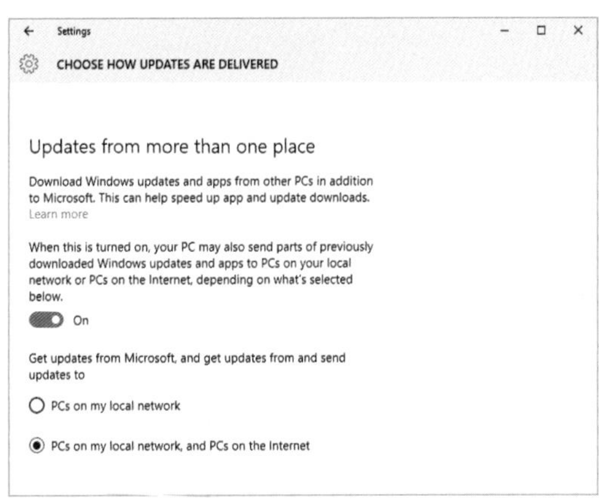

Allowing updates from more than one location can speed up the process.

Backing Up

The security settings in Windows 10 are designed to try to protect your laptop as much as possible and ensure that you don't lose any valuable data. However, no system is infallible and sometimes malicious programs, or human error, can cause the loss of files and documents on your laptop. Because of this, it is important that you have a robust procedure in place for backing up your information and also have the means to restore it if it does get deleted or corrupted. The first step is to make sure your computer files are backed up. To do this:

Backing up means copying your data to another location. One of the best options for doing this is to use an external hard drive.

1. Open the **Control Panel** and select **Save backup copies of your files with File History** in the **System and Security** category

System and Security
Review your computer's status
Save backup copies of your files with File History
Back up and Restore (Windows 7)
Find and fix problems

An external hard drive is one that can be connected to your laptop with a USB cable and then used as a backup device.

2. The first time you do this, you can select a drive such as an external hard drive or a network drive to use for the backup

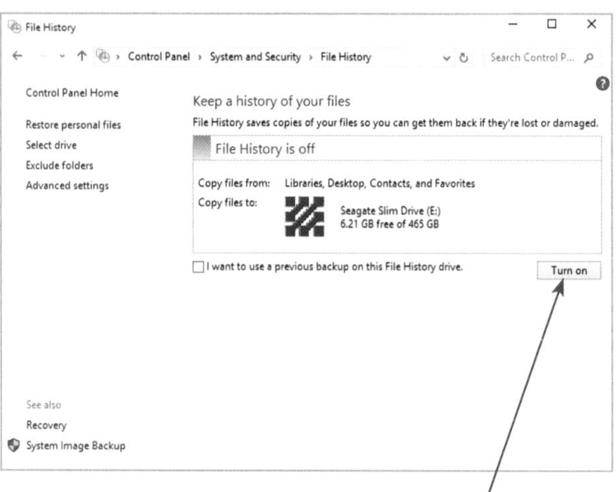

3. Make sure the selected device is connected, and click on the **Turn on** button to back up copies of your files

4. The backup runs and copies the files to the selected location, i.e. the external drive

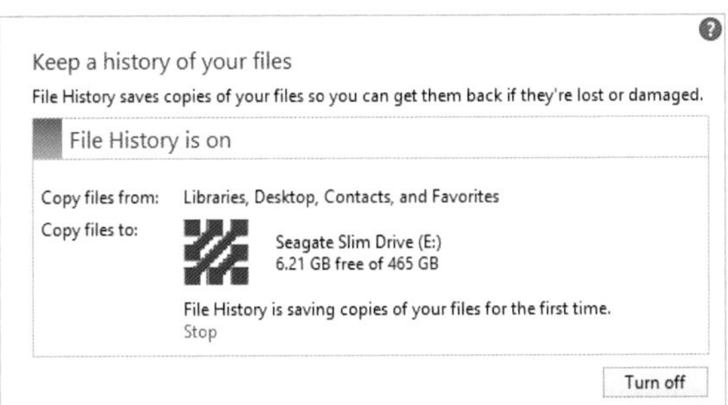

5. Click on the **Run now** link to perform another backup

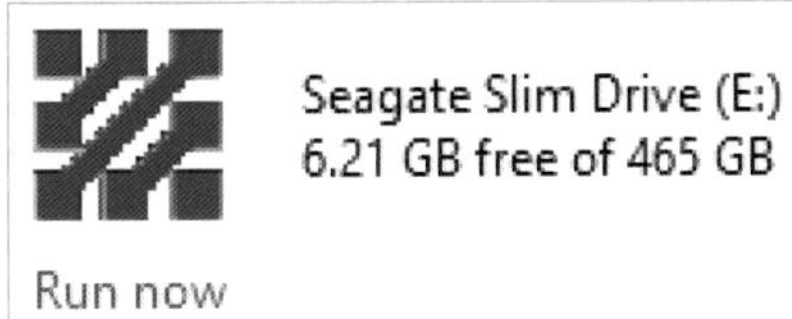

6. Click on the **Advanced settings** link to select additional options for how the backup is performed

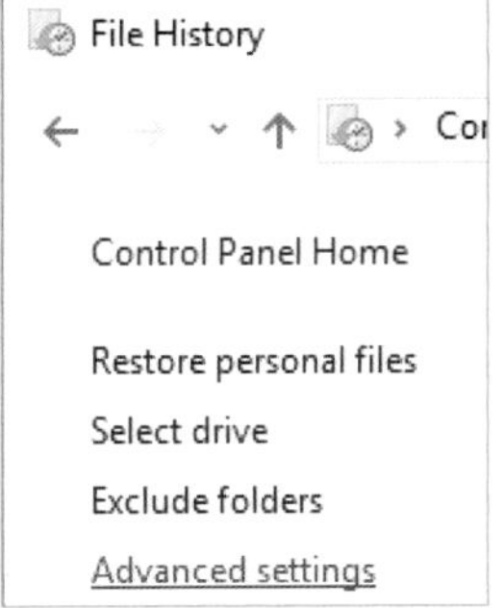

7. Select any additional options and click on the **Save changes** button at the bottom of the window

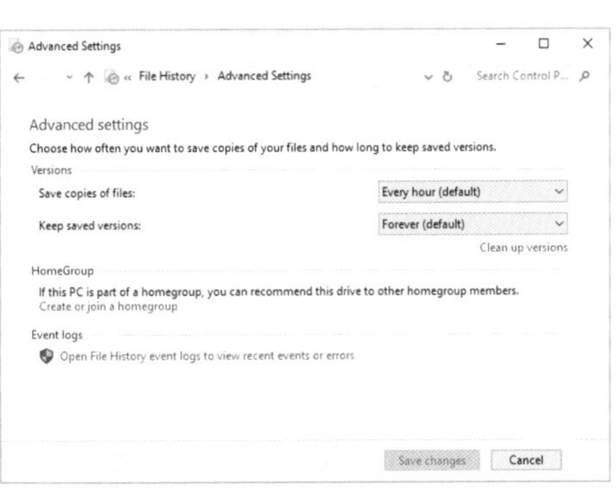

Restoring Files

Once files have been backed up they should be kept in a safe place, preferably in a different location from the original files, i.e. the laptop itself. If the original files ever get deleted or corrupted, they can be restored from the backup location. To do this:

1. Open the **Control Panel** and click on the **File History** section under **System and Security**

2. Click on the **Restore personal files** button

Control Panel Home

Restore personal files

3. The files for the current date are displayed

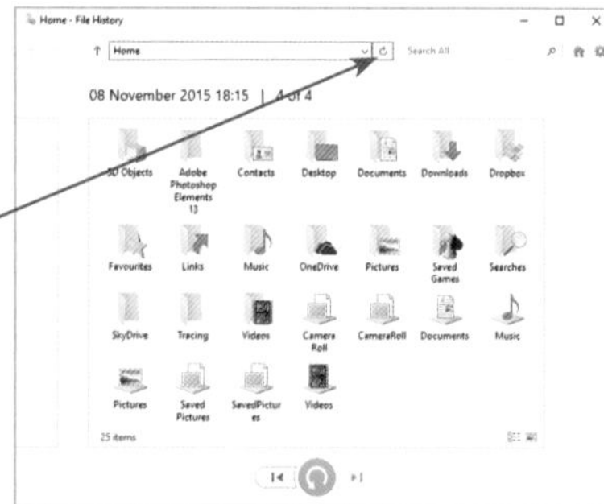

4. Click here to move back to an earlier date, if you want to restore files from here

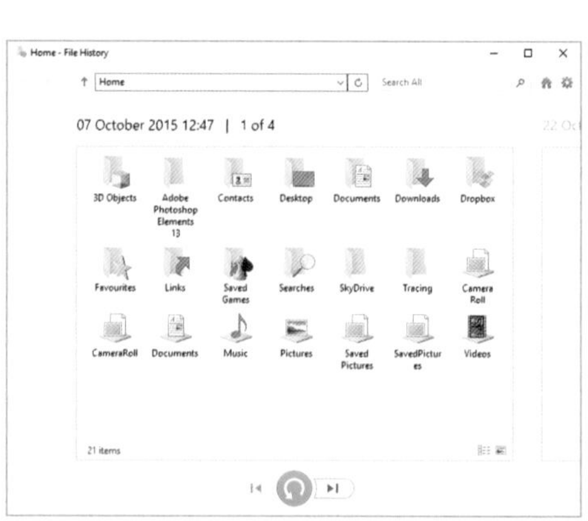

Depending on the types of files that you have selected for backing up, the process can take a considerable amount of time, so be prepared for a wait. Click on the Refresh button in the Control Panel window to see if the operation has been completed.

5. Select the items you want to restore by clicking on them. (Double-click on a folder to view its contents and select individual files)

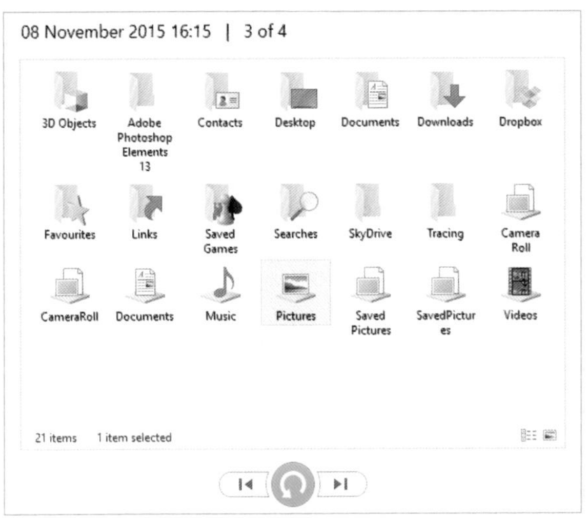

6. Click on this button to restore the selected items

7. If there is a file conflict with the ones that you are restoring, i.e. there is one with the same name already in the selected location, you will be presented with options for what to do with the files being restored

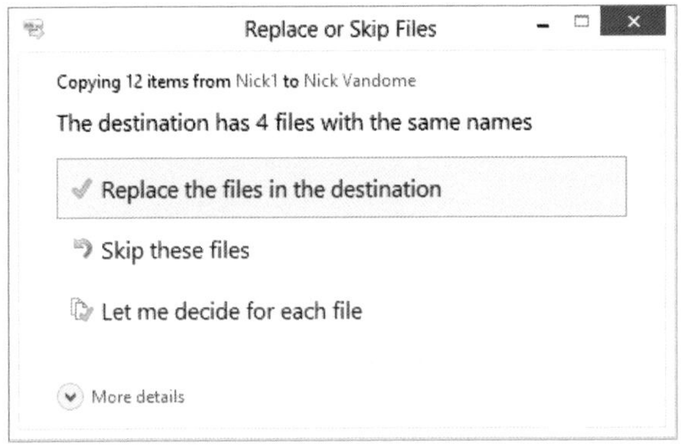

If you are at all worried about copying over existing files, restore the files from the backup disc to a different location from the original one.

System Restore

Inevitably, when working with your laptop you will come across occasions when it behaves erratically. This could be because of a program that has been loaded, or software (driver) that has been loaded for an external device, such as a printer. However, with Windows 10 it is possible to try to rectify the problem by restoring the settings of your laptop to an earlier date. This does not affect any of your personal files or folders, but it can help the laptop perform better by taking it back to a date before the problem started. To use System Restore, you have to first create a Restore Point from where you can then restore your settings:

System Restore is a good option to use if your laptop starts to perform erratically after you have installed a new app.

1. Access the **Control Panel** and click on the **System** link under **System and Security**

2. Click on the **System protection** link, to access this section within the System Properties window

3. Click on the **Create...** button, to create a restore point manually

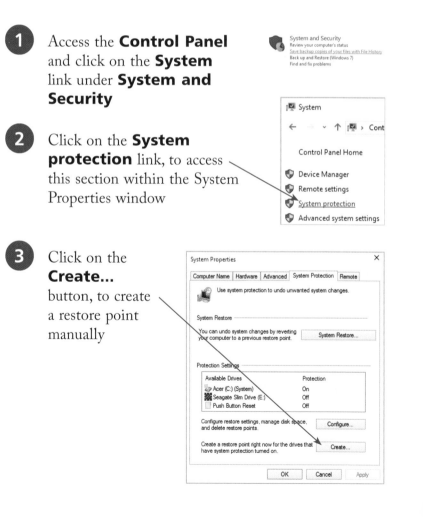

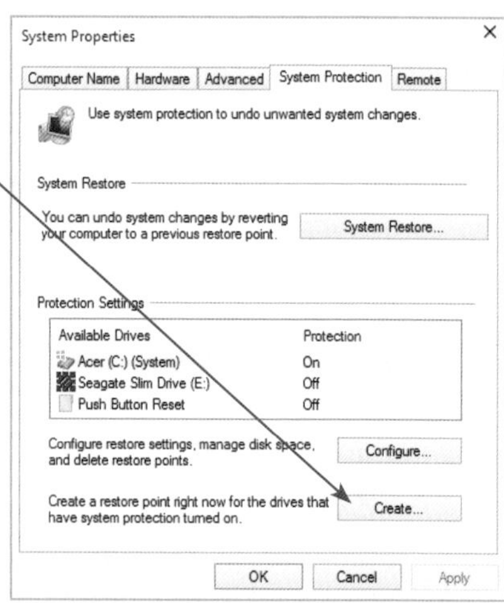

4. Enter a title for the restore point

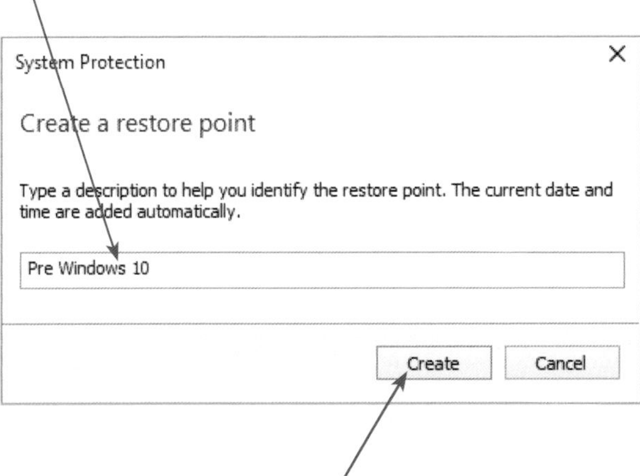
System Protection

Create a restore point

Type a description to help you identify the restore point. The current date and time are added automatically.

Pre Windows 10

Create Cancel

Always start with the most recent System Restore point to see if this fixes the problem. If not, use a more distant restore point.

5. Click on the **Create** button

6. The required data is written to the disk and the manual restore point is set up

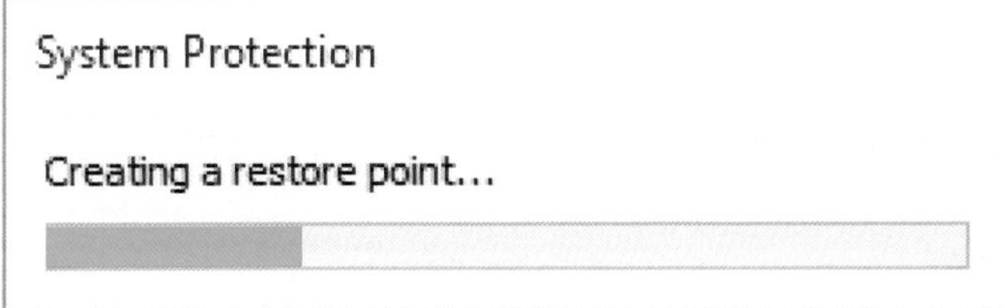
System Protection

Creating a restore point...

7. Once the restore point has been created, a notification box will appear. Click on the **Close** button to finish the process

System Protection

The restore point was created successfully.

Close

...cont'd

Using Restore Points

The installation of a new app or driver software may make Windows behave unpredictably or have other unexpected results. Usually, uninstalling the app or rolling back the driver will correct the situation. If this does not fix the problem, you can use an automatic or manual restore point to reset your system to an earlier date when everything worked correctly.

Hot tip

Whenever you install a new app, or a driver for an external device, it is always worth creating a custom restore point, so that you have a dated reference for everything you have added to your laptop.

1. Access **System Protection** and click on the **System Restore...** button

   System Restore...

2. Click on the **Next** button to move to the next stage of the System Restore process

   Next >

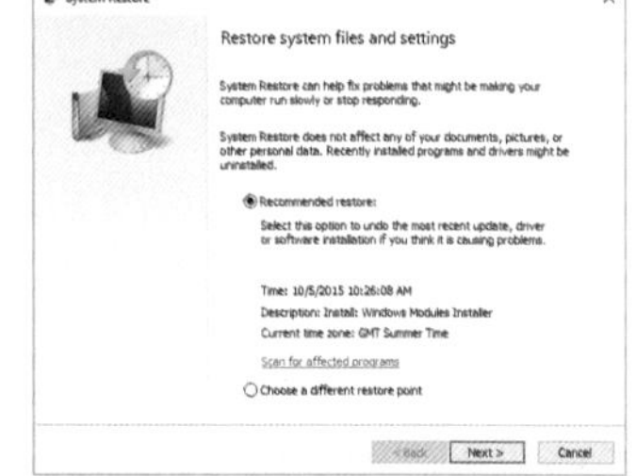

3. Select a restore point and click on the **Next** button

   Next >

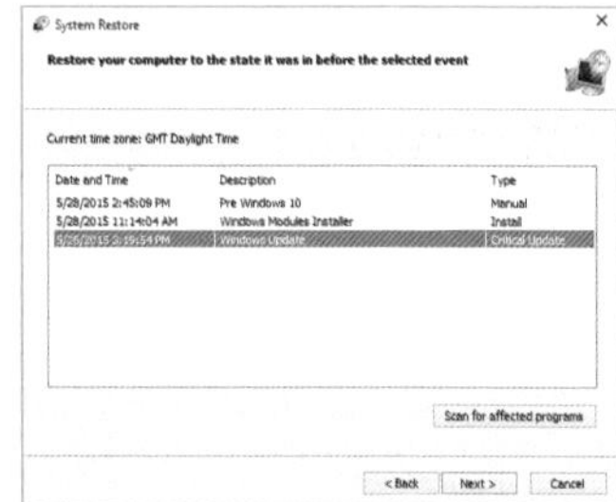

4. Details of the System Restore are displayed here. Click on the **Finish** button

   Finish

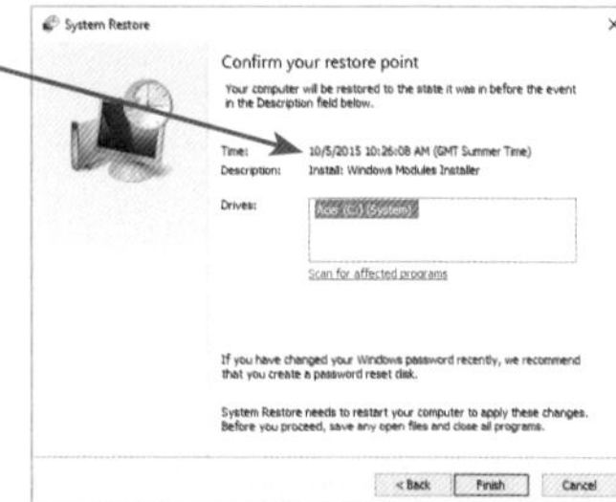

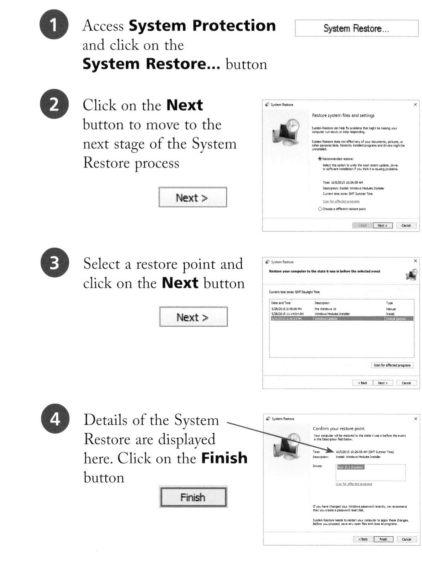

A

B

C

D

E

F

G

H

I

K

L

M

N

O

P

Q

R

V

W

X

Y